THE PEOPLING OF AFRICA

THE PEOPLING OF AFRICA

A GEOGRAPHIC INTERPRETATION

JAMES L. NEWMAN

Yale University Press New Haven and London

Set in Times Roman and Lithos types by The Composing Room
of Michigan, Inc. Printed in the United States of America by
Thomson-Shore, Dexter, Michigan.

Maps by Marcia J. Harrington.

Library of Congress Cataloging-in-Publication Data

Newman, James L.
The peopling of Africa : a geographic interpretation√
James L. Newman.
p.   cm.
Includes bibliographical references (p.   ) and index.
ISBN 0-300-06003-3 (cloth: acid-free paper)
0-300-07280-5 (pbk.: acid-free paper)
1. Human geography—Africa.   2. Africa—History.   3. Man,
Prehistoric—Africa.   4. Africa—Antiquities.   I. Title.
GF701.N48   1995
960′.1—dc20   94-38259
CIP

A catalogue record for this book is available from the British
Library.

The paper in this book meets the guidelines for permanence and
durability of the Committee on Production Guidelines for Book
Longevity of the Council on Library Resources.

3   5   7   10   8   6   4   2

TO THE MEMORY OF ALAN K. SMITH,
A TRUE FRIEND AND SCHOLAR OF AFRICA

CONTENTS

PART TWO: REGIONAL UNFOLDINGS

MAPS

PREFACE

I don't know exactly when the first seed for this book was planted, but my sophomore year at the University of Minnesota provides a good-enough starting point. It was then, while taking a course taught by John Borchert, that I decided to switch majors from geology to geography. He was a gifted and persuasive teacher who interwove the environmental geography of monsoonal climates, chernozem soils, and glaciated landscapes with their corresponding human responses. As we traveled via maps and diagrams, I found myself thinking in ways that made the world more understandable and, therefore, more interesting. I could appreciate what made Ukraine and Kansas both different and similar places. Nature provided the stage, but people did the acting. What a bachelor's degree in geography would lead to beyond increasing my enjoyment of life was not at all clear, but in the buoyant and optimistic late 1950s, planning the future did not matter as much as it does to students today. Some reasonable job would show up in due course.

Although the whole world comes within the purview of geography, even undergraduates at Minnesota commonly selected a region of specialization. I decided on Africa. True, a certain degree of romanticism influenced my thinking. There was the scenic grandeur of rift valleys, volcanoes, and vast plains that I had discovered in geology, besides, of course, the fabled wildlife. My choice, however, had a much more compelling motivation. The colonial era was coming to an end, and although a new Africa loomed on the horizon, to most Americans it still carried the dark continent image—that of a place little understood and negatively perceived. Fortunately, I had three professors who knew better, and they infused me with the desire to learn as much about Africa and Africans as I could. One, Philip Porter, became my adviser in geography, and the other two, James Gibbs and Luther Gerlach, taught me anthropology. Making my regional choice that much easier were the African students whom I met. Their warmth, graciousness, and hope for a future in which even a young, naive American would be welcome were irresistible lures.

As graduation approached, I faced a tough decision. By participating in a land survey being conducted by the Liberian American Mining Company I could go to Africa sooner rather than later. I decided, however, not to accept the job. Two things bothered me: my first experience in Africa would be colored by a corporate connection, and deep down, I knew I was not yet ready. I needed more preparation, so enrolling in graduate school seemed the wiser choice. A search for top African studies program at a place with a strong geography department led me to UCLA and Northwestern, but I stayed put at Minnesota. Philip Porter was preparing to join a multidisciplinary Culture and Ecology in East Africa project, and when he returned, I would have an adviser fresh from the field and actively researching matters of population and settlement, which I had decided would be my topical specialties. Furthermore, during his year's absence, Keith Buchanan would take his place, and he was unrivaled among contemporary geographers for the depth of his African experience. As it turned out, I had what amounted to a private tutorial in which he taught me many things, especially how the continent had been transformed by colonialism. To fully grasp the effects of colonialism, I would have to delve much deeper into the precolonial African experience. I was fortunate to have Ward Barrett as a supportive mentor.

As a part of my studies I read the book *Africa: Its Peoples and Their Culture History* by George Peter Murdock, which had a profound influence on my thinking and career. By synthesizing a diverse array of archeological, linguistic, biological, and cultural data, Murdock portrayed an Africa whose many peoples had complex and dynamic pasts in which they had adapted and readapted to varying human and natural environmental circumstances. Although Murdock was an anthropologist, the geography embedded in his interpretation could not be missed. Now I had better idea of what I wanted to do: join the effort to disclose Africa's rich past and maybe someday even write a book about it. But this would have to be preceded by a more modest accomplishment—my doctoral dissertation.

The subject came to me while I was working on a population map of eastern Africa that Philip Porter was putting together for the project. As we assembled quantitative and qualitative information, a roughly arrowhead-shaped area fewer than 300 kilometers from north to south and no more than 200 kilometers at its widest from east to west captured my attention. Here was the human diversity of the continent in microcosm. For starters, the area contained representatives of each of the four language phyla of Africa: the Khoisan-speaking Hadza and Sandawe; the southern Cushitic Iraqw, Gorowa, and Burunge; the Bantu Isanzu, Iramba, Rimi, Mbugwe, and Langi; and the Nilotic Barabaig and Baraguyu. Furthermore, each group appeared to occupy its own special place according to an array of economies: gathering and hunting, nomadic herding, mixed agro-pastoralism, shifting cultivation, and intensive subsistence farming. In the years ahead I planned to devote myself to discovering how this arrangement had all come to pass.

Because the Khoisan speakers were thought to be the oldest inhabitants, it seemed logical to begin my investigations with them. At the north end of the area near Lake Eyasi, the Hadza still lived by gathering and hunting, whereas to their south the Sandawe had, for the most part, given it up in favor of farming. The obvious question was, What had happened to cause one to change and not the other? and I framed my research to find the answer. In the field, the logistical and intellectual obstacles to a comparative study of this sort quickly assumed enormous proportions, and I dropped the Hadza part to concentrate on the hows and whys of change among the Sandawe. Confronting the realities of Africa in the mid-1960s and imbued with the desire to make a tangible contribution to newly independent Tanzania, I decided to deal not only with the Sandawe past but also with their future. I did so by adding an agricultural resources inventory to my study.

My dissertation, which carried the title "Geography and Subsistence Change among the Sandawe of Tanzania," helped me secure a job at Syracuse University with its well-known Program of Eastern African Studies. During my first several years I taught two courses— The Historical Geography of Africa and Africa: Problems and Prospects—that reflected my dual interests. But events were running against the continuation of the former course. Development-related issues increasingly captivated student attention, and when enrollments fell off to nearly single digits, I stopped teaching the historical course. Admittedly, I, too, was more caught up in the present and future as my work shifted toward issues of nutrition and fertility. The Tanzania project disappeared from my agenda, but the book idea lingered in my mind. I still wanted to write about the African past some day, probably toward the end of my career.

The time to do it came sooner than I had planned. In 1987, when I received my third straight rejection of a request for funds to support fieldwork in Africa, I took the plunge. I set about reading for and writing a temporally oriented geography of the peoples of Africa. Having no specific idea of what the book would look like, I simply let the pieces fall where they might. By 1989 the basic structure had taken shape.

Deciding on an audience took me a little longer. My initial thought was to address other academics, especially Africanists. Although much of the information would not be new to most of them, general syntheses are needed every so often in order to help put the accumulated, often disjointed specialized research into perspective. The more I thought about the matter, however, the more I became convinced that a wider audience should be targeted. The building blocks for understanding the African past have been strengthened enormously since Murdock wrote, but except for a few books dealing with human origins, what we have learned has, for the most part, remained rather narrowly confined. For the vast majority of people, even highly educated ones, the continent is still heavily shrouded in their minds. So I have written a book for both Africanists and an interested public. I hope that I have succeeded in informing the former about matters beyond their specializations and maybe even occasionally stimulated a few fresh research insights. For the nonspecialists my wish is to provide two things: a lifting of the shroud and an incentive to keep on learning about Africa and Africans. True knowledge requires constant revision—the work is always in progress. Should some readers be motivated to read further, then I will have made at least a small payment on the debt that I owe Africans for all they have provided me, including, of course, a career.

I have already acknowledged several people, but a few more need to be mentioned. A very important one is Marcia Harrington. I wanted the maps to be special, but I am not very good at making them. As you will see, she is. Text editing at Yale University Press was in the capable hands of Mary Pasti. Little escaped her eagle eye in the effort to ensure the book's accuracy and readability. What she and I missed was caught by Kay Steinmetz. David deLaubenfels also deserves a nod. His knowledge of prehistory is extraordinary, and I can't count the number of times I wandered into his office to seek some point of clarification or try out my latest interpretation. I never failed to come away enlightened. For over thirty years my wife Carole has had to put up with my bouts of inattention. I owe her more than I can say for all the patience and support she has provided. And I cannot forget Alan Smith, to whom this book is dedicated. I miss him as a friend and colleague who I could always count on for honest and sage opinions, whether about an idea, a recent book, a student problem, the curriculum, or basketball. Then there are those people who took the time to read various chapters and offer their comments and suggestions. The ones I know about are Doug Armstrong, Janet Crane, Chris DeCorse, Andrew Hill, Philip Porter, John Western, and Tom Whitmore. Thank you all.

THE PEOPLING OF AFRICA

1

INTRODUCTION

The title of a book should mirror its contents; thus I will use the four key words in *The Peopling of Africa: A Geographic Interpretation* as the foundation for my introductory remarks. We can begin with *Africa*. All places are constructs of one kind or another, and the construct employed here is the conventional map depiction of a land mass bounded by the Mediterranean and Red seas and the Atlantic and Indian oceans (map 1.1). I will also include nearby islands, such as Zanzibar and Bioko (formerly Fernando Po), but exclude several more distant ones that sometimes are made part of Africa. The more prominent are Madagascar, the Comoros, the Seychelles, and the Azores. That each carries a strong African cultural imprint cannot be denied; however, the same can be said about Jamaica, Brazil, and even the United States, and including them certainly would stretch the definition of Africa. As I see it, the essential issue is contiguity and what contiguity says about continuity. Once those of African descent either voluntarily or involuntarily departed for more distant lands, they lost direct involvement with happenings on the continent and became participants in other realms of experience.

Next we can look at *Peopling*. I use the word to highlight the dynamic nature of populations and, therefore, the necessity of considering the past if we seek to comprehend the present and anticipate the future. In Africa the past goes all the way back to the very origins of humanity, and so we will begin then and continue until just before the scramble for Africa in the late nineteenth century. This voracious land grab marks the onset of the colonial era, a

1

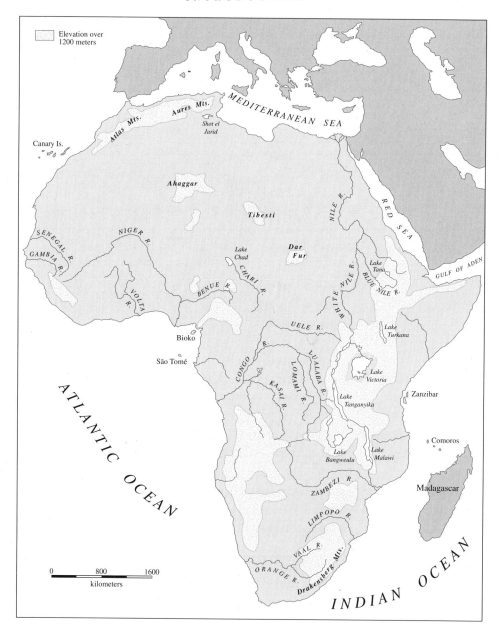

Elevation over
1200 meters

1.1 In this book Africa means the conventionally recognized continental
land mass and near-shore islands.

time when Europe-derived forces asserted themselves over African ones, and as these
forces intensified, an alien and often rigid order enveloped most of the continent's inhabitants. The workings of colonialism are detailed in a large body of scholarship, and the
aftermaths of political independence and neocolonialism have also been subjects of close

2

scrutiny. But Africa and Africans deserve to be known on their own terms, and to achieve this goal, we need to improve our understanding of what took place before colonialism rewrote many of life's rules.

Peopling implies the existence of distinctive peoples and hence highlights the issue of identity. All humanity shares a common Africa-forged genetic identity, and to see how and why this happened, we will have to examine the course of primate and hominid evolution. The rise and eventual success of *Homo sapiens* leads to a consideration of culture. Our first meeting with this hard-to-define yet essential feature of human existence will be through the stone tools unearthed by archeologists. Because little else has survived the workings of nature, they must suffice for defining how and where the earliest Africans lived. At the outset of the Stone Age the tools were simple and highly uniform from place to place, but as the millennia passed, they became increasingly complex and diverse. Different circumstances were producing different human responses, in other words, different cultures.

Humans were also diversifying genetically. There is little doubt that Africa is where the negroid genetic type originated. At least two early varieties existed: one developed within and around the Saharan region, then wetter than now, whereas the origin of the other is traceable to tropical woodland and forest habitats. A third early variety might also have existed—namely, those people often referred to as Bushmen and Hottentots. The open country of southern Africa is their established homeland. Experts disagree over whether they should be classified as negroids or put within a separate genetic grouping, and what to call them remains unresolved as well. The names Bushmen and Hottentots ought to be dropped because they carry less than flattering connotations in their original Afrikaans. San and Khoikhoi are widely used, but these are linguistic categories and should be kept as such. The only alternative proposed so far is *capoids,* so that is what I will call them.

There were caucasoids among the earliest modern Africans, too. They occupied the northernmost portion of the continent. Later, others came to Africa from elsewhere within the Mediterranean basin, from southwestern Asia, and, later still, from northwestern Europe.

Subsequent population interweaving created a highly complex African genetic cloth. Time and space have varied the circumstances, but Africa has been characterized more by human inclusion than by human exclusion, a circumstance that explains my avoidance of the word *race.* It is an imported concept implying a separation and a fixity of membership that is out of accord with African genetic facts and, indeed, with those of humankind generally.

Closer to an African concept of identity is language. Throughout the continent, a home or natal language is often the most important badge of a person's ethnicity, and thus you often see the coined word *ethnolinguistic* used by students of culture and society. In Nigeria, for example, there are people who refer to themselves as Yoruba and others who call themselves Igbo. Similarly, in South Africa we encounter Zulu and Xhosa. In both cases, the contrasted groups share numerous cultural affinities, but language is an impor-

3

tant perceived difference and says something to each people about who they are compared with others.

At a more abstract level, languages can reveal the past. They have origins, and they spread and change in reasonably predictable ways. By analyzing core vocabularies and grammars, linguists can reconstruct language relationships and occasionally even establish chronologies, at least in a relative sense. Although many classificatory details need to be worked out, there is general agreement that all of the more than one thousand African languages thus far enumerated can be arrayed within four phyla called Khoisan, Nilosaharan, Afroasiatic, and Niger Congo (table 1.1). The only major uncertainties surround several languages in the Kordofan area of the Sudan, which most often are linked to the Niger Congo phylum. With or without these languages, by the late nineteenth century Niger Congo was by far the largest phylum, in both number of speakers and size of area covered (map 1.2). Afroasiatic languages also spread over a substantial area, but since much of the land is desert or semidesert, its speakers were far fewer in number. Both had expanded their geographic ranges considerably, Afroasiatic largely at the expense of Nilosaharan, and Niger Congo at the expense of Khoisan.

The unfolding of Africa's language map will be a major theme of this book. We shall see the protoforms of the phyla taking shape toward the close of the Stone Age. The adoption of agriculture favored both population growth and more sedentary ways of life, and because the centers where people started raising crops and tending livestock were usually distant from one another, linguistic differentiation was the norm. Later, countervailing processes favoring convergence gained prominence. In a few instances, single languages,

Table 1.1 • Classification of African Languages

Phylum	Family	Language Examples
Khoisan	Khoikhoi	Nama, Korana, Griqua
	San	!Kung, //aikwe, /nu//en
Nilosaharan	Eastern Sudanic	Nuer, Karamojong, Nandi
	Central Sudanic	Bongo, Mangbetu, Madi
	Saharan	Kanuri, Teda, Zaghawa
	Songhai	Songhai
Afroasiatic	Semitic	Arabic, Amharic, Tigrinya
	Berber	Tuareg, Kabyle, Jerba
	Cushitic	Beja, Somali, Iraqw
	Chadic	Hausa, Logone, Fali
Niger	Kwa	Ewe, Yoruba, Kru
Congo	Mande	Soninke, Bambara, Kpelle
	Voltaic	Dogon, Senufo, Mossi
	Atlantic	Woloff, Fulbe, Dyula
	Bantu	Luganda, Xhosa, Herero
	Adamawa	Zande, Mbum, Kotoko

4

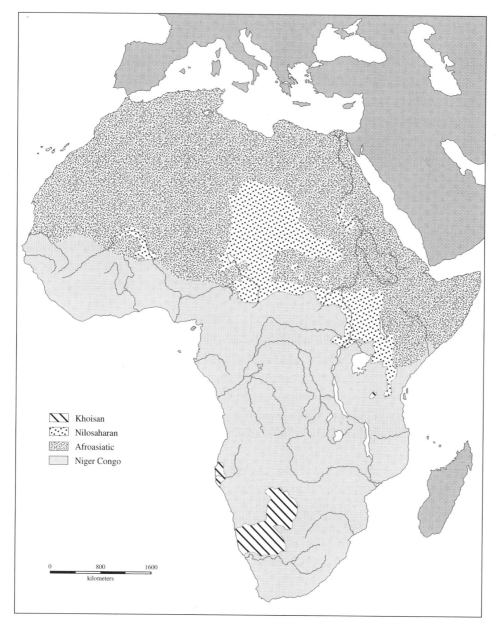

1.2 All African languages can be grouped into four phyla. By the end of the nineteenth century, peoples speaking Afroasiatic and Niger Congo languages had become predominant.

such as Arabic, Hausa, and Tswana, came to dominate large areas, whereas the diversity of other areas gave them something akin to a "shatterbelt" appearance—that is, the territories in which numerous languages are spoken—often even those from different phyla—abut and interdigitate with one another.

Occupation has also been an important aspect of African perceptions of identity. Whether people were gatherer-hunters, farmers, herders, traders, or craft workers could matter. To be a Maasai, for instance, has meant more than speaking Maa. It also has required possessing and herding cattle. A Maa speaker who took up farming assumed another identity, such as Arusha. Conversely, by giving up farming for herding a Kikuyu could join the Maasai. Speaking Maa would be required, but multilingualism has been a common feature of the African experience.

Several other factors have played crucial roles in creating varying African identities. Religion, for one, reinforces an individual's place in the world by linking present with past and future. Each of the so-called great religions—Judaism, Christianity, and Islam—did gain African converts, and frequently the choice of affiliation determined what people would be known as, in both their own eyes and those of others. Still, change was almost always possible, reflecting the nonexclusionary and nonmessianic traditions of indigenous African belief systems. Virtually everywhere on the continent, group boundaries, even religious ones, were flexible and permeable. The notion of rigid and unchanging "tribes" belongs to the minds of others; it is not evident in the actions of Africans.

There is also a quantitative side to the peopling story that informs us about where Africans chose to live. Trustworthy population totals and densities prior to the twentieth century are virtually nonexistent, and any that you see, including those in this book, must be treated with a great deal of caution. It is often possible, however, to make reasonable statements about relative distributions and densities, that is, to identify places supporting more people as compared to places supporting fewer. Once again, archeology provides a few clues, but inferences based on environment and economy can also yield useful information.

The third key word in the title is *Geographic*. It identifies the perspective of my profession, one imbued with notions about regions, spaces, and places. Together, these create maps, whether pictorial or mental. When using maps, scale is crucial. Taking a global view gives us the region of Africa that I have defined; it occupies a space different from, for instance, that of North or South America. Within Africa.itself, several macro regions, like northern and eastern, are generally recognized, and each of these can be divided into subregions of various types. The Sahel is an example, as is the Congo basin. Regions help us organize our maps, but they are abstractions. We impose them on the earth for convenience' sake. Places are something else. They are "real" in that they are defined by human experience. We were created as a species in certain places, and ever since then, places of all sorts have shaped and been shaped by us. Places encapsulate our interactions with nature and with one another, so their value is always relative. At any given time, places vary in what they mean to people and, therefore, in how attractive they are.

In the beginning, attractiveness was measured mainly by what the natural environment could supply for shelter, food, and water. Later, technological capabilities mattered, and their development changed how places came to be viewed, especially after agriculture replaced gathering and hunting as the primary means of subsistence. Variations in rainfall and soil quality now produced a much more varied map of population distribution. Occasionally other environmental features exerted strong influences. Of particular importance in Africa were places providing security from human aggressors, places free from some of the lethal diseases, especially malaria and sleeping sickness, and places where valuable minerals, such as iron ore and gold, could be mined.

The search for land and its valued resources fostered competition, which, in turn, kept populations on the move. The great spatial mobility of Africans will be a theme recurring throughout this book, and it introduces another important geographic consideration—routes. They channel populations, connecting regions and places with one another, and thus also become parts of maps.

At least three thousand years ago trade routes had begun altering the comparative value of places. In turn, trade fostered the development of more complex societies, and in several portions of the continent territorially expansive kingdoms and empires arose. Populations grew as never before, and towns and cities sprang into being. But trade has a fickle side, and when fortunes shifted, populations redistributed accordingly. Wars of competition erupted as elsewhere in the world, although it is unlikely that the numbers lost in battle approached the numbers associated with the outmigrations that usually ensued. In addition to causing shifts in numerical balances, migrations often led to wide-ranging ethnolinguistic changes.

The slave trade was of special significance to Africa. It began several thousand years ago and reached its apogee between the sixteenth and the middle of the nineteenth centuries. Very few places remained untouched; and in general, the slave trade ushered in an era of social volatility that had multifarious population outcomes. Numerous migrations changed the locations of peoples, and while some places were all but depopulated, others experienced significant numerical growth.

Finally we come to the word *Interpretation,* which is all that a book covering so much space and time can ever be. In essence, I am creating a narrative from what I know, and I want the narrative to be interesting, as well as informative. I have not lowered my scholarly standards in striving to intrigue readers. On the contrary, I have built my interpretation by scouring a vast literature in many academic disciplines, including biology, archeology, linguistics, history, anthropology, and demography, as well as geography. To keep the narrative flowing as smoothly as possible, I decided against employing either footnotes or in-text citations. Instead I have appended a Bibliographical Essay to the end of the book. Following a review of general sources comes a chapter-by-chapter listing of sources, so that readers can both identify key references and seek out additional readings.

As you read through the text you will notice the absence of individual people. I do not deny their importance in the shaping of larger events, but because most of this book deals with time before the advent of writing, the huge preponderance of actors are unknowable. To give recognition to those few whose names we are aware of—people who came along later and whose existence happens to have been recorded by someone—overstates their importance relative to the anonymous many who are responsible for the peopling of Africa.

I need to inform you about two other matters as well. First is the rather difficult problem of dates. With regard to long-ago times, for which precision is impossible, I will count from the present and, because there is no widely agreed-on format for abbreviations, simply give the time in years ago, as in "2 million years ago." This style will be maintained until we approach 3,000 years ago, when I will switch to the conventional B.C. and A.D. abbreviations; I will drop A.D. when the era is obvious. I realize that these designations have the force of cultural imperialism behind them, but I can find no satisfactory replacements. Most people, including me, still refer to the centuries as, for example, the eighteenth—a style based on the B.C. and A.D. dichotomy, and I doubt that this way of thinking will change anytime soon.

The second matter involves the spellings of places and peoples. Renditions are a morass of confusion, and to provide all of the variations would be unproductive. So I have had to make choices using accuracy, currency, and consistency as my primary guides.

PART ONE

BEGINNINGS

2

BECOMING HUMAN

Consensus holds that the hominid lineage—of which the subspecies that we chauvin-istically call *Homo sapiens sapiens* is the lone living representative—originated some-where along the eastern side of Africa between the Horn and the Transvaal. There is less agreement about the timing of the event. Not too long ago, the only available dates came from paleontology, and these suggested that the hominids diverged from their closest pongid or great ape relatives, the chimpanzee and gorilla, during mid-Miocene times—15 million years ago. In contrast, more recently available biochemical data indicate later dates: 8 million years ago for the split from gorillas and only 5 million years ago for the split from chimpanzees. Although the laboratory-derived findings have won increasing numbers of converts, full confirmation must await the unearthing of skeletal remains from the "great fossil gap"—the latter half of the Miocene and early Pliocene. To the misfortune of those who study hominid origins, the earth has yielded precious little to examine for that span of nearly 9 million years.

EVOLUTIONARY TRENDS

With the appearance of the australopithecines during the mid-Pliocene the great fossil gap reaches an abrupt end. First discovered in South Africa during the 1920s, the austra-lopithecines are now represented by a wide range of diverse skeletal parts, with eastern

11

Africa at center stage since the 1960s (map 2.1). From Hadar in Ethiopia come the famous Lucy and First Family. In conjunction with several hominids whose remains were unearthed at Laetoli in northern Tanzania, and possibly Middle Awash and Omo as well, Lucy and family make up the species known as *Australopithecus afarensis*. Although there is still a little uncertainty about dating, *A. afarensis* probably appeared no later than 3.9

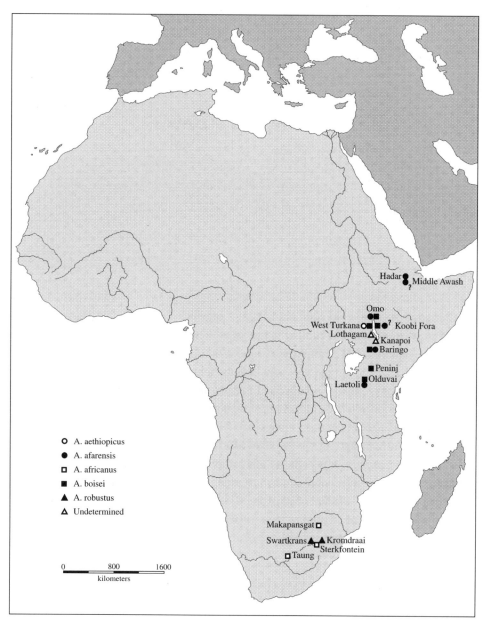

2.1 The first australopithecine fossils were discovered in South Africa, but since 1959, sites in Tanzania, Kenya, and Ethiopia have come to the fore.

million years ago. The dentition is distinctly apelike: the species has large canines, a massive face, and a brain the average size of a gorilla's (415 cubic centimeters). Considerable sexual dimorphism is detected, with adult males up to 1.7 meters in height and 68 kilograms in weight existing side by side with adult females no more than 1.0 meter in height and 33 kilograms in weight. Still, postcranial remains and the remarkable footprints preserved in the volcanic ash at Laetoli show that *A. afarensis* possessed one distinctive non-apelike characteristic. It was bipedal, at least part of the time.

After *A. afarensis* the hominid picture becomes more complex. A possible descendant is *A. africanus,* whose remains date back 3–2.5 million years and show some progress in the human direction. Although possessed of a marginally larger brain (mean size, 440 cubic centimeters) than *A. afarensis,* specimens have the considerably smaller cheek teeth associated with a less massive and protruding face. The beginnings of a forehead can be seen, and sexual dimorphism is not as marked. We cannot be sure of a lineal relationship, however, because the two species have never been found in proximity. Indeed, they are separated by thousands of kilometers, with *A. afarensis* so far confined to eastern Africa and fully confirmed specimens of *A. africanus* restricted to the three sites of Taung, Sterkfontein, and Makapansgat in the Transvaal of South Africa.

So-called robust australopithecines struck out in a different evolutionary direction. The oldest specimen thus far recorded, known as the Black Skull and designated by some as *A. aethiopicus,* was found a few kilometers west of Lake Turkana in sediments dating back 2.5 million years. The braincase measures only 410 cubic centimeters, and in general the skull and face exhibit extremely "primitive" characteristics. Especially noteworthy are the lack of a forehead and the presence of a saggital crest for attaching what must have been huge jaw muscles, given the enormous root size of the grinding molars. The type represented by the Black Skull is a likely ancestral candidate for *A. boisei,* found at several sites in eastern Africa—including Olduvai Gorge, where the famous Nutcracker Man was discovered in 1959. Currently available dates put *A. boisei* between 1.8 and 1.4 million years ago, and there is some speculation that the span may have to be extended forward. A comparison with *A. aethiopicus* shows an expanded cranial capacity—a mean of 520 cubic centimeters—and some diminution of facial features.

Similar finds from Kromdraai and Swartkrans in South Africa are thought to date from 2–1 million years ago. They show quite a few similarities to *A. boisei* but are usually given their own species category, *A. robustus.*

All the accumulated evidence supports the view that these robust australopithecines stood at evolutionary dead ends. They left no living descendants, and their parentage remains a mystery. It is possible that *A. afarensis* is ancestral to *A. aethiopicus,* but both could have an unknown ancestor in common. A candidate is the owner of the australopithecine-like molars found at Baringo and Lothagam in Kenya that are 6.5 to 5 million years old. Or perhaps there were two *A. afarensis* subspecies, one leading to *A. africanus* and the other heading in the robust direction. Minimally, *A. afarensis* lasted for 0.9 million years, and more than one branching could have taken place.

13

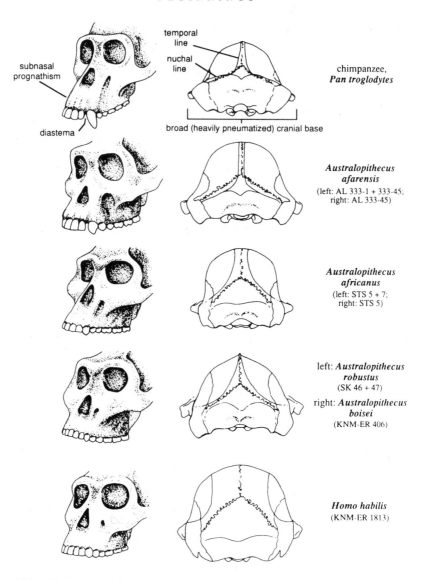

subnasal
prognathism

temporal
line

nuchal
line

chimpanzee,
Pan troglodytes

diastema

broad (heavily pneumatized) cranial base

*Australopithecus
afarensis*
(left: AL 333-1 + 333-45;
right: AL 333-45)

*Australopithecus
africanus*
(left: STS 5 + 7;
right: STS 5)

left: *Australopithecus
robustus*
(SK 46 + 47)

right: *Australopithecus
boisei*
(KNM-ER 406)

Homo habilis
(KNM-ER 1813)

Although *Australopithecus afarensis* could walk upright, its facial and cranial characteristics resembled those of chimpanzees. Continuing evolution in the direction of *Homo habilis* produced a shortening of the face in conjunction with smaller cheek teeth and an enlargement and rounding of the cranium. (Reprinted from Richard G. Klein, *The Human Career: Human Biological and Cultural Origins,* University of Chicago Press, 1989, p. 144.)

Overlapping in time and space with the later australopithecines were other hominids categorized within the genus *Homo.* The oldest is termed *H. habilis,* the remains of which have been found at a number of sites in eastern Africa (map 2.2). Dentition and face were more humanlike, and cranial capacity had grown to 630 cubic centimeters or so, while the

The first australopithecine from eastern Africa was discovered at Olduvai Gorge in 1959. Since then the site has yielded a number of other finds critical to understanding the course of hominid evolution. (Photo by author.)

rest of the skeleton looks much like an australopithecine's. Assigned dates generally go back 2 million years or slightly less, although a recent reevaluation of a skull fragment from Lake Baringo has determined an age of nearly 2.5 million years.

Following in the evolutionary sequence is *Homo erectus,* with the Koobi Fora dates of 1.8–1.3 million years being the oldest on record. A few hundred thousand years later, sites become numerous, and we can see that *H. erectus* occupied an area from Morocco through eastern Africa to South Africa. In dental morphology and craniofacial features *H. erectus* exhibits major advances toward modern human appearance. Brain size averaged between 800 and 900 cubic centimeters for early representatives and nearly 1,100 cubic centimeters for later ones, and the postcranial skeleton reached essentially modern form. Some adult males may have been over 1.8 meters—nearly six feet— tall. Nevertheless, *H. erectus* still had a massive and protruding brow ridge, only the barest sign of a forehead, marked prognathism (that is, a jutting jaw), and no chin.

Although most family trees presuppose a line of descent from *A. africanus* through *H. habilis* to *H. erectus,* several problems make the connections highly tenuous. One is familiar —that of spatial discontinuity. As with *A. afarensis,* no *H. habilis* has been found in southern Africa. Another problem is the considerable variability of *H. habilis,* suggesting that more than one species might be included among the remains. Third, the evolutionary leap from *H. habilis* to *H. erectus* is a large one, much larger than that from *A. africanus* to *H. habilis.* Not only brain size but also growth trends show substantial differences. Whereas *H. erectus* displays the distinctively humanlike tendency of delayed maturation, *H. habilis*

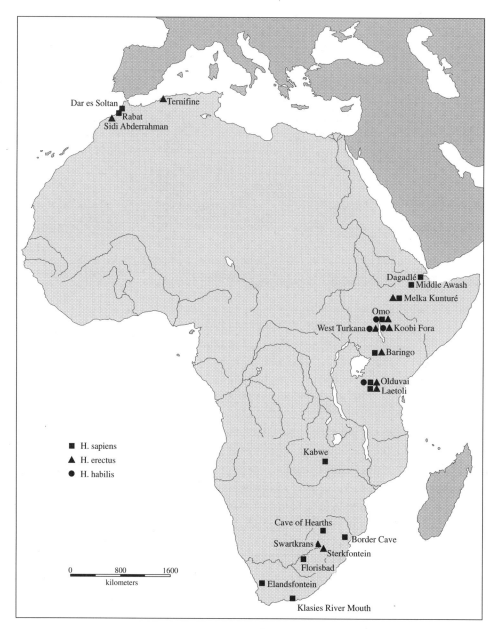

Dar es Soltan ▲Ternifine
Rabat
Sidi Abderrahman

Dagadlé■
■ Middle Awash
▲■ Melka Kunturé
Omo
●■▲
West Turkana●▲ ●▲ ▲Koobi Fora
■▲Baringo
●■▲Olduvai
■▲Laetoli

■ H. sapiens
▲ H. erectus
● H. habilis

Kabwe
■

Cave of Hearths
■
Swartkrans ▲ ■ Border Cave
■Sterkfontein
Florisbad
■ Elandsfontein
■
Klasies River Mouth

0   800   1600
kilometers

2.2 The fossil record indicates that the transition from *Homo habilis* to *Homo erectus* probably took place in eastern Africa, whereas *Homo sapiens* may have arisen at the very southern tip of the continent.

evidently took the much more rapid developmental path characteristic of apes. Finally, at Omo there is a complicating overlap of the two species 1.5 million years ago, which implies that some *H. habilis* evolved into *H. erectus* while others remained as they were.

Given all this uncertainty, we could plausibly make *H. habilis* an advanced australopithecine and produce a sequence leading from *A. afarensis* through *A. africanus* to *A. habilis*. The change leaves the ancestor of *H. erectus* undetermined, and thus in violation of the current sense of parsimony, but it is important to understand that the data one can muster to support a particular evolutionary scheme are meager at best. At the moment, conclusions about human origins rest as much on opinion as on fact, and the history of paleoanthropology amply demonstrates how personalities and careerism can supersede what the data reasonably allow.

No matter who the immediate ancestor may have been, *H. erectus* was a huge success. All other African hominids eventually disappeared, and the human geographic range was extended northward into Europe and eastward as far as China and Indonesia. If the date of 1.6 million years ago for a jawbone discovered near Tblisi, Georgia, and the even older date of 1.8 million years ago for finds in Java prove correct, this out-of-Africa dispersal must have taken place much earlier and much more rapidly than the usual estimate putting it between 1 million and 500,000 years ago. And there is a more radical hypothesis to contemplate: that *H. erectus* originated in Asia rather than Africa. Only further discoveries will tell which version is closer to the truth.

In a reversal of previous spatial and temporal directions, convention has held that the appearance of *Homo sapiens* in Africa, especially south of the Sahara, was late relative to its appearance in Europe and Asia. To some extent this view can be explained by the location of the first fossils discovered, but it rests primarily on long-held Eurocentric and Asiacentric biases. Where else could *H. sapiens* have arisen other than in a presumed hearth of "civilization"? An array of evidence has now invited a reconsideration of the question, and Africa is once again moving to center stage.

The transition from *H. erectus* seems to have been very gradual. Craniofacial characteristics, especially brain size (usually put at 1,400 cubic centimeters or so), are used to differentiate *H. erectus* from *H. sapiens*, although no sharp dividing line can readily be drawn. A variety of skull parts indicative of larger brains, dating back perhaps as far as 400,000 to 150,000 years, have been unearthed from sites in southern, eastern, and northern Africa. The most famous specimen is Rhodesian Man from Kabwe (formerly Broken Hill) in Zambia, which, along with others of its type, is often considered representative of an archaic *H. sapiens*.

A direct line from the archaic type to modern *H. sapiens sapiens* is apparent south of the Sahara. According to finds spread from Klasies River Mouth and Border Cave in South Africa to Laetoli in Tanzania and Omo in Ethiopia, modern *H. sapiens* may have existed as long as 150,000 to 100,000 years ago. This is a much earlier date than those recorded so far in Europe and Asia, and attention has therefore shifted to Africa as the likely home of modern *H. sapiens*. Giving greater credence to this interpretation are mitochondrial DNA data that connect all contemporary humans to an African source within the same general time frame, although, contrary to a widely publicized report, no specific "Eve" can, or likely will, be pinpointed.

In northern Africa the picture is complicated by the possible presence of some Neanderthals, whose origins and placement within the human lineage continue to be hotly debated. Neanderthals are best considered a regional branch of the evolving *H. sapiens* line and thus deserving of the designation *H. sapiens neanderthalensis* as opposed to being classified as a totally separate species. That is, they are another of the several archaic *Homo* types. If Neanderthals did extend into northern Africa, they would have been at the extreme southwestern margin of their distribution, and, in fact, the few skeletal remains from the region indicate the presence of the modern human type, *H. sapiens sapiens,* 90,000 years ago. In any event, by 35,000 years ago distinct Neanderthals had disappeared throughout their former range. They were either absorbed or displaced by expanding *H. sapiens sapiens* populations.

Although hominids can be differentiated on the basis of a set of anatomical characteristics, the real measure of humanity is the possession of culture, that unique ability to communicate a patterned set of values and behaviors and then to modify and build on them as circumstances demand. Indeed, it is precisely the capacity to adapt that separates cultural behavior from the routinized behavior of other social animals, which are dependent on their genetic heritages and therefore largely at the mercy of environmental forces. Culture, on the other hand, allows the shaping of both genes and the environment, creating an interaction across space and time that ultimately makes environment, biology, and culture inseparable. Still, we must go back to the paleoenvironment, and particularly to changes in it, to see how humanity had its African start.

PRECULTURAL ORIGINS

The Miocene is the critical period for hominid beginnings. At its outset 23 million years ago, much of intertropical Eurasia and Africa was covered by lush forests inhabited by numerous species of arboreal primates, most classified as hominoids. Their relations are with modern African apes rather than monkeys, whose ancestors had already departed on other evolutionary pathways. The data are still too fragmentary to sort out who gave rise to whom, but one variety, going by the name Proconsul, which lived in what is now the Lake Victoria Basin 18 million years ago, might be a candidate for inclusion on the main hominid branch. A possible successor is the type labeled *Kenyapithecus,* represented by several specimens from the same general area as Proconsul and dated back 14–12 million years.

By mid-Miocene times (16–15 million years ago), the global climate had become cooler and drier; as a result, the dense forests retreated in favor of woodland and other areas of more open vegetation, creating a complex mosaic of habitats throughout eastern and southern Africa. Later developments prove that the hominoids responded to these changes, but after Kenyapithecus we reach the heart of the great fossil gap and cannot trace the hominid branchings.

Still, a few matters related to these later developments are worth speculating about. The

During the early Miocene, dense rain forests covered much of tropical Africa. The onset of cooler and drier climatic conditions led to the establishment of more open vegetative habitats that supported the rise of the hominids. (Photo courtesy of Philip W. Porter.)

new habitats provided environmental niches containing a variety of foodstuffs, including animals, and hominoids with omnivorous feeding habits would have been favored over those whose diets were more restricted. Strong selective pressures were clearly operative: by mid-Pliocene times, when the fossil record can be read again, the number of hominoids had declined considerably.

Proto-australopithecines, whatever their kinship with later *Homo* species, probably lived in small groups at ecotones, using the cover of forests and woodlands for protection upon return from foraging expeditions in more open country. In all likelihood, the key anatomical adaptation to such foraging was an increasingly upright posture. With the forelimbs freed from the requirements of locomotion, more food could be carried back to the safer forest and woodland abodes. Standing upright would also have aided in viewing things far away, and evidence indicates that bipedalism is more energy-efficient than quadrupedalism for traversing long distances. Some scientists even suggest that bipedalism fostered pair bonding and the evolution of human sexuality, including the unique loss of female estrus, although this conclusion may be stretching the data a bit too far. In any event, cooperation among group members would have facilitated the food search, as well as provided for greater protection; and the more involved the cooperation became, the more valuable intelligence would have been. The seeds of an evolutionary relation between upright posture, social interaction, and brain size had thus been planted; they would bear fruit in *Homo*.

Still, the combination had advanced enough among australopithecines to allow them to expand their geographic range. Lake basins and river valleys within open, savannalike country seem to have been the preferred habitats; there, groups could find water, shade, fruit trees, and soft sand to sit and sleep on. They do not seem to have occupied caves and rock shelters, but Olduvai Gorge contains evidence suggesting that later australopithecines may have put up windbreaks and other crude shelters. A good guess is that hilltops were also frequently used habitation sites. They would have provided excellent vantage points for spotting game and predators. Unfortunately, the unlikelihood of preservation augurs against such sites ever being discovered.

No matter where situated, the camps must have been temporary. Reoccupation of favorite places on a seasonal basis undoubtedly occurred, but groups could not tarry anywhere for fear of attracting the attention of predators, particularly hyenas and big cats. The use of fire was still a long way off, and sticks and stones would have been the only weapons that the earliest australopithecines had at their disposal.

Diet is the factor that best explains the differences between the two basic australopithecine types. The robust varieties, with their massive jaws and grinding-style molars, must have been predominantly, if not exclusively, vegetarians. This specialization is one reason why they overlapped in space and time for so long with *Homo*. For the most part, the two were not in direct competition. In contrast, the more gracile forms, like *Homo,* were

Before the development of more advanced hunting technologies, humans scavenged for much of the meat in their diets. An important source would have been the bone marrow that remained after other scavengers had picked carcasses clean. (Photo by author.)

20

omnivorous and hence competed for the same foods. The lack of technology severely limited australopithecines' ability to hunt, although they may have captured rodents, lizards, and other small animals as chimpanzees and baboons have been observed to do. In all probability, scavenging the leftovers of predator kills was a more common activity. Other scavengers would have taken most of the meat, but by breaking open the bones, marrow could be had.

The growing importance of meat and marrow in the diet appears to have been crucial to hominid evolution. Not only did dentition and therefore the shape of the skull change—the face became less prognathous—but the brain also enlarged. Part of the explanation undoubtedly relates to the need for enhanced tracking abilities, particularly given the rather poor hominid sense of smell. Visual acuity and cunning defined success. Social cooperation would likely have made advances; perhaps an incipient division of labor between the sexes even existed. Finally, because meat and marrow are nutrient-rich and energy-dense sources of food, those hominids who added them to their diet could be relieved of the necessity of continually searching for food, as apes do. Time for other activities was available, bringing a freedom that unleased the potential for culture. And with culture, hominids reached the stage of becoming fully human.

POSTSCRIPT. Discoveries near Lake Turkana have revealed a likely ancestor to *A. afarensis*. Called *A. anamensis,* they have been dated to between 3.9–4.2 million years ago. How the 4.4 million year old finds from Hadar, now called *Ardipithecus ramidus,* fit into the hominid picture is uncertain.

3

CULTURAL ORIGINS

Although culture is much more than its material conditions, tools are about all that remain as testimony to how and where our ancestors lived. Because the debris at several australopithecine sites in South Africa contained fragmented animal parts, some paleo-anthropologists have concluded that the first tools were made from osteodontokeratic (bone, tooth, horn) resources. We can reasonably infer that even *A. afarensis* picked up such objects to use in a toollike manner, but the crucial cultural issue is manufacture. That the animal parts were selected and shaped for specific uses has not been demonstrated; in fact, the fragments are now generally thought to be leftovers, dragged to caches by porcupines, from kills by hyenas, leopards, and other predators. Convenient pieces of wood were undoubtedly used as well, but time and the elements have prevented their preservation. Consequently, work in stone must do for information about human cultural beginnings.

In European archeology the conventionally recognized eras are Lower Paleolithic, Middle Paleolithic, Upper Paleolithic, and Mesolithic, which are closely tied to Pleistocene glacial and interglacial periods. The eras were initially applied to Africa, where the oscillation was between pluvial (wet) and interpluvial (dry) phases. Connections between climatic events on the two continents existed, but the sequences of local changes are far more complex than people originally realized. Consequently, to avoid confusion and correlational errors, most Africanists now use the divisions Old Stone Age, Middle Stone

Age, and Late Stone Age and do not concern themselves about linkages to Europe. Furthermore, these divisions are employed more to label general toolmaking traditions than to specify a necessary chronological sequence.

THE OLD STONE AGE

The first clearly recognizable stone tools have been given the name Oldowan after the eponymous site of Olduvai Gorge. Other discoveries have been made elsewhere in eastern Africa, as well as in the Maghrib and along the Nile valley. Their oldest date so far is 2.5– 2.6 million years ago from the Gona River valley in Ethiopia. The main implements constituting the industry are crudely hewn choppers, apparently used for stripping meat from bones. Often accompanying them are various polyhedrons, discoids, and scrapers, whose functions are more problematic. All the tools fit comfortably in the hand and were made by striking off a few flakes from any convenient stone core. The Oldowan tool kit shows considerable spatial and temporal uniformity because of its technological simplicity. Most of the minor variations noted by specialists are best explained by the differing raw materials and the sizes and shapes of the original cores. Interestingly, the striking angles

The Oldowan tool kit is exclusively African and the oldest one on record. It consists of crudely hewn choppers, discoids, scrapers, and polyhedrons that show little spatial or temporal stylistic variation. (Photo courtesy of Andrew Hill.)

23

indicate that the fashioners of the tools were predominantly right-handed, implying significant brain lateralization as an early human trait.

Succeeding the Oldowan industry around 1.5 million years ago was the Developed Oldowan, which is characterized by the first bifacial tools and a more diverse array of flakes. At Koobi Fora a variant on the Developed Oldowan theme known as Karari has been identified. Its distinctive core scrapers and lack of discoids indicate at least a minor degree of regional toolmaking specialization. Both Oldowan and Developed Oldowan tools were uniquely African. No examples have been found elsewhere, although some of the early chopper and core industries of Europe and Asia could be their descendants.

Slightly less than 1.5 million years ago, Acheulian tools made their appearance, establishing a tradition that lasted until 200,000–100,000 years ago. Characterizing the kit is increasing functional differentiation; the most distinctive implements are multipurpose hand axes and cleavers, which replication experiments have shown to be quite effective for butchering animals, even large ones. Their abundance and advance over Oldowan choppers lend support to the skeletal evidence pointing to the important role played by meat eating in the formative phases of human cultural development.

Acheulian sites are scattered over a large portion of Africa, extending from the Maghrib to the Cape of Good Hope (map 3.1). They are correlated with semiarid and subhumid savanna and open woodland environments, and the settlements cluster around sources of water, whether coastal, riverine, lacustrine, or artesian. In western Africa, Acheulian tools

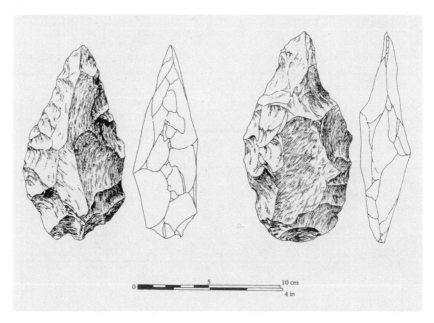

The Acheulian tool kit featured hand axes and cleavers. Its *Homo erectus* fashioners had spread beyond Africa into Europe and Asia. (Reprinted from Kathy D. Schick and Nicholas Toth, *Making Silent Stones Speak: Human Evolution and the Dawn of Technology,* Simon and Schuster, 1993, p. 232.)

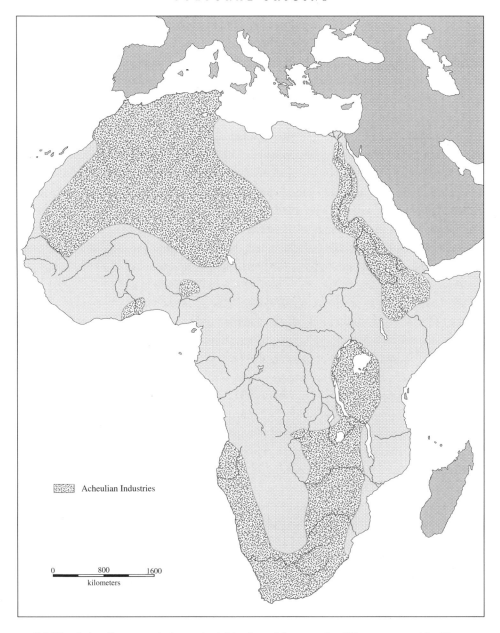

3.1 The Acheulian stone industry in Africa lasted for over 1 million years, and its *Homo erectus* makers seem to have preferred open vegetative habitats.

have been discovered along the Volta River in Ghana and on the Jos Plateau in Nigeria; in both areas, however, dating has been next to impossible. Apparently the toolmakers did not invade tropical rain forest habitats until near the very end of the Acheulian time span. In spite of vegetative luxuriance, tropical forests have a low edible plant biomass, and meat would have been scarce as well. Although birds and monkeys abound, they live high in the canopy and thus are mostly inaccessible to people. In addition, many of the larger ground-dwelling animals lead solitary and widely dispersed lives, while small mammals, such as rodents, are hard to spot in the diffuse, highly shaded light. If some people did manage to penetrate the rain forests during earlier times, we will probably never find their traces because of the destruction wrought by high humidity and acid soils.

The Acheulian tool kit was almost as conservative as the Oldowan for virtually all of its tenure. Toward the end, however, two distinct regional variants can be detected. The Fauresmith tools continued in the tradition of savanna dwellers, while the Sangoan has been found mostly in more heavily wooded areas (map 3.2). The short and wide Sangoan tools look crude next to those of the Fauresmith, but crudity does not necessarily imply technological retrogression. With trees as an abundant source of raw materials in many Sangoan habitats, at least some of the stone tools were probably used for making finer wood implements, which have not endured. More important, the Sangoan kit demonstrates that humans were no longer inhabitants mainly—or exclusively—of savanna-type country.

Unlike the Oldowan and Developed Oldowan, the Acheulian did not remain confined to Africa. The tool type spread throughout much of Europe—the name Acheulian comes from the site of Saint Acheul in France—although no dates earlier than 700,000 years ago have been recorded. The Acheulian can also be found as far east as India, where it may have been present more than 1 million years ago. If this still-tentative date is accurate, then a substantial reinterpretation of the diffusion of the Acheulian and its makers will be required.

An "advanced" Acheulian technique known as the Levallois appears at later Old Stone Age sites from the Nile valley southward into the highlands of Ethiopia. The simple but more standardized flakes of all shapes and sizes suggest that the artisans were employing a greater degree of calculation with regard to the functions and shapes of their finished products. Can we take standardization as a clue of more evolved hominid conceptual abilities, perhaps those of *H. sapiens?*

This brings us to the issue of who created the various tool industries. The most widely held opinion is that all were made by *Homo* and not by any of the australopithecines. Indeed, for many paleoanthropologists it is the appearance of tools that marks the emergence of *Homo* as a genus. They give *H. habilis* credit for the Oldowan and possibly the Developed Oldowan, and *H. erectus* credit for the Acheulian.

Still, we should not be so quick to dismiss the australopithecines. In at least a few instances, most notably cases involving robust varieties at Olduvai Gorge, their remains have been found in close enough proximity to Oldowan tools to warrant considering them the makers. True, *Homo* specimens have been located nearby, but attributing the creation of the tools to them may be nothing more than a "man the tool maker" bias (to borrow from the title of a once prominent book) intruding itself on the data. In fact, an ability to make tools might help explain why the robust australopithecines survived as long as they did. Of some significance in this regard is the rather abrupt appearance of the Acheulian industry at

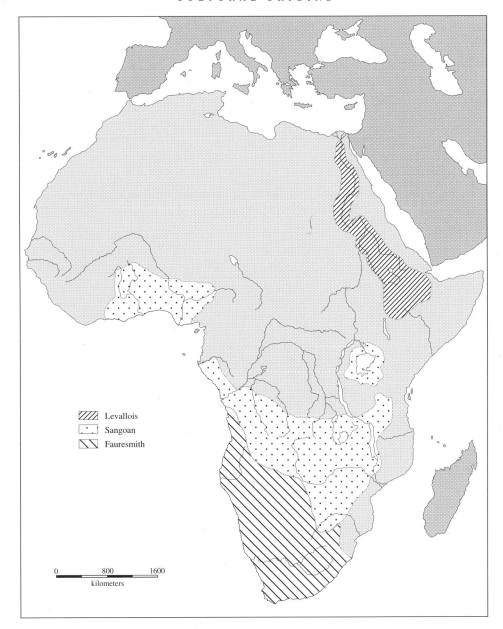

3.2 Three variants of the late African Acheulian indicate a speeding-up of cultural evolution and the extension of humans into wooded environments.

Olduvai Gorge. There are no signs of its having developed from the existing Oldowan industry, and the two types existed side by side for thousands of years. Similarly, at Koobi Fora the Karari tradition extends into Acheulian time for several hundred thousand years.

The Old Stone Age was a time of very slow cultural change, including little advance in the technologies for procuring food. Hunting efficiency may have improved slightly, but the tool kits imply a continued reliance on scavenging for animal foods. Overall, there is little doubt that gathering fruits and vegetables provided for most of people's dietary needs. As a result, population numbers do not seem to have increased to any appreciable extent, and they probably waxed and waned with climatic conditions. Little in the way of distributional change occurred until near the very end of the Acheulian period, when wooded habitats were settled and caves were occupied, at least on a temporary basis. Carbonized remains at the Cave of Hearths point to the making of fire, and the lack of carbonization at other later Acheulian sites may once again be a function of the difficulties associated with preservation in the tropics.

Qualitatively, population events proved far more dramatic than toolmaking events, for relatively early in the Old Stone Age *Homo* achieved ascendance over the remaining australopithecines. There is no evidence of hostile replacement; instead, competitive exclusion probably best explains what happened. Being more thoroughly omnivorous, *H. erectus* was a more efficient user of food resources and, therefore, superior at reproducing its kind. Whether language was important beyond simple forms of communication will never be known with complete certainty.

THE MIDDLE STONE AGE

Characteristic Middle Stone Age industries are defined by prepared cores and retouched flakes. These appear earlier than 100,000 years ago and may go as far back as 200,000 years in South Africa; with a few exceptions, they stopped being made 35,000 years ago. The Middle Stone Age also had distinctive regional industries, which probably mirror other cultural changes (map 3.3).

One such regional industry is the Mousterian of northern Africa. Part of the wider Mousterian of southwestern Asia and Europe, it seems to have accompanied a westward migration of its makers. After the Mousterian came the Aterian, the tools of which have been found in the Maghrib and throughout much of the Sahara. During most of Aterian time, the Saharan region was far less arid than it is today and thus more suited to human occupancy. It contained numerous lakes and swamps and supported a rich faunal assemblage, including the rhinoceros, hippopotamus, elephant, buffalo, warthog, crocodile, gazelle, and zebra. By persisting until severe aridity returned 20,000 years ago to reestablish desert conditions, the Aterian constitutes a major exception to the Middle Stone Age temporal rule.

South of the Sahara, toolmaking styles reflect the locational differences established during the Old Stone Age. The Stillbay label applies to a variety of savanna-based light flake industries, whereas Lupemban encompasses heavy core tools associated with woodland habitats. Variations within each industry can be detected, but these are best seen as resulting from differences in raw materials and subsistence strategies. Between 100,000 and 80,000 years ago considerable habitat modification took place as glaciers once again

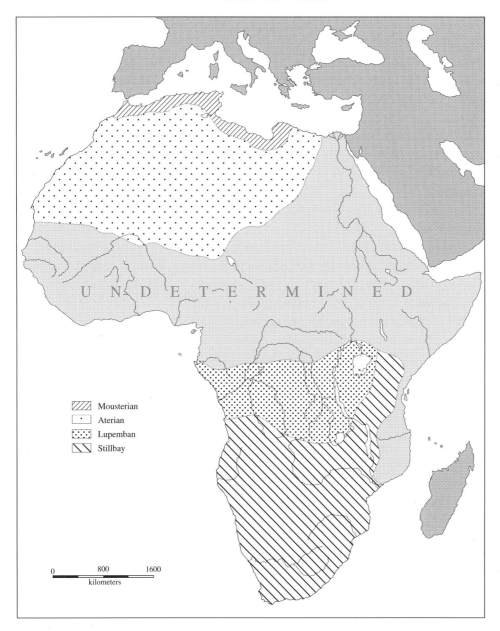

3.3 The African Middle Stone Age was characterized by the emergence of regionally distinctive toolmaking traditions.

moved southward in Eurasia and North America. As sea levels declined, African climatic conditions generally became drier, causing forests to retreat and fauna to change.

Cultural trends in western Africa are poorly known. Developments seem to have derived from the Sangoan in many areas, but almost no dates are available. As might be expected, the interior beyond the woodlands has yielded some signs of Aterian influences. The highlands and the arid plateaus of Ethiopia and the Horn were definitely occupied, but once again details are lacking.

Although the transition from *H. erectus* to *H. sapiens* started during the later phases of the Old Stone Age, it was not completed until the Middle Stone Age. In southern Africa the Rhodesian types have been found in association with the Stillbay and with several of the South African flake industries, whereas in the Maghrib the existence of Mousterian tools is the reason that some analysts infer the presence of Neanderthals. The makers of the Aterian tool kit remain a mystery, but given the timing, the most feasible candidate is *H. sapiens sapiens*.

The ability to hunt improved in the Middle Stone Age, as we can see from the bones of hares, warthogs, wild asses, cattle, Barbary sheep, and antelopes that have been unearthed, but tracking the likes of the elephant, rhinoceros, giant buffalo, and bush pig was probably still too dangerous an activity. Remains along the coastal areas of both northern and southern Africa show a considerable use of sea foods, particularly mollusks. Evidence for fishing is sparse, however; the necessary technologies apparently had yet to be developed.

Besides further movement into wooded and forested habitats and greater occupancy of caves and rock shelters, population distribution patterns remained much as before. Ecotones were the preferred settlement sites, and camp sizes did not depart from the long

Although when home bases first arose remains in doubt, they were an important part of human development during the Stone Age. They not only provided physical protection for band members but also served vital social functions. (Photo by author.)

established range of thirty to fifty persons. Favored sites may been occupied for longer periods of time, and some may have served as home bases. Such bases are characteristic of contemporary gatherer-hunters and provide congregation points for a variety of social activities, including sharing food, contracting marriages, and passing on information.

Overall, population grew imperceptibly as periods of expansion and decline tied to climatic fluctuations succeeded one another. A nadir was reached 50,000–40,000 years ago, when hyperaridity became widespread, but even during more buoyant times, humans remained a rather insignificant part of the biotic landscape, with most people dying young. What evidence can be gleaned from skeletons suggests that many environmental hazards and accidents took their toll, and very few individuals could have lived past the age of forty.

Layers of ash and carbonized materials indicate that meat was dried, an important process for both diet and trade. In general, fire was more widely used for food preparation than before, and it provided requisite warmth and protection. Remains of hematite, ocher, and manganese bespeak painting, probably of the body, as well as of weapons and utensils, but there are no rock paintings such as exist at Mousterian sites in Europe. The pace of technological and cultural change definitely quickened during the Middle Stone Age, but it looks slow next to what was about to come.

THE LATE STONE AGE

Microliths and increasingly specialized economies signify the arrival of the Late Stone Age. The microliths were made using refined techniques designed to produce tools for a broad array of tasks: awls, burins, scrapers of various kinds, needles, punches, and points for arrows and harpoons, which were more often hafted than not. Finer work was done in chert and obsidian, whereas granite provided the raw material for cruder tools. Besides stone tools, dry cave sites have yielded wooden arrow shafts, digging sticks, and pegs. Bark trays were made, leather bags were sewed, leaves were used as wrappings, and, significantly, toward the end of the period, pottery was fired. Once considered a manufacture of food-producing societies only, pottery is now viewed by more and more paleoanthropologists as an independent development that preceded crop and animal husbandry in many places. Late Stone Age burial sites suggest concern about an afterlife, and artwork flourished, especially rock paintings and engravings. Barely perceptible during the Middle Stone Age, regional lithic diversity multiplied.

The Mediterranean littoral from Morocco to Tunisia was home to a tradition known as the Iberomaurusian, which spanned a time between 22,000 and 9,500 years ago (map 3.4). It does not seem to follow from either the Mousterian or the Aterian. Digging sticks have been identified, and grindstones attest to the processing of gathered grains into food or pigments. Marine resources, including fish, were exploited, but no nets or boats have yet been found. Skulls exhibit the medical practice of treppaning, as well as purposeful dental mutilations. Personal art (such as jewelry) and mural art are missing.

Farther inland and at living sites in a variety of habitats, including desert margins, lake

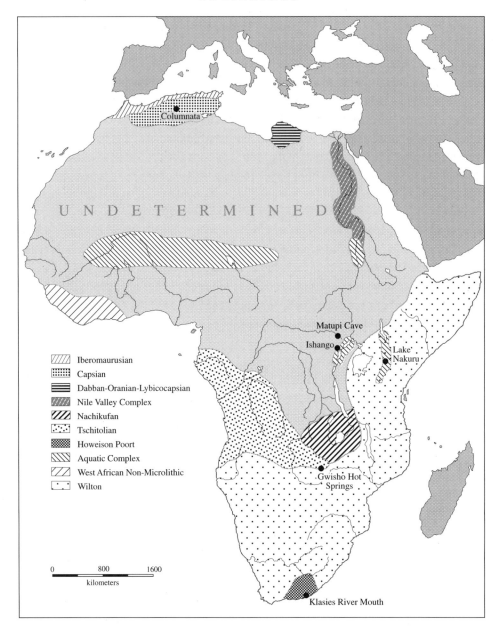

3.4 The plethora of Late Stone Age industries in Africa shows *Homo sapiens sapiens* adapting to a wide array of different environments.

shores, savannas, and mountain parklands, one finds evidence of the Capsian industry. It flourished between 10,000 and 6,000 years ago, and by all indications, communities were both larger and more sedentary than before. Plant foods played the major role in Capsian diets, while just a few species, notably Barbary sheep and large bovids, were the targets of hunters. Of far greater food importance were land mollusks, as we can judge from the huge middens left behind. Pottery and numerous small art forms in stone and ostrich egg shells have been found. Some rock paintings appear to date from this time, and an impressive funeral monument at Columnata in Algeria has been assigned to the Capsian.

A more localized industry, known as the Dabban, arose in Cyrenaica perhaps as early as 40,000 years ago. It lasted for 26,000 years and, like the Iberomaurusian, exhibits no earlier cultural connections. Its successor was the Oranian, which does show some Ibero-maurusian affinities. Then, 4,000 years later, a Capsian derivative called the Libycocapsian appeared on the scene. It continued the trends of manufacturing diverse and refined tools, using plant foods more intensively, and having a greater degree of settlement stability.

Between 20,000 and 12,000 years ago the Sahara was very arid and largely depopulated, except in highland retreats such as the Aïr where there were springs and surface pools fed by large aquifers. Even today, the reliable water supply in the Aïr supports relict populations of mouflons, ostriches, baboons, and monkeys. So few and widely spaced were inhabitable sites that the Late Stone Age did not occur in the Sahara until gatherers and fishers reoccupied the shores along replenished lakes, streams, and swamps 10,000 years ago. The new inhabitants made pottery, but the techniques show neither Aterian nor Capsian influences.

Largely because annual floods destroyed or buried most post-Acheulian materials downstream from Luxor, the Nile valley presents an incomplete Late Stone Age picture. Indications are that a growing population included a plethora of communities that followed rather conservative technological traditions. The river level was higher than it is today, a larger floodplain existed, and most of the time the adjacent countryside had a more semiarid than desertlike climate. Even in years with poor rainfall, food resources would have been fairly plentiful, so older technologies seem to have generally sufficed. Still, the communities in Upper Egypt and Nubia were changing, as is evident in the use of grind-stones and flat-bladed implements, whose glossy edges indicate their possible employment in cutting wild grains. Fish were important foods, and the abundance of debris suggests an increasing population, although signs of permanent settlements are lacking.

South of the Sahara five well-established toolmaking traditions are widely recognized. The makers do not appear to have been in close contact with one another, so the assumption is that developments were largely independent. This view could be modified, however, as researchers refine procedures and fill in the gaps in poorly known traditions.

Nachikufan tools have been found in open woodland and savanna country between Lakes Mweru and Bangweulu and the headwaters of the Zambezi River. Although highly localized, the tradition had considerable durability, dating back 17,000 years and lasting to as late as A.D. 1000 in a few locales. Farther west, in what is now northeastern Angola and adjacent Zaire, was the Tschitolian industry. With only minor modifications, it carried on the large-core tradition of the Sangoan and Lupemban from 13,000 to 2,000 years ago. In the Congo basin proper, only a few crude chopping tools have been located and, therefore, nothing conclusive can be said about cultural affinities. On the margins of the basin, however, just to the southwest of Lake Edward, is Matupi Cave. It was occupied for a very long span of time and contains tools with microlithic tendencies dating possibly as far back as 50,000 years.

Even earlier microlithic trends have been found at Klasies River Mouth and several other South African sites. The tools in this Howeison Poort industry are at least 50,000 and maybe as much as 100,000 years old. It is tempting to attribute their manufacture to the

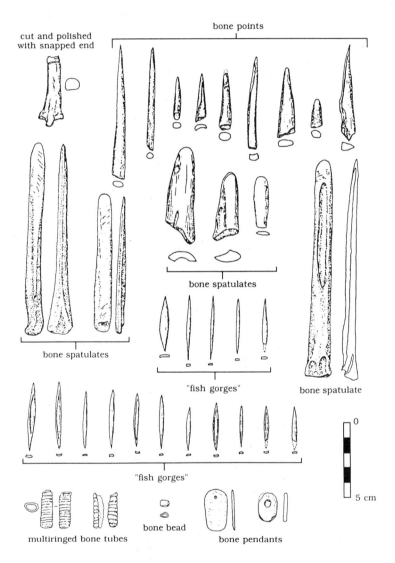

The microlithic tools from a Late Stone Age site in South Africa show considerable refinement and specialization for hunting and fishing. (Reprinted from Richard G. Klein, *The Human Career: Human Biological and Cultural Origins,* University of Chicago Press, 1989, p. 377.)

early *H. sapiens sapiens* from the same area, although so far the two have not been found in association. After the Howeison Poort period there was a temporary return to Middle Stone Age blade traditions. This could signify either the adaptation of toolmaking strategies to changing environmental conditions or the northward migration of the Howeison Poort makers.

Is there a connection between Howeison Poort, Matupi Cave, and Dabban industries? Did Late Stone Age traditions and *Homo sapiens sapiens* accompany one another on a northerly migration? Although such an interpretation is more than the available evidence will support, the possibility is tempting to contemplate.

The Wilton is the most widespread Late Stone Age industry on the continent. First appearing 8,000 years ago in the river valleys and along the coast of south-central Africa, it was later carried onto the plateau lands as far away as Ethiopia and the Horn. The many sites and spatial range indicate a rapidly expanding population, and by managing to hold out in the Drakensberg Mountains until the nineteenth century, the Wilton tool makers also have the distinction of belonging to the latest surviving true Stone Age culture in Africa. To the northwest, along the Upper Zambezi valley, the blade tradition continued without ever incorporating microlithic tendencies, probably because of the lack of stone in this dominantly floodplain area. If there were prior cultural links, they were most likely with the Tschitolian.

A distinct industry known as the Eburran (formerly Kenya Capsian) has been identified in the rift valleys of eastern Africa. An especially well developed version was found around Lake Nakuru; it dates back 12,000 years, but hints of microlithic tendencies can be detected in even earlier tool specimens. An almost exclusive use of obsidian characterizes the Eburran, and since 8,000 years ago, sedentary tendencies based on fishing are evident. A very wet period set in 10,000 years ago, and Lake Nakuru was much larger than it is now. Supported by bountiful food, the population grew and settlements became more permanent.

These trends are evident at other sites: at Ishango on the shores of Lake Edward, at Lake Turkana, and near the confluence of the White and Blue Niles. Indeed, the same subsistence and population trajectories can be described along the replenished lakes, streams, and swamps of the Sahel and the margins of the southern Sahara. Similar pottery styles and similar techniques of fashioning bone harpoons are evident; they are quite distinct from styles and techniques found in the Maghrib and along the Lower Nile. Although the large and discontinuous area involved makes the existence of a single culture highly improbable, the commonalities—plus, as we shall see, later developments—do provide some justification for putting the traditions together into an evolving aquatic-based complex.

Reconstructions of the latter stages of the Late Stone Age throughout the rest of western Africa are hindered by a paucity of archeological data; nevertheless, 12,000–10,000 years ago at least two broad regional toolmaking traditions can be discerned. Some microlithic tools have been found in the interior to the south of the Sahelian lakes. The area was rich in game, and nomadic gathering and hunting supported the population. By way of contrast, the prevailing industries in the forest and coastal zones continued to be basically non-

Ten thousand years ago, the shores of a much larger and deeper Lake Nakuru supported semipermanent settlements with economies focused on fishing and intensive gathering. (Photo courtesy of Philip W. Porter.)

microlithic. The prevalence of lagoonal and riverine locations indicates that fishing opportunities must have been an important settlement criterion. A variety of sites across the region show that pottery was manufactured no later than 7,000 years ago.

Between 15,000 and 10,000 years ago the early modern *Homo sapiens sapiens* had evolved into the immediate forerunner of almost all contemporary Africans (map 3.5). South-central and southern Africa belonged to capoids. Their remains have been found in conjunction with the Nachikufan and Wilton industries, and by inference they are thought to have been responsible for the Wilton in eastern Africa, although finds that are conclusively capoid have yet to be made in this area. An especially interesting and important archeological site exists at Gwisho Hot Springs in southern Zambia. Thirty-three skeletons have been unearthed, all showing definite capoid affinities, with the exception of being somewhat larger than later representatives. Two possibilities for this reversal of the general human growth trend come to mind. One is later physical diminution resulting from movement into limited food environments, which actually did occur. Or maybe larger and smaller capoid varieties already existed, with the former eventually disappearing as a distinct type. The puzzle awaits a solution.

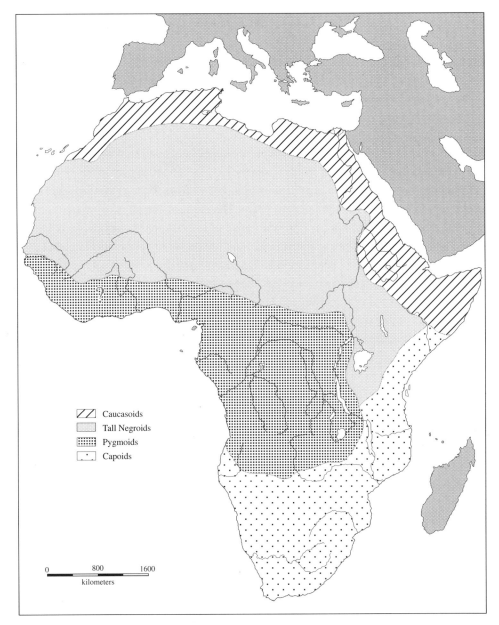

3.5 The four regional genetic populations from which virtually all Africans are descended had formed by the close of the Late Stone Age.

At the northern end of the continent, skeletal remains indicate that Cro-Magnon precursors to modern Mediterranean caucasoids inhabited the area from the Lower Nile into the Maghrib. They seem to have been the makers of the Lybicocapsian industries and probably all the others extending back to the Iberomaurusian.

Dwelling between the capoids and the Cro-Magnon caucasoids were at least two

37

different types of negroids. One was very tall and slender, and although skeletons are few, those that do exist indicate an association with the sedentarizing lakeside and riverine peoples of the Sahara, the Sahel, the Middle Nile, and eastern Africa. The other was much shorter and was in all probability ancestral to the people referred to as pygmoids. No definitive Late Stone Age pygmoid skeletons have been discovered, but the surviving groups are often described as displaying "ultra-African" genetic characteristics of considerable antiquity, perhaps dating as far back as 20,000 years. If so, pygmoids were the first negroids to emerge from proto–*Homo sapiens sapiens* stock—which would make them the likely fashioners of the Tschitolian industry and place their origins in the woodlands surrounding the rain forest, where various groups known as Twa, to the east and south of the rain forest, survived into modern times. The cultures and physical characteristics of some pygmoids indicate long-term occupancy of the rain forest, especially so for the Mbuti and Efe of Zaire. Because of the extreme shortness of Mbuti and Efe stature— males average 145 and 142 centimeters in height and females 137 and 134 centimeters, respectively—and certain genetic markers, the two groups are often cited as true pygmies in comparision with the pygmoids.

Improved hunting technologies, especially the ability to make nets, snares, and traps, facilitated the occupancy of tropical rain forests, but perhaps even more crucial was fishing, which made it possible to exploit a valuable source of animal protein. Still, the food sources were comparatively limited, which is a likely explanation for the true pygmy status of the Mbuti and Efe, among other deep forest dwellers.

If we accept the existence of two base populations, then the later negroids of western and equatorial Africa were descended from both; that is, they must have developed from genetic blending along the woodland-savanna boundary. The openness and gentle environmental gradients that then characterized, and still characterize, Africa between the Sahara and the rain forest would virtually guarantee that populations met and mixed with one another.

Similar genetic blendings undoubtedly went on elsewhere. Tall negroids, capoids, and pygmoids were all present in eastern Africa, and who interacted with whom would have been determined by location. In open country the probabilities favored the intermingling of tall negroids and capoids, whereas around the lakes in the western rift valley all three could have met. Pygmoids and capoids would have encountered one another in the woodlands of central Africa, and some contact between tall negroids and Cro-Magnon caucasoids must have occurred along the valley of the Nile. By way of contrast, the caucasoids inhabiting the Maghrib were largely isolated from other Africans, a situation that did not change for many thousands of years.

Before writing was invented, language left no traces on the archeological record, but linguistic research can still provide some clues to the past, and the work so far suggests that each of the four African phyla (table 1.1) had its roots within one of these four populations. The clearest relation is between Khoisan and the capoids in southern Africa. No plausible alternative exists. The next most certain correspondence is between Afroasiatic and the

38

Cro-Magnon caucasoids. The search for the origins of Afroasiatic goes on, but a likely locale was the grasslands east of the Nile valley in what is now the northern Sudan; however, somewhere in adjacent southwestern Asia is also a possibility. Nilosaharan is best seen as originating among the tall negroids, probably in the central portion of the Sahara, from where it spread in all directions except north.

That leaves the need to account for Niger Congo. The evidence points to its having developed in the lands just north of the equatorial rain forest in what are now Nigeria and Cameroon. If this is indeed correct, then the original speakers of Niger Congo may very well have been pygmoids. Or the language could have arisen among the peoples derived from the blending of pygmoids and tall negroids. But, in that case, what did the pygmoids speak? We shall return to this question in Chapter 8.

4

THE AGRICULTURAL TRANSFORMATION

Growth in human numbers and corresponding institutional development would have stagnated without agriculture, so the revolutionary status often attached to its origins is certainly deserved. Yet transformation better describes the pace of change. Agriculture had to be preceded by domestication—a set of processes altering plants and animals in ways to suit human use—and these alterations must have proceeded very gradually at first.

The initial steps toward domestication would not have been taken intentionally. Instead, they probably followed accidentally induced microenvironmental changes within and around regularly inhabited Late Stone Age/Paleolithic sites. The repeated clearing of vegetation, frequent fires, the accumulation of wastes, and intensified trampling of the soil created niches that favored particular plants at the expense of others. Similarly, some animal species proved more adept than others at living in close proximity to humans. With increasing exposure, people eventually recognized which of these plants and animals yielded the greatest benefits, and made them the focus of attention, which included providing protection from competitors. Ever so slowly, selected varieties replaced wild foods in the diet until they required purposeful breeding and planting to maintain reliable levels of productivity. The intentional control of plant and animal growth for food is what defines agriculture, and once under way, it eventually gained ascendancy over gathering and hunting. In most places, population size, settlement type, production, and the environment became too interdependent for reversion to occur, short of that brought on by catastrophe.

People in a number of places in both hemispheres participated in the agricultural transformation. Over time, some experiments proved more successful than others, and through cultural diffusion certain domesticates and practices won out. Products and ideas were spread by the transfer of information among peoples, which was itself facilitated by population growth and the consequent filling of spaces between communities. In some instances, agriculture followed human migration, and although some migrations led to the rapid displacement of gatherer-hunters, the general advance of the agricultural frontier is better depicted as an amoebalike movement, with those in the path being slowly absorbed.

That Africans participated in the early stages of domestication is no longer open to much doubt. Indigenous varieties of yams, millets, rice, sorghums, and cattle have been identified, and some unique African cultigens—notably teff, ensete, and noog—are still grown in Ethiopia (table 4.1). Nevertheless, it is difficult to be precise about exact whens and wheres. Crops are perishable, especially tuberous ones, and were seldom preserved. Carbonized seeds and seed impressions are usually the best evidence that paleobotanists have at their disposal. The presence of pottery, sickles, and grindstones in archeological debris was once thought to indicate crop cultivation, but these implements are now known to have been adopted independently by gatherer-hunters for other than agriculturally related purposes. Grindstones, for example, have often been used in the preparation of pigments and medicines.

Yet another problem is the difficulty of differentiating the skeletal remains of the earliest domesticated animals from those of their wild progenitors. Morphological changes proceeded slowly and in different directions. Consequently, the existence of early domestication usually has to be inferred from indirect evidence such as the frequency of a species's bones and the age structure of kills. An unusually high proportion of cattle bones, for example, serves as a sign that the animals were probably domesticated varieties, and such

Table 4.1 • Important Food Crops of African Origin

Common Name	Latin Binomial	Area of Origin
Sorghum	Sorghum vulgare	Sahel-savanna
Bulrush millet	Pennisetum typhoideum	Sahel-savanna
Finger millet	Eleusine coracana	Ethiopian highlands
African rice	Oryza glabberima	Upper Niger valley
Hungry rice	Digitaria exilis	Upper Niger valley
Teff	Eragrostif tef	Ethiopian highlands
Cowpea	Vigna unguiculata	Forest-savanna ecotone
Pigeon pea	Cajanus cajan	Forest-savanna ecotone
Bambara groundnut	Voandzeia subterranea	West African savanna
Guinea yam	Dioscorea rotundata	Forest-savanna ecotone
Watermelon	Citrullus lanatus	West African rain forest
Okra	Hibiscus esculentus	West African rain forest
Ensete	Ensete ventricosa	Ethiopian humid forest

41

an inference is strengthened if the bones are of juveniles, because ethnographic studies have shown a tendency among herders to slaughter livestock at younger ages than those at which wildlife is killed.

Linguistic evidence can also add to our knowledge of agricultural developments. It is possible to estimate the antiquity of a core vocabulary that relates to crop growing and livestock raising, and the analysis of loanwords helps point to likely directions and sequences of borrowings. Although these methods do not yield precise dates, rough chronologies can usually be constructed.

What the various bits of information show is that 7,000 to 5,000 years ago experiments with plant and animal domestication reached or were about to reach the agricultural stage in a number of places north of the equatorial rain forest. The Lower Nile valley was the site of the most rapid developments, but the pace of subsistence change picked up momentum among communities elsewhere—in the Maghrib and the Sahara, in the Ethiopian highlands, and between the desert and the rain forest in western and central Africa. The peopling of Africa was on the verge of a new era.

THE NILE VALLEY

Egypt

The Fayum depression, located just west of the Nile before the river branches to form its delta, contains the oldest confirmed agricultural site in Africa, with a date of approximately 7,000 years ago. Although wild varieties of barley and einkorn wheat have been discovered in Egypt, the agriculture being practiced at Fayum was identical to that developed 2,000 years earlier in southwestern Asia, and the only reasonable conclusion is that it came from there. The predominant crops were barley (*Hordeum vulgare*), emmer wheat (*Triticum dicocuum*), and flax (*Linum usitatissimum*), which were cultivated with both digging sticks and wooden hoes. The livestock included cattle, sheep, goats, pigs, and dogs, and from all indications, the Fayum settlements were occupied seasonally rather than permanently.

Direct evidence for similarly dated developments along the floodplain of the Nile River itself has yet to appear and indeed may never be forthcoming because of the sediment that has accumulated over the intervening millennia. Still, a connection between Fayum and the floodplain is a logical inference, particularly given the fully sedentary farming villages discovered at Merimde near the western margin of the delta and at El Omari just outside Cairo. Dated to 5,700 years ago, they produced the same crops and animals as at Fayum and must have arisen from prior developments. Shortly thereafter many more villages appeared on the scene, creating the base for the Predynastic era in Egypt.

Agriculture seems to have reached Egypt through contact diffusion rather than through immigrants or invaders. The material cultural continuity from preceding times is considerable, and cemeteries have yielded comparable skeletal remains. Consequently, a fairly safe conclusion is that the language spoken was the immediate ancestor of the Egyptian branch

A page from a codex written in Coptic containing the portions of the *Apocryphon of John* and the *Gospel of Thomas*. (Reprinted from Alan Bowman, *Egypt after the Pharaohs, 332 B.C.–A.D. 642,* University of California Press, 1986, p. 200.)

of Afroasiatic represented in the hieroglyphics. It evolved into the demotic script, which in turn became Coptic.

By late Predynastic times Lower Egypt was being differentiated from Upper Egypt; the former designated the lands immediately south of the delta, and the latter, everything beyond it to the vicinity of the First Cataract. Apparently the unification of separate village communities under a single administration started about 5,500 years ago in Upper Egypt during the so-called Gerzean period and spread north. When the whole territory came under one rule 500 years later, the Dynastic era began (table 4.2). Although there would be

43

Table 4.2 • Periods of Ancient Egypt

Predynastic (3500–2920 B.C.)
Early Dynastic: 1st–3rd Dynasties (2920–2575 B.C.)
Old Kingdom: 4th–8th Dynasties (2575–2134 B.C.)
First Intermediate: 9th–11th Dynasties (2134–2040 B.C.)
Middle Kingdom: 11th–14th Dynasties (2040–1640 B.C.)
Second Intermediate: 15th–17th Dynasties (1640–1550 B.C.)
New Kingdom: 18th–20th Dynasties (1550–1070 B.C.)
Third Intermediate: 21st–24th Dynasties (1070–712 B.C.)
Late Dynastic: 25th–30th Dynasties (712–343 B.C.)

Source and note: Uncertain dates have led to differing chronologies. This one follows *The Encyclopedia of Ancient Egypt* by Margaret Bunson (New York: Factson File, 1991).

periods of disorganization and even decline, the Egypt of the pharaohs endured for nearly 3,000 years. This record of political and cultural continuity is unparalleled and helps explain the remarkable monument building and other technological achievements of the state, all made without the benefit of bronze and iron until near the very end of the era.

From the outset, Egypt's wealth depended on the Nile. The annual floods were more reliable than those along any other major river valley in the world where early irrigation was established, and until the completion of the Aswan High Dam in the twentieth century the floods brought rich alluvial sediments from the volcanic highlands of the African interior to restore soil fertility. During Early Dynastic times artificial basin irrigation techniques were introduced to ensure a regular supply of water over a large area. To maintain and upgrade the water flow system required a huge and continual expenditure of labor, especially in the effort to minimize flood damage—a much more common hazard than low floodwaters. Sometime during the first centuries of the New Kingdom, the *shaduf*, a counterweighted lift-bucket, was introduced from eastern sources and quickly became a prominent part of Egyptian agriculture. Its value lay not so much in expanding the area under cultivation as in increasing yields on small garden plots adjacent to the irrigation channels. The gardens provided the bulk of the vegetables for the local population, and the shaduf allowed farmers to water them year round with fair reliability.

Occasional severe food crises, even famines, struck Egypt, but over the long run productivity was high enough to support both a growing population and a larger body of nonagriculturalists. Estimates for the late Predynastic period place the total population at no more than 340,000; by the onset of the Old Kingdom it had reached 1.5 million, and the sparsely inhabited delta was being actively settled. A figure of 3 million seems reasonable for the late New Kingdom, and densities for several of the provinces may have reached as high as 500 people per square kilometer. The vast majority of the population consisted of peasant cultivators, with members of the royal family, provincial nobility, priests, artisans, traders, and military personnel above them and slaves beneath.

Although agricultural villages dominated the settlement landscape, they were tied

The adoption of the shaduf provided farmers in Egypt with a reliable way to
water their vegetable gardens. (Reprinted from Barry J. Kemp, *Ancient
Egypt: Anatomy of a Civilization*, Routledge, 1989, p. 12.)

together by a network of cities and towns, which were created from those villages housing
major temple and trade functions. Religion was the glue holding dynastic society together,
and the economic prosperity of the state depended on a regular flow of internal and
international trade. Memphis was the initial capital, but because of the need to display the
royal presence throughout the realm, Thebes, Pi-Ramesse, and Tell el-Amarna became co-
capitals by New Kingdom times (map 4.1). Each was connected to a set of provincial
capitals, which, in turn, were surrounded by smaller towns with their respective satellite
villages. Today this configuration would be called a central place network, although river
and desert gave the one in Egypt an elongated shape; in contrast, more or less hexagonal
ones have been documented for areas of relative environmental uniformity, such as the
midwestern United States. But no matter its overall shape, a central place network indicates an advanced and highly integrated economy and polity.

Nubia

The name Nubia identifies the Nile valley between the First and Fifth cataracts, home to
a range of poorly described Stone Age cultures. The formation of Nubia rested on people's
ability to absorb and synthesize a wide range of externally derived cultural influences. A
particularly significant set of such influences emanated from lands surrounding the conflu-

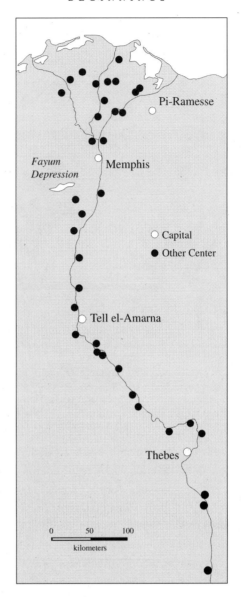

4.1 By New Kingdom times Egypt had
four regional capitals with numerous other
cities and towns linked to them.

ence of the White and Blue Niles. Here, evidence from the two archeological sites of
Kadero and Esh Shaheinab show livestock keeping and possibly sorghum cultivation having been incorporated into an aquatic-style economy 7,000 years ago. By this time, significant linguistic differentiation within the Nilosaharan phylum had taken place, and the
people involved were most likely the immediate ancestors of those now known as Nilotes,
or at least their cousins.

Some of the people moved downstream, where, 5,500 years ago in the vicinity of the Second Cataract, they encountered the Stone Age Abkan culture. Its fashioners, who were closely related to the Egyptians, absorbed the immigrants, and 500 years later they emerged with their own agriculture-based way of life modeled on that of their northern neighbors. This so-called A Culture served as the nucleus around which Nubia formed.

Nubia never matched Egypt in its demographic and technological developments, largely because of its severely limited agricultural potential. South of the First Cataract, the floodplain of the Nile is discontinuous and usually less than two kilometers wide. Between the Second and Dal cataracts and the Fourth and Fifth cataracts it disappears almost completely as the river cuts through ancient granites to form steep-sided gorges. Only in the area known as the Dongola Reach were basin irrigation techniques and, therefore, multicropping possible; elsewhere just one harvest could be produced after each year's flood.

Location was both the wealth and curse of Nubia. It lay next to Egypt, with its demands for such items as gold, ivory, semiprecious stones, ebony, fragrances, oils, skins, slaves, and mercenaries. Some of these could be had within Nubia, but the richest supplies existed in lands to the south, which it could access. During late A Culture times, 4,700 years ago, trade brought considerable prosperity and population growth to Lower Nubia (the riverine area between the First and Second cataracts), at least as measured by material remains and the number of settlement sites. The society was still agrarian and pastorally based, however, with the maximum settlement size averaging fewer than 100 individuals. Nothing resembling villages or towns seems to have existed. Quite suddenly, the A Culture disappeared, and Lower Nubia was virtually depopulated for several hundred years. Although the reasons for such a dramatic change in fortune are not entirely clear, they probably involve increasing Egyptian exploitation centered on slave raiding. Some of the A Culture people may have sought refuge in the desert, where they became nomads, while others followed the Nile southward into Upper Nubia.

Resettlement of Lower Nubia came with the rise of the C Culture 4,300 years. Once thought to have been brought in by a wave of immigrants coming from either the east or west, the C Culture now looks to have been a direct descendant of the A Culture, with no intervening and different B Culture. In other words, the former inhabitants returned, and with them came renewed prosperity. The population in Lower Nubia reached its height during the early New Kingdom: there were at least 15,000 inhabitants, up from a maximum of 8,000 during A Culture times, with increasing numbers living in larger villages. But the Egyptians also returned, this time as conquerors. They established agricultural estates and mined the gold of the ancient basement-complex rocks exposed in the desert east of the Second and Third cataracts. Some Lower Nubians were forced into slavery, others became virtual serfs on Egyptian estates, and still others once again fled south into Upper Nubia. By 3,200 years ago, all signs of the C Culture had disappeared; only Egyptians seem to have remained behind.

Within a hundred years the Egyptians also departed, leaving Lower Nubia abandoned

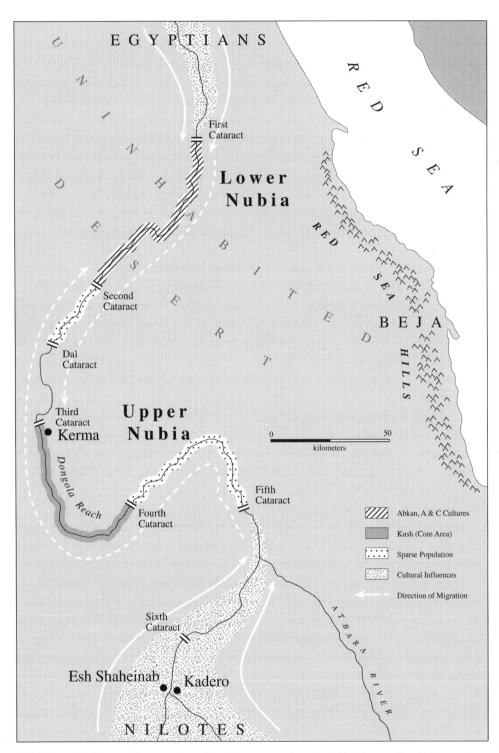

4.2 Cultural influences from north and south converged on the Nile River valley between the First and Fifth cataracts to create Nubia, where the Kingdom of Kush arose.

one more time. A reduction in the level of the Nile flood may have caused the exodus, but no geological evidence has been found to support this hypothesis. Instead, we can look to changing economic and political fortunes as the more likely reasons for evacuation. The gold had given out, and a shortage of labor to work the estates followed from the population decline. In addition, Egypt was under siege from Asian invaders known as the Hyksos and could spare few reinforcements for its southern frontier.

The remaining Nubian population consolidated itself farther south in the area of the Dongola Reach. In fact, the area, because of its agricultural potential, had already become the new core of Nubian settlement. Egyptian texts initially refer to it as the Land of Yam, and it later became Kush (map 4.2). Very little archeological work has been done in Upper Nubia, but excavations of grave sites at Kerma suggest that a stratified and possibly politically centralized society had arisen by 3,800 years ago. Kush was conquered by Egypt during the New Kingdom period, though without undergoing appreciable colonization. What happened instead was the adoption by Kushites of much of Egyptian culture, including language, as surviving inscriptions reveal. There must have been a Nubian language at one time, but it has left no traces. In keeping with an oft-repeated human pattern, cultural changes started at the top of Nubian society and filtered downward to the population at large. The result was an imperial civilization that would soon challenge Egypt for Nile hegemony.

NORTHERN AFRICA AND THE SAHARA

At Hanu Fteah in Cyrenaica the Libycocapsian gatherer-hunters were succeeded 7,000 years ago by people whose economy included sheep and goat raising. Shortly thereafter, similar developments took place along the Maghrib coast and soon appeared within and around the Atlas and Aures mountains, making up what has become known as the Neolithic of Capsian Tradition (hereafter Capsian Neolithic). Cattle do not seem to have been present, nor are there indications of grain cultivation. Because no wild ancestors have been identified so far, it is assumed that the sheep and goats were introduced from elsewhere. Overland diffusion from Egypt was the most likely route of entry, but maritime contacts from across the Mediterranean are also a possibility. Agricultural sites dating back 8,000 and 7,000 years have been located on the European side of the Mediterranean, and boats capable of sailing the sea existed by this time. Pottery affinities also point in the direction of likely cross-Mediterranean contacts.

The Capsian Neolithic furnished the base for all later Maghrib developments. Five thousand years ago the people had evolved a transhumance-type herding economy; animals grazed in upland pastures in the summer and valleys during the winter. Cattle were now being kept, and, unlike the sheep and goats, they could have been domesticated from local varieties of *Bos primigenius*, whose natural range included northern Africa. Wheat and barley cultivation had also become part of an expanding agricultural inventory.

The changes first occurred at the margins of the mountains, whereas the richer natural

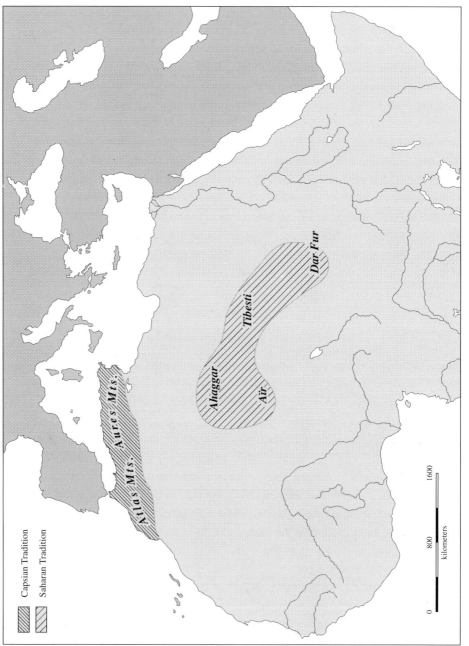

4.3 Early agriculture in the Maghrib took the form of transhumant herding and grain cultivation (Capsian Tradition), whereas the highlands in the Sahara supported the development of nomadic herding systems (Saharan Tradition).

Capsian Tradition

Saharan Tradition

Atlas Mts.

Aures Mts.

Ahaggar

Tibesti

Aïr

Dar Fur

0   800   1600

kilometers

resources of interior valleys and lower slopes supported gatherer-hunter economies for a while longer. As herder numbers grew, however, and the superior quality of mountain pasturage was established, the complete displacement of Stone Age occupants was all but inevitable. Still, changes came about slowly and without discernible cultural discontinuities. The most plausible conclusion is that these developments relate to the origins and dispersals of proto-Berber-speaking peoples.

Several traces of early agriculture have been found within the Sahara, although only from playas in the western desert of Egypt can cereal cultivation be confirmed. Here emmer wheat has been dated to approximately the same time as at Fayum, whence it undoubtedly came. On the other hand, barley was apparently grown before 8,000 years ago, and it could have had a different source. Lending weight to this possibility are pottery styles that demonstrate broad Saharan-Sudanic affinities, instead of associations with the Nile. The only other evidence of very early cereal cultivation in the desert comes from the Ahaggar Mountains, where several pollen grains, possibly millet (*Pennisetum* sp.), have also been dated to 8,000 years ago. The climate was moister then, and cereals may in fact have been grown; however, considerably more evidence is needed before the timing and extent of initial Saharan crop cultivation can be confirmed.

More certain is the presence of cattle keeping by 7,000 years ago. The evidence comes from dated rock art (both paintings and engravings) at Tassili-n-Ajer in the Ahaggar. Shown in considerable detail are indisputable scenes of cattle herding, along with those depicting wild fauna that would eventually disappear from the Saharan region with deepening aridity. There might have been several different sources for cattle, including the Maghrib, and possibly even the domestication of a local shorthorn variety, *Bos brachyceros*. Shortly thereafter, signs of domesticated cattle can be detected within and around the other desert highlands of Dar Fur, Tibesti, and the Aïr (map 4.3).

Skeletal remains indicate that the herders were negroid; they were thus connected to peoples of the Sahel-Sudan instead of Egypt and the Maghrib. Historical linguistic patterning points in the direction of Nilosaharans, an inference given support by the importance that livestock, particularly cattle, attained among so many of its speakers. As climatic conditions deteriorated, livestock herding provided a viable response for those inhabiting the Sahara and its immediate environs. Unlike the Nilotes, many found their water sources drying up and had to abandon an aquatic economy in favor of one much more centered on livestock.

HIGHLAND ETHIOPIA

Since the 1920s highland Ethiopia has been recognized as a place of early plant domestication. Two environmental settings were involved. One encompassed the grassy northern and eastern margins of the highlands, where teff (*Eragrostis tef*), finger millet (*Eleusine coracana*), noog (*Guizotia abyssinica*), sesame (*Sesamum indica*), mustard (*Brassica juncea*), and several other minor crops were brought under cultivation. The other was the

A portion of a fresco from Tassili-n-Ajer showing a herd of domesticated cattle prior to the onset of modern hyperaridity in the Sahara. (Reprinted from Henri Lhote, *The Search for the Tassili Frescoes,* trans. Alan Houghton Brodrick, Hutchinson of London, 1959, pl. 46. Photo by Gérard Franceschi.)

heavily forested uplands of the southwest, with ensete (*Ensete ventricosa*), or false banana, as the primary staple food. Coffee (*Coffea arabica*) also appears to have originated there. Exactly when these crops became important enough to support agricultural communities remains unclear. The date often suggested for the grains, around 5,000 years ago, is largely conjectural because archeological data are lacking, but it is probably not too far off the mark. Wheat and barley, the eventual staple foods of much of highland Ethiopia, are thought to have been introduced from across the Red Sea sometime just prior to 3,000 years ago, and they were joined to already well established systems of cultivation, which included such practices as manuring and irrigation.

As in the Sahara, we see a much clearer picture of the use of livestock. There are signs that cattle, sheep, and goats were herded in combination in the highlands around 5,000 years ago; with the Blue Nile, Atbara, and other river valleys providing avenues of communication, the animals could have arrived in an extension of the same diffusion that brought them to Esh Shaheinab and Kadero. Cultural remains indicate that gathering and hunting continued to be important subsistence activities, but events definitely favored nomadic herding, particularly in the more arid rift valleys and eastern lowlands.

Distinct economies were thus developing in different environments, and each can be

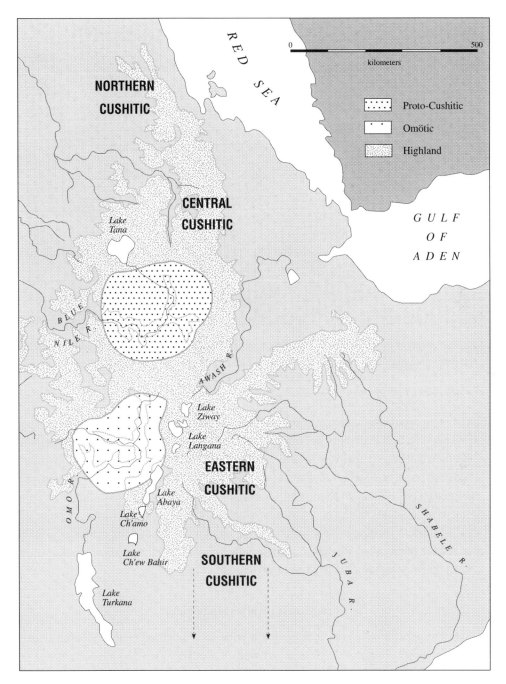

4.4 Agricultural developments prompted the rise and spread of Central, Northern, Eastern, and Southern branches of proto-Cushitic. In contrast, the Omötic languages remained confined to a localized niche.

Eleusine or finger millet seems to have first been domesticated along the grassy margins of the Ethiopian highlands. From here it spread southward with the migrations of Southern Cushites. (Photo courtesy of Philip W. Porter.)

linked to a particular language within Afroasiatic (map 4.4). Proto-Cushitic has a time depth of at least 9,000 years in central Ethiopia, and with the coming of agriculture, it differentiated into its major branches. Central Cushitic developed among the highland grain cultivators and herders, and it sprouted a Southern branch, which is associated with emigrants who headed into Kenya and Tanzania. Those elaborating the herding way of life in the arid lowlands of the north became Northern Cushites; those in the southern rift valleys, Eastern Cushites. Who, then, were the ensete cultivators? Not too long ago they would have been called Western Cushites. Now, however, their languages are thought to constitute an Afroasiatic family known as Omötic.

THE SAHEL AND THE SUDAN

Several agricultural systems involving a wide variety of indigenously domesticated plants developed south of the Sahara and west of the Nile. Two systems were based on seeds—one on sorghums and millets and the other on African rice (*Oryza glaberrima*) and fonio (*Digitaria exilis*). Secondary crops included Bambara nuts (*Voandzeia subterranea*), cowpeas (*Vigna unguiculata*), and Kersting's groundnuts (*Kerstingiella geocarpa*). Agriculture-based communities may have formed in this part of the continent as early as 6,000 years ago, although so far the oldest archeologically confirmed date comes in connection with bulrush (pearl) millet at Dhar Tichitt in south-central Mauretania, 3,100 years ago. The presence of millet evidences the transition from a classic aquatic economy focused on several small but shrinking freshwater lakes to an economy in which crops, along with cattle, sheep, and goats, were gaining prominence.

Dhar Tichitt undoubtedly exemplifies happenings at other sites immediately south of the desert. By the end of a wet phase beginning 7,500 years ago and lasting 3,000 years, the Sahel was four to five degrees of latitude farther north than it is now and contained a series of lakes, just as it had during prior pluvial episodes. These lakes flooded annually with waters brought by streams draining the Saharan highlands and were rich sites for wild grasses and fish. Several of the grasses changed status from being protected to being planted; and as climatic conditions worsened, more attention was paid to cultivating the grasses until they became fully domesticated. Just as we can see along some of the local rivers today, the sowing probably accompanied the retreat of the annual floods.

As aridity intensified and the lakes dried up, the sites for grain cultivators became fewer and fewer. The best available ones would have been within the valleys of the Senegal and Niger rivers and around Lake Chad. Filtering between the cultivators were nomadic herders, pushed southward by the same worsening aridity. Ironically, their expansion may have been facilitated by the retreat of tsetse, which also found conditions over much of the region increasingly unfavorable to survival. When they departed, so, too, did sleeping sickness, and its departure opened large expanses of land to pasture- and water-seeking nomads.

Farther south, in an area extending from the western Ivory Coast to Cameroon, is the Yam Belt. Today Asiatic yams (*Dioscorea alata* and *D. esculenta*) are the predominant varieties, but they are fairly recent adoptions, having been brought to western Africa by the Portuguese early in their voyages. They replaced, though not completely, indigenous yam varieties, notably *D. cayenensis* and *D. rotundata*. Both of these seem to have been domesticated initially in the forest-savanna ecotone that marks the northern boundary of the Yam Belt; when the process started and when cultivated yams became important enough to support agricultural communities are unknowns, however. That these mysteries will ever be solved is highly doubtful because of the unlikelihood of finding preserved specimens so far back in time. An educated guess is that domestication of yams and also oil palm (*Elaeis guineensis*) had advanced far enough to become agriculture 5,000–4,000 years ago.

Lending some support for this date are the several archeological sites associated with the Kintampo culture in Ghana and adjacent areas of Ivory Coast and Togo. No early yams have been unearthed, but there is evidence of permanent settlement, cowpea cultivation, and the keeping of dwarf cattle and goats by 3,800 years ago. These findings raise the possibility that yam domestication may have proceeded under the influence of southward-moving cereal growers, although a strong case also can be made for the independent domestication of yams. The techniques of vegetative propagation and digging stick culti-

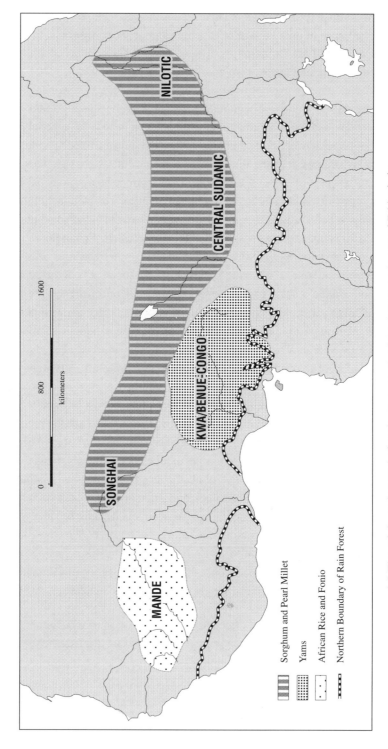

4.5 The origin and spread of agriculture south of the Sahara and west of Ethiopia is associated with distinctive language families.

vation associated with yams are distinct from those used in seed agriculture, and Kintampo may represent a fusion of the two traditions.

The combination of botanical, linguistic, and geographic evidence points to Nilosaharan origins for the agricultural systems based on sorghums, millets, and livestock. As noted, developments correspond with the distribution of the Late Stone Age aquatic tradition, so we can postulate the existence of early Nilosaharan agricultural communities scattered in a bandlike pattern immediately south of the desert (map 4.5). Later migrations by other peoples cut off the western portion and left the Songhai linguistic family the only surviving representative of Nilosaharan. By way of contrast, the eastern half of the band was relatively isolated and remained Nilosaharan territory. Two branches can be identified with some degree of assurance: extending from the Nile into the swamps and grasslands of the Sudd and Bahr al-Ghazal were yet other Nilotes, whereas the open woodlands and savannas westward provided a home for the first Central Sudanic–speaking peoples.

One of the earliest migrations to impinge on the western Nilosaharans involved the ancestors of the Mande branch of Niger Congo, who were the likely domesticators of fonio and African rice. Over the course of the next several millennia various Mande peoples claimed most of the better-watered sites between the headwaters and the bend of the Niger River.

The initial development of the yam and oil palm agricultural tradition appears to be associated with the rise and spread of two other Niger Congo language families, Kwa and Benue-Congo. Both originated somewhere in the vicinity of the Benue River valley, but speakers of Kwa were poised to expand westward, whereas speakers of Benue-Congo later headed east and south.

AGRICULTURE AND POPULATION CHANGE

The adoption of agriculture triggered humanity's first major demographic transition. The conventional explanation is that larger numbers were possible because increased food availability lessened the toll of famine-induced mortality, which had kept Stone Age gatherer-hunters in check. The evidence, however, contradicts this line of reasoning. At low population densities, gathering and hunting can meet basic subsistence needs with reasonable assurance and usually with no more than a couple of hours' effort per day. Starvation was not a constant companion of Stone Age peoples, nor, for that matter, was malnutrition, so the adoption of agriculture would have had little or no positive effect on death rates and life expectancy. Indeed, agriculture may have had at least one substantially negative impact on health. It disturbs the environment in and around settlements in ways that allow numerous small pools of water to collect. These provided ideal breeding grounds for anopheles mosquitoes, which multiplied and, for the first time, became people's constant neighbor. Accordingly, the chances of being bitten by a mosquito carrying the plasmodia that cause malaria rose considerably. Once a minor hazard, malaria was now on the way to becoming tropical Africa's number one health threat.

If mortality declines are ruled out, then population could have grown only by increases in fertility. Archeological data will never be able to document precisely how fertility increased, but some interesting biological and anthropological evidence suggests a likely combination of earlier births and shorter birth intervals as the principal factors. The onset of puberty in women and then the maintenance of regular ovulatory cycles were at least partially dependent on achieving minimum stores of body fat, which the calorie-rich carbohydrate foods of agriculture-based diets could better accomplish than the diets of gatherer-hunters.

In addition, cultural factors seem to have played a role in limiting gatherer-hunter birthrates. Contemporary !Kung San women consider closely spaced births highly undesirable because of the burden imposed on them by having to carry young children during moves and while foraging. The goal is to have no more than one child who cannot walk fast enough to keep up with the group. How is family planning accomplished without modern contraceptives? The answer is a combination of induced abortion, infanticide, sexual abstinence, and very prolonged breast feeding, a phenomenon that extends the period of postpartum amenorrhea. None of these methods is new to the !Kung, and they may have been common among many gatherer-hunters during at least the latter stages of the Stone Age.

A more sedentary agriculture-based way of life would have eliminated the concern about limiting births and actually brought with it an increased desire for children. Productivity in nonmechanized agricultural systems is largely a function of the available labor supply, and the easiest way to ensure enough hands to do the work is to bear more children. A synergism is created: population and food supply depend on one another. No such relation exists for gatherer-hunters. Nature's bounty limits group size, and extra hands do not mean greater productivity. If numbers grow, band segmentation results as surplus members seek out new lands from which to secure their subsistence.

The initial impact of agriculture on population number and density was highly variable. By far the most dramatic increases took place along the Nile River in Egypt, where by Old Kingdom times the provision of food had become almost completely dependent on domesticated crops and animals. Nubia also became essentially agricultural 4,000 years ago and, in consequence, experienced a noteworthy numerical growth.

Far less is known about population trends elsewhere in Africa, but for the most part, increases were bound to have been gradual. Along the Maghrib coast an economy based on crops, livestock, fishing, and maritime trade eventually developed. Local pockets with higher population density undoubtedly existed, and small trade centers may have come into being, although these are not fully attested to until the arrival of the Phoenicians 3,000 years ago. Within the nearby Atlas and Aures mountains, transhumance dominated, and the favored valley sites became comparatively well populated. In contrast, 4,000–3,000 years ago the Sahara had already undergone extensive depopulation; only in the highlands and at oases where permanent water supplies could be found was life possible. In the Sahel, population densities probably increased in those few areas where natural irrigation still occurred. Elsewhere, densities may have declined as the sedentary aquatic economy disappeared.

The least extreme numerical changes took place along the forest-savanna ecotone and in the highlands of Ethiopia. Agriculture was spreading, but in the forms of shifting cultivation and nomadic herding. Gathering and hunting remained important ways to obtain food, as they did into modern times in much of the area. Still, as events show, even very small increments to population growth can have substantial ramifications.

PART TWO

REGIONAL UNFOLDINGS

5

NORTHERN AFRICA

Three thousand years ago virtually all of Africa from the Sahara to the Mediterranean was firmly entrenched within the wider Afroasiatic linguistic realm. Although Egypt was in decline from the heights of prosperity reached during New Kingdom times, the Nile valley south to the First Cataract remained in Egyptian hands, and nothing indicates that any qualitative population change had yet taken place in Nubia. To the east, in the Red Sea Hills and the adjacent desert, the Northern Cushitic Beja herders, who had immigrated from the lowlands of Eritrea, held sway. Inhabiting the country directly west of the Nile all the way to the Atlantic were the peoples whom classical writers termed Libyans. Comprising a plethora of localized, autonomous groupings known by such names as Garamantes, Bavares, Troglodytes, Nasamones, Mauri, Lotophagi, Giligamai, Marmaridai, Masaesylii, Gaetuli, and Pharusii, they represent the immediate ancestors of the modern-day Berbers.

Most of the Libyans, or Libyco-Berbers, as many prefer to call them, lived along the Mediterranean coast and within the Atlas-Aures mountain chain, pursuing mixed agricultural economies involving grain farming and transhumance herding developed during the Capsian Neolithic period. Others, however, had moved into the Sahara. Some groups occupied oases in the northern and central portions, relying on the cultivation of figs, dates, and olives for subsistence, whereas others became nomadic herders. Libyco-Berber expansion occurred at the expense of Nilosaharans, who, save those who held out in the highlands of Tibesti and Dar Fur, were confined to the southernmost oases.

63

Up to this point, non-African immigrants had scarcely influenced regional population trends. Change was imminent, however, as one such group after another made its presence felt. The sequence started with the arrival of Mediterranean-based colonists—Phoenicians, Ionians, and Romans—and reached its apex when northern Africa became part of the Arab world, an integration that is still going on. Finally, various other Europeans entered the population mélange from time to time. What looks like considerable ethnolinguistic uniformity today compared with the diveristy of the rest of Africa has in fact been built from numerous sources.

MEDITERRANEAN ORIENTATIONS

Phoenician Colonization

During the later centuries of the second millennium B.C., the Phoenicians developed a highly successful mercantile-based economy centered on the Levantine coast. They operated from the cities of Tyre and Sidon, whence they sailed westward seeking gold, silver, copper, and tin (map 5.1). Greek and Roman accounts suggest that their first outpost on the coast of northern Africa was established at Utica about 1100 B.C., but archeological research has confirmed dates 300 years later, none earlier. Whatever time is closer to the truth, the initial Phoenician settlements were all small trading and revictualing stations designed to support the traffic with Spain, where large silver deposits had been discovered and where tin from Britain could be obtained. Colonization does not seem to have been an objective. The early sites—all on offshore islands and peninsulas—were chosen for their relative security, and the ruins found there indicate populations of no more than a few hundred at any given time.

Although most Phoenician settlements never grew much larger, a few did, especially after the decline of Tyre, which had been weakened both by Babylonian invasion and by the rise of Ionian commercial activity in the eastern Mediterranean. Among the settlements Carthage was preeminent. By the sixth century B.C., it had gone well beyond its trading and revictualing functions to become one of the major economic and political centers of the ancient world, and at the height of its prosperity it may have contained a population in excess of 400,000.

Carthaginian-owned *latifundia* (estates) were established on the adjacent fertile plains of the Bon Peninsula, with dispossessed Libyco-Berbers often serving as slave laborers. The latifundia produced wheat, barley, livestock, and the many new or improved crops that the Phoenicians brought with them—fig, olive, plum, peach, pomegranate, almond, pistachio, grape, and filbert, among others. Although Libyco-Berber groups to the south remained in possession of their lands, they had to pay tribute in grain or else risk retribution. Agricultural produce became a vital part of Carthaginian trade and was crucial to the support of its armies, particularly those stationed in Sicily, where wars with the competing Ionian colonies verged on endemic.

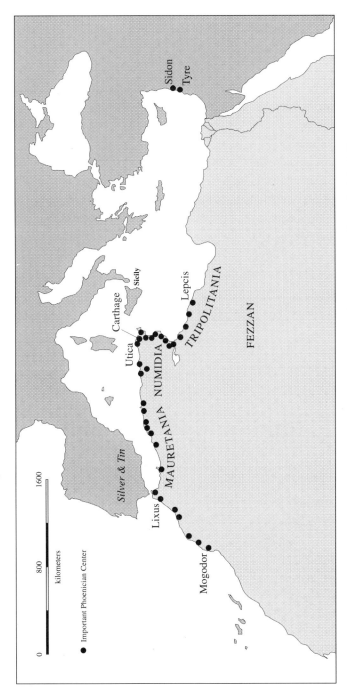

5.1 The Phoenicians established an enduring urban settlement pattern along the Maghrib coast.

Phoenician agricultural colonies also spread into Tripolitania, although on a considerably lesser scale because of the limited area available for cultivation. Lepcis was the dominant city, and its merchants carried on some trans-Saharan trade via the Garamantes who occupied the Fezzan region of southwestern Libya. Carbuncle (debatable, but most likely red garnet) and small numbers of slaves were the main commodities going north in exchange for manufactured items like pottery, glassware, and metal tools. The most likely source of slaves was apparently the nearby Nilosaharan oases dwellers, not peoples south of the desert. The camel had not yet replaced the horse as the Libyco-Berbers' pack animal, so long journeys across the Sahara would have been difficult, if not virtually impossible to negotiate.

No indications of gold or ivory reaching Lepcis via the Fezzan route have been found. These items were obtained from trade with other Libyco-Berbers farther to the west, in areas known as Numidia and Mauretania. The latter was reached from several trade centers on the Atlantic coast, meaning that Phoenicians regularly passed through the Strait of Gibraltar. Lixus and Mogodor are the best-known centers, and although several others supposedly existed beyond Mogodor, their locations have never been identified. Unresolved as well is whether or not the Phoenicians had direct contact with Africans south of the Sahara.

Even if contact was direct, it would have been fleeting as far as the Africans were

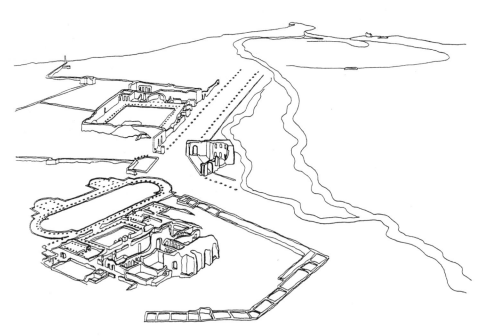

Sketch of the ruins of Lepcis Magna, an important Mediterranean seaport in Roman North Africa. (Reprinted from William L. MacDonald, *The Architecture of the Roman Empire,* vol. 2, Yale University Press, 1986, fig. 52.)

concerned. For the Maghrib, however, the story is different. The sacking of Carthage by Rome in 146 B.C. did not bring the Phoenician presence to an end, as is often thought. Other cities, like Utica and Lixus, housed considerable numbers of Carthaginian descendants for many years thereafter, and the Phoenician language, Punic, remained in widespread use. But the real measure of the Phoenicians cum Carthaginians lies in their legacy. They brought northwestern Africa into the Iron Age and instituted many agricultural innovations. The crops that they introduced were planted throughout the Maghrib, furthering sedentarization among the Libyco-Berbers of Numidia in particular, where a series of states modeled along Carthaginian lines sprang up. In addition, the Phoenicians imposed a city-based settlement pattern on the northwest African coast that integrated the area into the Mediterranean world. The seaward orientation endured and, as much as the desert did, separated the Maghrib from the rest of Africa to the south.

Ionian Colonization

A significant Ionian (Greek and Macedonian) presence in Africa dates from the seventh century B.C., when the Saite dynasty in Egypt recruited large numbers of mercenaries to help with campaigns against Assyrian invaders. Shortly thereafter, Ionian traders founded Naukratis as a center from which to do business along the Nile. Grain, linen, and papyrus were in demand, and some gold, ivory, and ebony could be procured from Nubia. The pace of Ionian settlement gained momentum after the Ionians conquered Egypt's Persian overlords in 332 B.C. They immediately undertook the construction of Alexandria at the western end of the Nile Delta to serve both as a victory monument and as a direct point of contact between Egypt and Greece.

With the installation of the Ptolemies as the new dynasty in 323 B.C., the official language of Egypt changed from demotic Egyptian to Greek. The switch brought in Ionians seeking their fortune, and although trade remained a favored form of employment, some of the newcomers filled positions in the bureaucracy and military, and still others became landholders. Soon more Ionian-dominated cities appeared, the two most important being Ptolemais and the port of Paraetonium.

As the immigrant population increased and spread upstream, Hellenistic influences made their way into the circles of the Egyptian elite. The Egyptians, too, often joined the bureaucracy, and some intermarriages were contracted, mostly involving Egyptian women and Ionian men. The number of hellenized Egyptians never grew very large, however, and the Ionians generally kept themselves apart. As a result, Hellenism had little impact on the population at large.

Egypt nevertheless underwent considerable change during the Ionian era. Alexandria superseded Memphis as the foremost city, and through its port passed not only commerce of Mediterranean origin but also goods from an expanded Red Sea trade. Expeditions ventured to the Horn of Africa in search of war elephants, and the discovery of the monsoon winds allowed ships to complete quick voyages to and from India. In addition, several important manufacturing industries, including cloth, papyrus, and glass, were concentrated in Alexandria; and remarkable libraries made the city the premier center of scholarship in the Mediterranean world.

The combination of sea-borne trade and Alexandria's rise to prominence led to a change in population distribution. By freeing land for agricultural colonization, marsh drainage in both the delta and the Fayum depression also boosted the attraction of Lower Egypt. Further augmenting crop production, still the main revenue earner for the state, were the adoption of the Syria-derived *saqiya*—a wheel-driven, animal-powered water-lift, which extended the area under irrigation—and sorghum and durum wheat, which expanded the crop inventory. The population of Egypt reached at least 4 million during late Ptolemaic times, and Alexandria may have had as many as 300,000 inhabitants, including sizable foreign communities other than those of Ionian extraction.

West of Egypt, Ionian settlement was confined to the al-Jebel al-Akhdar Plateau in Cyrenaica, where enough winter rain fell to support wheat and barley cultivation. Unlike in Egypt, ample land could be found to accommodate a growing population of colonists. Apparently, only small numbers of seminomadic Libyco-Berbers were present when the Ionians arrived. Although some lost their land and fled, others were absorbed into the colonial population—again, often through intermarriage. The first colony was Cyrene, founded in 631 B.C., and all the others were evidently offshoots. In typical Ionian fashion, each operated as an independent city-state, although the Ptolemies, when they came to power, managed to bring all of the colonies under a single administrative umbrella, at least nominally. Several attempts were made to establish outposts farther west, and some Ionians did settle among Libyco-Berbers, but beyond the Gulf of Sidra the firm entrenchment of the Phoenicians blocked Ionian territorial expansion.

Roman North Africa

The fall of Carthage in 146 B.C., the conquest of Egypt in 30 B.C., and the incorporation of Mauretania in A.D. 40 were the events that created Roman North Africa (map 5.2). How firmly the Romans held this vast area varied, but effective control persisted until the Vandal invasion of the Maghrib in A.D. 429. Roman rule under the aegis of Byzantium held out longer in Egypt, finally succumbing to the Arab advance in A.D. 639.

The Roman presence in Egypt was largely administrative; the chief concerns involved extracting grain and collecting taxes. Only the most senior officials came from Rome, and, in fact, Greek remained the official language, as it did in Cyrenaica. At the outset, the stability brought to Egypt by the Roman legions renewed its prosperity, with enhanced Red Sea and Indian Ocean commerce playing a crucial role. By the end of the first century A.D. the population reached slightly more than 5 million—the high point for some centuries to come. Alexandria was still the dominant city, but an additional thirty to forty sizable urban centers have been identified. Then decline set in, as the economy weakened under heavy-handed Roman requisitions to support the legions. During the latter half of the second century and again in the middle of the third century, epidemics swept cities and countryside alike. By A.D. 300 the population of Egypt had fallen to 3.25 million.

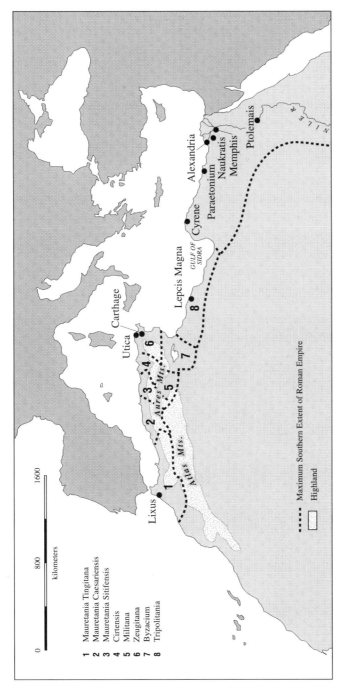

0   **800**   **1600**

kilometers

1 Mauretania Tingitana
2 Mauretania Caesariensis
3 Mauretania Sitifensis
4 Cirtensis
5 Militana
6 Zeugitana
7 Byzacium
8 Tripolitania

Lixus

Atlas Mts.

Aures Mts.

Utica

Carthage

Lepcis Magna

GULF OF SIDRA

Cyrene

Alexandria

Paraetonium

Naukratis

Memphis

Ptolemais

NILE R.

- - - - Maximum Southern Extent of Roman Empire

☐ Highland

5.2 The Roman presence in northern Africa extended from Egypt through the Maghrib and was characterized by separately administered provinces.

The Roman presence eventually loomed much larger in the Maghrib. At the outset, there was no immediate rush to fill the Carthaginian administrative vacuum. Instead, the Romans went about establishing their rule in the cities, surveying the land, and building an infrastructure of roads, harbors, and aqueducts. Toward the middle of the last century B.C., with the arrival of sizable numbers of colonists, the pace of development quickened. The Romans reestablished latifundia in Tunisia and augmented the legions to protect the estates from Libyco-Berber attacks. During the first century A.D. four political divisions were established, each governed somewhat differently. From east to west they were Africa Proconsularis, Numidia, Mauretania Caesariensis, and Mauretania Tingitana. In the late third century, the four provinces became eight: Africa Proconsularis became Tripolitania, Byzacium, and Zeugitana; Numidia became Cirtensis and Militiana; and a third Mauretania, Sitifensis, was created.

A series of trenches and roads known as the limes guarded the southern frontier of Roman agricultural settlement, which roughly followed the 400 millimeter isohyet. The limes were discontinuous and therefore were unlikely to have served as a fortification against potential Libyco-Berber incursions. Instead, they probably helped funnel the migrations of herders along specific routes as they moved back and forth from winter pastures

An estate of a Roman seigneur depicted in a mosaic found at Carthage.
(Reprinted from Susan Raven, *Rome in Africa,* Evans Brothers, 1969, p. 129.
Photo by Susan Raven.)

at chotts (lakes) at the desert margin to summer pastures in the mountains. In this way, a watchful eye could be kept and taxes collected.

Most of the first colonists were either retired legionnaires or Italians who had been re-settled in Africa as a result of growing land shortages on the peninsula. A new Roman-Berber segment of the population was created when increasing numbers of Libyco-Berbers were drawn by the lures of Roman wealth and culture. As with the Phoenicians, a prefer-ence for urban residence is evident. More than 500 towns and cities have been identified, with a heavy concentration on the agriculturally rich Tunisian Plain. Most were small, with no more than 10,000 inhabitants, and served primarily as local trade centers. At the other end of the continuum, a restored Carthage grew to nearly its former size, while the population of Lepcis Magna may have approached 100,000 at its height. All told, the urban population of the Roman Maghrib numbered between a third to a half of the total population, which probably exceeded 6 million by the turn of the third century.

Agriculture, however, was the cornerstone of the regional economy, with the Maghrib earning the label "granary of Rome" because of the large quantities of wheat and barley regularly exported from there. The Romans introduced improved irrigation systems with terraces, dams, and canals; soil conservation methods; and a variety of tree and vegetable crops. The export of olive oil was especially important and brought prosperity to many large landowners, if not to the growing numbers of small farmers and landless laborers. With its many uses, for cooking, soaps and perfumes, and lamp fuel, the demand for olive oil surpassed what the Italian Peninsula could supply. Plantations sprang up wherever available land existed, even along the desert margin, where the drought-tolerant olive tree prospered as no other crop could.

Some trans-Saharan trade for gold and slaves also took place, although these goods were outranked by the wild animals required for the spectacles held in forums in all major Roman cities. By the beginning of the fourth century A.D. much of the indigenous wildlife of the Maghrib had been been pushed to the brink of extinction, so sources were sought farther afield.

Although many factors can be implicated in Rome's eventual collapse, the spread of infectious diseases was one of the most significant. Two particularly devastating outbreaks struck throughout the empire, including the Maghrib and Egypt. One disease occurred episodically between A.D. 165 and 266 and, though difficult to pinpoint from extant descriptions, looks to have been a combination of measles and smallpox. Whatever caused the epidemics, they took their toll on the population and severely weakened Rome's political and economic capacity to govern. The second outbreak began with the even more devastating Justinian Plague of 542–43 and may have administered the coup de grace to Rome as an imperial power. Although precise numbers are impossible to determine, the death toll was substantial across the northern African littoral, striking the cities hardest. Everything points to bubonic plague (*Pasteurella pestis*) as the culprit.

The vulnerability of the Roman Empire to epidemics was, to a great extent, a function of

71

population density, which, especially in the cities, had reached such levels that rapid transmission became a virtual certainty once infectious diseases made their appearance. And the prospects of transmission increased as caravan and sea contacts with distant lands in Asia and Africa intensified; new diseases were passed on to previously unexposed populations. Bubonic plague, for example, was not endemic to the Mediterranean region but came from one of two hearths—either the northern foothills of the Himalayas or the great lakes region of eastern Africa. For the Justinian Plague the foothills are the most likely source. Contacts were far more regular than with the lakes region, and the most important host for human bubonic plague, the black rat, also seems to have come from this direction. Plague-carrying rats probably boarded ships bound for Alexandria. Nubia was apparently spared, which would not have been the case if the lakes region had been the source.

Nubian Developments

Lower Nubia, as we have discussed, was devoid of population 3,000 years ago, and the settlement of Upper Nubia remains a mystery. Something of note must have occurred, however, because 250 years later, sources describe an already substantial Kingdom of Kush, with its capital at Napata. Although monarchical institutions and architecture were modeled along pharaonic lines, cemetery excavations indicate indigenous origins and thus suggest a retention of Egyptian traditions rather than their reintroduction. Nevertheless, a period of heightened direct contact with Egypt was imminent, though this time as a result of Nubian initiatives. Taking advantage of internal factionalism within Egypt, Kush advanced northward, quelling various dissident groups and eventually installing Egypt's Twenty-fifth Dynasty. Founded in 751 B.C., the dynasty lasted until an Assyrian invasion in 636 B.C. The era of Kush had ended in Egypt, but not in Nubia; Kush persisted with remarkable stability into the first centuries A.D. and for a time flourished as no other Nubia-based political entity before or since.

Reconsolidation took place around the city of Meroë, on the other side of the great bend in the Nile from Napata (map 5.3). The location had several distinct advantages: it was further removed from possible Egyptian invasion, such as the one that occurred around 590 B.C., and its hinterland had considerably greater agricultural potential. Enough summer rain fell to support the cultivation of sorghum in nearby wadis (seasonally flooded drainage channels), and the Butana Steppe, lying between the Atbara and Nile rivers, provided rich grazing for cattle and other livestock. Of even greater significance, however, were Meroë's trading advantages. The Red Sea coast was within easy reach, the Ethiopian highlands were accessible by road, both the White and Blue Niles could be followed upstream without too much difficulty, and, using overland routes, the great Nile bend could be bypassed. Avoiding the navigational difficulties of upstream travel posed by currents and prevailing headwinds cut the distance to Egypt, and hence the wider Mediterranean world, even more in journey time than in kilometers.

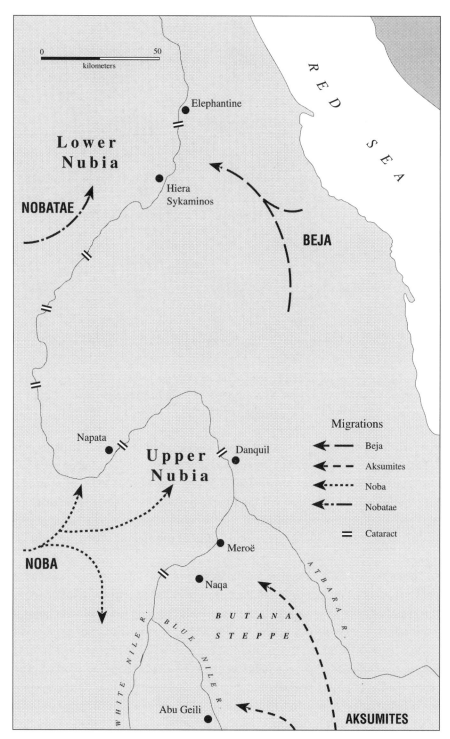

5.3 From the fifth century B.C. to the fourth century A.D. population developments in Nubia were tied to the rise of Meroë and a series of later invasions and in-migrations.

The cultural influence of Egypt can be seen in the dress of the Nubian nobility shown in this fresco. (Reprinted from Bruce Trigger, *Nubia under the Pharaohs,* Westview Press, 1976, pl. 53.)

The replacement of oxen by dromedary (one-humped) camels revolutionized overland travel. The origins of the camel as a domesticated species have been traced back 5,000 years to southern Arabia. The Babylonians knew of the camel's existence, but early Egyptian sources are silent, in spite of the Egyptian tendency to describe animals, both domestic and wild, in considerable detail. Nor is there other evidence to suggest that camels were kept. Perhaps the Egyptians had adopted the Hebrew view that they were unclean.

If so, then attitudes must have changed, because by the middle of the first century B.C. the camel had assumed increasing importance, not only as a mode of transportation for both riders and bundles but also as a source of milk and meat. The conventional view holds that use of the camel quickly spread up the Nile to Nubia. It is possible, however, that the Nubians used camels before the Egyptians. Another route of entry into Africa is across the Red Sea, and considerable evidence suggests that the nomadic Beja had adopted camels well before the Egyptians. How else could they have exploited the desert lands around the Red Sea Hills? Whatever the source of camels, once they came into widespread use, north-south journeys were much easier and quicker. Because of the camel, Meroë expanded to just beyond the Second Cataract and at least as far south as Abu Geili on the Blue Nile. How much territory it controlled in a westerly direction cannot be determined.

Meroë is often credited with being the center for the development of iron smelting, indeed, the place responsible for its spread elsewhere in Africa south of the Sahara. It has even been termed the Birmingham of ancient Africa. The site around the city does indeed contain impressive slag heaps, but these seem to have accumulated over several centuries of activity. Artifactual assemblages give no indication that iron working was an exceptionally prominent industry, so the Birmingham epitaph is unwarranted. And, as we shall see, the diffusion of iron smelting had more likely sources.

Nevertheless, Meroitic craft specialization attained a high level of sophistication: there were potters, jewelers, woodworkers, and smiths of various kinds. Also, by 200 B.C., cotton was being grown—well before it appeared in Egypt—and finished cloth constituted an important export.

The Ptolemies initiated the repopulation of Lower Nubia. Settlements appeared from Elephantine (Aswan) southward to Hiera Sykaminos (Makarraqa), and the area continued to grow during Roman times, such that a number of garrisons had to be built for security. Settlers from Meroë came primarily during the second and third centuries A.D., and they dominated the southern half of Lower Nubia. Gold and emerald deposits in the eastern desert lured traders, but the new wealth of Lower Nubia depended mainly on agriculture. The adoption of the saqiya increased the cultivable area, allowing the floodplain to support numerous and, from the evidence, fairly prosperous agricultural villages. A few towns have been identified, but no major cities existed. Still, the balance of power shifted back to Lower Nubia, and according to estimates, its population eclipsed that of Upper Nubia, reaching 60,000 during the second century A.D.

Accomplishments notwithstanding, the millennium of Kush-Meroë came to an end. The declining prosperity of Egypt meant a reduction in the volume of Mediterranean trade. The rise of the Aksumite kingdom in Ethiopia also hurt trade. Aksum, which launched an invasion into Upper Nubia in A.D. 350, controlled the interior sources of such commodities as gold, ivory, slaves, oils, and fragrances and had direct access to the Red Sea for their export. Nomadic incursions undermined trade as well, especially those by the Beja, or Blemmeys. Their attacks became so troublesome that at the end of the third century A.D. the Romans moved their settlers to the other side of the First Cataract.

The collapse of Meroë came during the first part of the next century, and with it the population of Nubia changed in several important ways. Archeologists and linguists still dispute who exactly the Meroites were. We know that they did have a script that replaced Egyptian, but the surviving texts are not fully decipherable, and from what can be determined, the script has no apparent connection to any known language, dead or living.

Whatever the language may have been, when Meroë disappeared, it did as well, to be replaced by the precursors of modern Nubian languages. These had Eastern Sudanic affinities and thus fall within the Nilosaharan grouping. The peoples using them seem to have originated in the vicinity of Dar Fur, and sometime during the last millennium B.C. they began working their way eastward. One group known since antiquity as the Nobatae populated Lower Nubia. Its members probably made up the majority of the settlers who arrived during the second and third centuries A.D. and were the ones responsible for the so-called Ballama culture, which followed upon the demise of Kush, between the First and Third cataracts. Another group, the Noba, gained control of Upper Nubia. It was they who suffered the Aksumite raids in A.D. 350, not Meroë, which had already disintegrated.

THE CHRISTIAN FACTOR

By the middle of the first millennium A.D., much of northern Africa had been brought within the expanding Christian world. No major population movements are implicated; instead, people converted in situ in response to changing political, economic, and social conditions within the wider Roman-Byzantine Empire. In the Maghrib, Christianity was a fleeting presence, but along the Nile its influence endured.

In Egypt during the first and second centuries interest in Christianity was confined mainly to educated Greeks residing in Alexandria and other cities who found the asceticism of the prevailing gnostic doctrine intellectually appealing. During the third century more orthodox beliefs attracted increasing numbers of converts; by the end of the fourth century 80–90 percent of the Egyptian population considered themselves Christian.

The dramatic break with the past was apparently caused by the decline of the Egyptian economy, which led the Roman administration and local landowners to impose more onerous exactions. As conditions worsened, the old deities lost their appeal and were replaced by a new, untainted god whose worship symbolized protest against the existing order. Crucial to the triumph of Christianity were monasteries. They provided the peasantry with an alternative to laboring for Rome; people could work at monasteries for God and salvation and, at the same time, shield themselves from taxes and military conscription. As monasteries brought more and more of the population within their orbit, they supplanted landlord-held estates as the dominant social and economic institution in the Egyptian countryside.

Competing for spiritual ascendancy were the Melkite and Monophysite doctrines of eastern Christiandom. The Monophysites won because they dominated the monasteries, whereas the Melkite doctrine was followed mainly by wealthy Greek speakers in Alexandria and Cyrenaica, the very people who represented unpopular Byzantium. Through the missionary zeal of Monophysite monks, Coptic Christianity, as it became known, followed Egyptian trade routes south. It reached the Red Sea port of Adulis, whence it was carried into the highlands of Eritrea, there to become the state religion of the rising Aksumite kingdom.

By the fifth century, elements of Christianity had entered Nubia, and over the course of the next several hundred years conversions became commonplace, until nearly the whole population was Christian. Nubian fortunes had revived yet again, this time within the context of three kingdoms—Nobatia, Makouria, and Alwa. Nobatia came within the Coptic fold in the 540s, and was joined by Alwa, centered on the Gezira, only a few years later. Makouria developed within the Dongola Reach. In competition with Nobatia, it accepted the Melkite doctrine around 570. The Melkite hold on the population, however, must have been weak, because after Makouria absorbed Nobatia to form Greater Nubia in the seventh century, the Coptic faith totally replaced it.

The Christian influence in the Maghrib was virtually nonexistent until the end of the second century, when small bands of adherents formed in Carthage and other major cities. Unlike in Egypt, there do not appear to have been any major economic or political crises behind the conversions. Instead, protest against the hedonism of Roman life and a desire among Punic speakers, Libyco-Berbers, and Jews to resist romanization were clear motivations. In spite of repeated persecutions, the number of Christians grew during the third century, and over the next hundred years many poor, rural Numidians and Mauretanians adopted Christian beliefs. Competing for souls were Catholics and Donatists, the latter challenging the authority of the "render unto Caesar" edict obeyed by the former. Which side someone chose marked that person's primary social identity, and although the Catholics eventually prevailed, decades of disputes, often escalating into violence, weakened the political and social fabric of the Roman Maghrib.

The Vandal invasions of 429–32 caused further weakening. The Vandals, part of the great Germanic outpourings of the fourth and fifth centuries, in this instance worked their way through Gaul and Iberia and then crossed into Africa at the Strait of Gibraltar. They came in the tens of thousands looking for land, and although the Vandals did some plundering along the way, it was the disruption brought by their sudden arrival that was critical. Many of them, in fact, quickly settled on the Tunisian Plain, taking up a way of life reminiscent of that of Roman gentry. A Vandal kingship developed there, but it never gained much of a territorial hold. Into the power vacuum stepped mountain and desert Libyco-Berbers, who chipped away at what remained of the Roman Maghrib. By this time they, too, had acquired the camel and the desert mobility that it provided.

Byzantium came to the rescue of the Maghrib in 533. The Byzantines defeated the Vandals and, after several decades of strife with recalcitrant Libyco-Berbers, reestablished order over much of former Numidia and Proconsularis. Some degree of prosperity returned, but the Christian days of the Maghrib were numbered.

THE ARAB ADVANCE

Egypt

The linking of northern Africa to the wider Arab world began with the Muslim armies that entered Egypt from Palestine in 639. Byzantine authority had become increasingly corrupt and oppressive, and the Coptic population more than welcomed its overthrow (map 5.4). By 642 Egypt was effectively secured, which basically meant the replacement of Greek-speaking with Arab-speaking rulers. Some administrative reforms were instituted, but these had little immediate impact on the Egyptian population. Still, the processes through which Egypt became increasingly Arab and Muslim were initiated. They started in

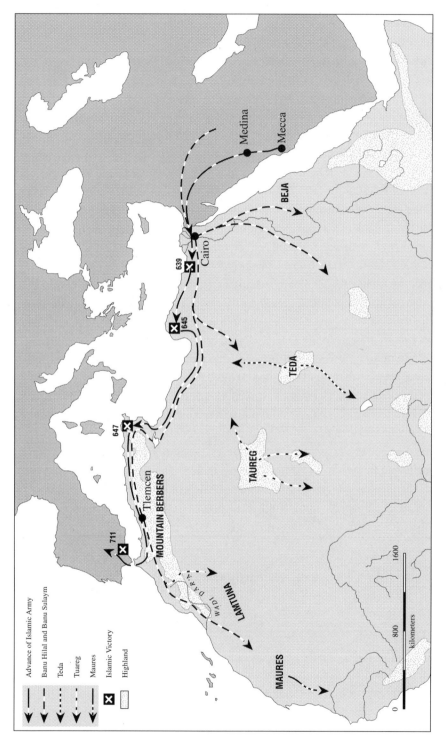

5.4 The Arab advance through northern Africa started with military victories over Byzantine forces in the seventh century. Later came the Banu Hilal and Banu Sulaym migrations, as well as the expansion of other desert-dwelling peoples, notably the Maures, Tuareg, and Teda.

the larger cities, where the Arab presence was most pronounced, and slowly spread to towns and villages. Although some bedouin (nomads) settled along the Nile during the ninth century, notably in the vicinity of Aswan and along both sides of the delta, arabization came about largely by way of adopting what was becoming the dominant cultural tradition. Within 300 years Arabic had replaced Greek and Coptic for both writing and speaking. Islam, however, did not advance quite so rapidly, as the continuing presence of Coptic Christians demonstrates. In Egypt one could become an Arab without being a Muslim. Arab rule was what counted, not conversions, which, according to the Quran, should never be compulsory.

It was not that Arabs physically displaced Egyptians. Instead, the Egyptians were transformed by relatively small numbers of immigrants bringing in new ideas, which, when disseminated, created a wider ethnic identity. Still, the inauguration of Arab-Muslim control could not halt the population slide begun in the third century. Losses continued until the middle of the eighth century, when the population reached a nadir of 2–2.25 million people. Political and religious turmoil were endemic and, in combination with repeated outbreaks of disease and recurrent low Nile floods, rendered life in Egypt highly precarious.

Following this low point, the population once again began to grow, albeit slowly. A reasonable degree of political stability was restored, and increased agricultural productivity followed from the adoption of a wide array of new crops, including rice, bananas, cotton, sugar cane, taro, and eggplant, along with improved varieties of older ones. Most of the introductions came from the Indian subcontinent; and together with refurbished irrigation systems and systematic crop rotation, the new crops helped to stimulate an Arab-induced agricultural revolution throughout Egypt and the Islamic world generally.

Economic conditions improved further when the Fatamid dynasty came to power in the late tenth century. The Fatamids were Isma'ili Shi'a Muslims who built Cairo as their capital for an empire that at its height stretched between Mesopotamia and the Maghrib, the original home of the Fatamids. Prosperity returned to Egypt with its new centrality within the Arab world, and the country withstood several epidemics and serious famines, brought on by repeated Nile floods in the 1060s and 1070s. Trade was revitalized, and goods went across the Indian Ocean to southern China and Indonesia and into Ethiopia and the Sudanic zone of western Africa. Slaves were in great demand for military and domestic service, including concubinage, and large numbers of other Africans joined the Egyptian population. The Fatamids put considerable pressure on the Coptic population to convert or else risk losing economic status, perhaps even their lives, and many chose to embrace Islam. The orthodox Sunni Muslims also faced discrimination, but few seem to have changed sectarian loyalties.

Egypt was formally restored to the Sunni Islamic world—where it has remained firmly entrenched—when the Ayyubids drove the Fatamids from power in 1169. By this time, the population had reached 5 million. The Ayyubids were succeeded by the Mamluks in 1250. Composed of an elite military corps of Turkish and Circassian manumitted slaves who had revolted against their masters, the Mamluks instituted a dictatorial regime that lasted until the Ottoman arrival in 1517. That the Egyptian economy remained buoyant under the Ayyubids and during the early stages of Mamluk rule is evidenced by population growth; the total exceeded 5 million shortly before the middle of the fourteenth century, with Cairo having perhaps as many as half a million inhabitants. Then it plummeted once again. The Black Death arrived in 1348, setting off a series of bubonic-pneumonic plague outbreaks; and a succession of famines caused by low Nile floods and locust invasions also caused havoc. As misery intensified, so, too, did the Mamluks' despotism as they sought to hold power no matter what the cost. The result was a second population nadir at the end of the sixteenth century, when there were just over 2 million people. Some recovery took place in the seventeenth century, but not until the late nineteenth century did the population of Egypt start on its modern explosive trajectory of growth.

The Maghrib and the Sahara

The Arab armies, not having to worry about protecting their position in Egypt, advanced quickly westward. Cyrenaica fell in 645, and the Tunisian Plain was invaded in 647. Here the Byzantine forces stood their ground and were not completely driven out until 670. Latin-speaking Christians, known to the Arabs as al-Afaria, managed to hold out much longer, but their number decreased, and by the fifteenth century only a few scattered groups remained.

As in Egypt, the first Arab immigrants were attracted to the cities. Their presence led to a revival of urban fortunes, and the cities served as centers from which the forces of arabization and islamization reached into the countryside. By the ninth century the Tunisian Plain, now called Ifriqiya, had become one of the most prosperous and progressive regions in the Islamic world. Part of its wealth was based on agricultural products—grain, olive oil, dates, meat, and skins—which came from the latifundia, now taken over by Arabs, and from numerous small peasant plots farmed by Berbers. To an ever increasing extent, however, the economic well-being of the area depended on trade. Ifriqiya figured prominently in Mediterranean commerce, with the cloth a specialty, and it drew on an expanding trans-Saharan trade involving primarily the African triumvirate of gold, ivory, and slaves. Slaves were particularly important; most went on to the eastern Islamic states, but some remained in Ifriqiya to serve as domestics, concubines, eunuch guards, laborers, and soldiers in the corps known as the 'abad.

The Arab troops sped westward through Mauretania, bypassing the Berber-held mountains, and reached their prime target, Visogothic Spain, in 711. In the wake of the troops, Islam spread inland, carried by numerous holy men and merchants, whose proselytizing created a patchwork of different sects—Ibadis, Sufis, Shi'as, Sunnis, and so on—that generated competing dynasties. In the Maghrib it was possible to accept Islam, and even learn Arabic, without assuming an Arab identity, although being a Berber meant second-class citizenship in a political culture that favored Arabs, especially in matters relating to taxation and prospects for economic advancement. In fact, until the eleventh century the number of resident Arabs was quite small, with most in the larger cities of Qayrawan, Tahert, Fes, and Sijilmasa.

For a time the desert remained under Berber control. The only major exception centered on the area surrounding the Tibesti Mountains, where the Nilosaharan Teda (Tibbu) held sway. Elsewhere, two broad and, for the most part, hostile groupings of Saharan Berbers, the Sanhadja and Zanata, competed for dominance. Both had a servile population known as the Haratin, who were not of Berber origin, but most likely remnants of earlier Nilosaharans and later slaves imported from farther south.

During the mid-eleventh century the Lamtuna Sanhadja, located between the Wadi Dar'a and the Senegal River, came under the rule of the puritanical Sunni Malikites. The Arabs found a responsive audience; the Lamtuna had been losing economic ground to Zanata and Arab traders, and soon a superficial Islam was transformed into the Almoravid jihad (literally, struggle to uphold the faith and not holy war), designed to enforce community prayer, the prohibitions against alcohol and unclean foods, Quranic education, the pilgrimage to Mecca, and fasting. The Lamtuna won over other Sanhadja Berbers and took the Almoravid movement northward. It reached its zenith during the early twelfth century, when all of present-day Morocco, half of Algeria and Mauretania, one-third of Spain, and portions of the Sahel were within its territory. Marrakesh was constructed to symbolize the Almoravid usurpation of Ifriqiya's role as the western bastion of Islam, and it became a major center of finance and scholarship.

The Almoravid era did not last for long, however. A revolt among dissident Berbers in the High Atlas region gave rise to the Almohad dynasty, which displaced the Almoravids in 1147. During the latter half of the twelfth century the Almohads united much of Spain, the Maghrib, and the western desert, but they, too, had trouble consolidating their position, and factions broke away. The Almohads were succeeded by the Marinides in Morocco, the Hafsids in Ifriqiya, and, in between, the Zayyanids, with their center at the rich trade city of Tlemcen. Within the High Atlas and the Sahara, political control reverted to many different autonomous Berber chiefs.

All the while, processes favoring arabization and islamization had been gaining momentum. An important boost came with the Banu Hilal and Banu Sulaym migrations that began in the late tenth century and continued for several hundred years. Consisting of a succession of bedouin peoples who left the interior of the Arabian Peninsula because of population pressure, which was the product of intensifying aridity, the immigrants first settled in Egypt, but the shortage of grazing lands there, plus military persuasion by the Fatamids and then the Mamluks, impelled most of them westward. Unlike earlier Arab immigrants, who were largely from urban areas, the bedouin had little experience with, or tolerance for, settled ways of life; their destinations were watering places and grazing grounds.

As more bedouin arrived, the population of the Sahara was reconfigured. The Beja held on to the Red Sea Hills, but the Berber-inhabited areas from Egypt through the Fezzan were overrun and became part of Arab-occupied Africa. So did the western desert. During

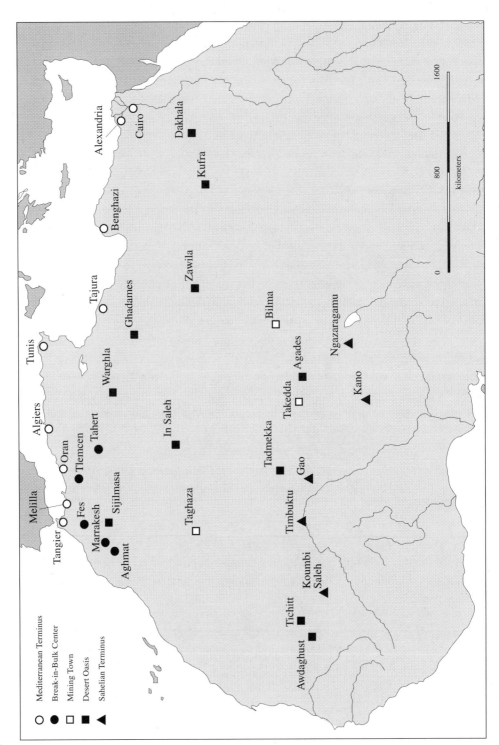

5.5 Most of the towns and cities involved in the trans-Saharan trade played specialized roles.

Almohad times, a number of bedouin were resettled in the lowlands of Morocco to relieve some of the pressure that they had been exerting on Ifriqiya. Soon after their arrival, they moved against the resident Berbers, and from these interactions arose the Maures, who proceeded southward toward the Senegal River. Much of the central desert, however, was beyond reach of the bedouin. The Teda remained inviolate, while the Sanhadja-speaking Tuareg actually expanded from the Ahaggar into the Aïr and Adrar. Both peoples accepted Islam but resisted arabization.

The arrival of bedouin often meant agricultural decline, especially in Ifriqiya, as live-stock herding replaced crop cultivation. Neglect of the *foggaras,* or underground water systems, that supplied many of the oases was particularly deleterious. Without regular maintenance, they quickly became choked with sand. On the other hand, the bedouin stimulated the trans-Saharan trade. Exceptionally skilled at herding camels, they arrived just when the traffic was expanding in response to a growing demand for gold in the Islamic world. Various routes were followed at different times, but most had one of three orienta-tions (map 5.5). One route connected Morocco with the region between the Senegal and Niger rivers; another went from the Niger bend to Morocco and Ifriqiya; and the third linked Tripoli to northern Nigeria, especially around Lake Chad. A fourth route connected Egypt with the Lake Chad area via Dar Fur, but it was less commonly traveled.

By the fourteenth century a highly prosperous and involved trading pattern supported the expansion of a number of urban centers. Those along the Mediterranean coast, like Tripoli, Algiers, Oran, Melilla, and Tangier, served as transshipment points for products from Europe, Asia, their own hinterlands, and Africa south of the Sahara. Jews often played the role of intermediaries between Christians and Muslims. The families of many Jews could be traced back to a second-century diaspora out of Egypt, whereas others relocated in the cities and towns of the Maghrib after being expelled from the Iberian Peninsula after the Christian reconquest. Locations toward the interior, such as Tahert, Tlemcen, Fes, Marrakesh, and Aghmat, were break-in-bulk points—places where goods were repackaged and reloaded—between the mountains and the coast; within the desert itself, towns sprang up at strategic oases, the most important being Sijilmasa, Ghadames, Zawila, Tadmekka, Agades, and Awdaghust. Several towns also developed around mines—Bilma and Taghaza for salt and Takedda for copper. A number of other centers also arose within the Sahel at strategic locations where desert economy met that of the savanna, as we shall see later.

As the cities flourished because of the trans-Saharan trade, the Maghrib countryside suffered. Agriculture lost its attraction, and slaves brought more immediate value when sold abroad. A labor shortage resulted, and as the irrigation systems fell into disrepair and the wells filled with sediment, the land was abandoned. No longer was Ifriqiya a granary for others: to an ever increasing extent it could not feed itself.

Nubia and the Sudan

The most formidable obstacle to the advance of Islam up the Nile was Christian Nubia. It had a well-equipped military, including horse cavalry and skilled archers, with which it repelled two invasions from Egypt in the mid-seventh century. The standoff resulted in a *bakt* (treaty) guaranteeing the autonomy of Nubia in exchange for an annual quota of slaves. Nubia thus gained the unique status of being neither within Dar-el-Islam, the realm of the faithful, nor within Dar-el-Harb, the realm of the enemy. In the centuries immediately thereafter, Lower Nubia became especially prosperous and populous. Barley, millet, dates, and livestock supported self-sufficiency, and the bakt allowed for a flourishing trade with both Egypt and Byzantium. Three towns—Qsar Ibrim, Gebel Adda, and Faras—contained at least several thousand inhabitants each, and there were numerous villages whose populations were in the hundreds. In Upper Nubia, Dongola and Soba seem to have been much larger than the towns of Lower Nubia, but they were the only centers of note in an area inhabited mostly by a dispersed rural population about which little is known.

Once again, however, Nubia found itself on the verge of a dramatic shift in fortune. Key among the internal forces at play was factionalism, prompted in large measure by an economy ever more dependent on the slave trade, and it eroded the authority of monarch and church. In the thirteenth century local secular warlords operated out of fortified castles, and they controlled territories and populations of varying sizes. Into this setting flowed the bedouin. They migrated southward to escape Mamluk pressure, traveling mainly through the Beja-occupied Red Sea Hills (map 5.6), causing the formation of several new Arab-Beja groupings. One amalgamation, known as the Banu Kaz, regularly invaded the region between the First and Second cataracts during the thirteenth century, taking many Nubian lives and forcing others to seek refuge in the rocky inhospitable Batn-el-Hajar, between the Second and Dal cataracts.

The area between the Third and Fifth cataracts also underwent repeated bedouin incursions. In conjunction with Mamluk attacks, these incursions exacted a heavy toll, and, as a result, the Greater Nubia of Nobatia and Makouria faded from history. The last reference to a king dates to 1397. Other Arab groups headed for better grazing lands farther south, and it was only a matter of time before Alwa collapsed, evidently toward the end of the fifteenth century. Christianity held on in localized communities for a while longer, but it, too, disappeared from the scene.

The whole of Nubia reverted to a tribal level of organization, and arabization and islamization proceeded apace. Culture and religion were spread not by the sword, nor in most instances by a numerical preponderance of Arabs, but through alliances and intermarriages between Nubians and Arabs from the surrounding groups. Arab identity prevailed in such circumstances, and to be an Arab meant becoming a Muslim. To justify the new ethnicity, fictive lineage ties to Saudi Arabia were constructed, ones that have come to define Nubian historical reality today.

Acculturation was not uniform. People from Aswan to just beyond Dongola retained a sense of Nubian identity because of their continuing everyday use of the Nubian language, whereas farther south, Nubian identity disappeared completely. Although the people there came predominantly from a Nubian background, they spoke Arabic exclusively and therefore considered themselves Arabs, belonging specifically to the Ja'aliyin lineage.

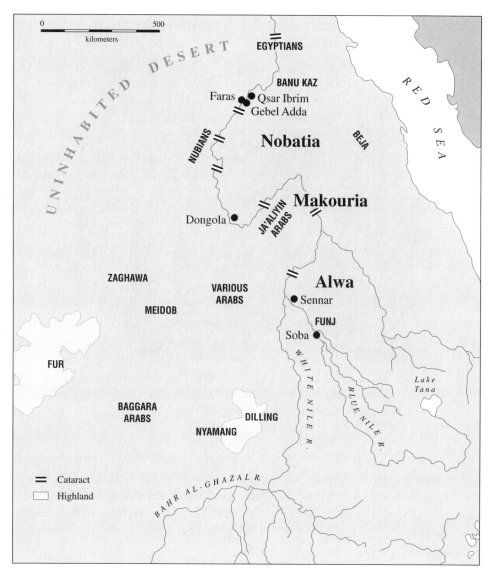

5.6 Continuing migrations and conversions eventually made Christian Nubia and most of the lands to its west parts of the Arab-Islamic cultural world. Only peoples occupying highland refuges remained outside its orbit.

A similar adoption of Arab identity took place among the founders of the Funj Sultanate, centered on the Gezira and Butana regions, with Sennar as its capital. The identity of the founders of Funj is uncertain, except for their nomadic background. If they were indigenes, then a Cushitic origin seems probable. The possibility of derivation from Eastern Sudanic migrants cannot, however, be dismissed. Whoever they might have been originally, they quickly became Muslim and perceived themselves as Arab. Other identity shifts like these explain such groups as the Baggara, or so-called Cattle Arabs, and the

Church ruins tell of the once important role of Christianity in Nubia.
(Reprinted from William Y. Adams, *Nubia Corridor to Africa,*
Princeton University Press, 1977, pl. xxb.)

Zaghawa, and shifts are still going on today among the Meidob, who at the moment claim both Nubian and Arab origins. By and large, the only peoples managing to maintain their previous identity in the face of the Arab advance were those inhabiting defensible highland sanctuaries. Examples include the Fur in the Jebel Mara and the Dilling and Nyamang of the Nuba Hills.

FROM OTTOMANS TO EUROPEANS

The Arabs were not the last invaders of northern Africa. Next came the Ottomans, who had conquered Egypt in 1517. Their political presence reached into Nubia as far as the Third Cataract, while to the west the provinces of Tripolitania, Tunisia, and Algeria became administrative divisions of the Ottoman Maghrib al-Adna. These African territories were peripheral to Ottoman imperial concerns, however; control from Istanbul tended to be weak and was already on the wane during the seventeenth century. Still, the Ottomans left their imprint on the population. They added yet another element of ethnic diversity to the northern African mix, especially, again, in the urban centers. Ottoman Turks took over prominent government and military positions, and many joined the local population through intermarriage. In the Maghrib such Turkish-Arab mixes became so common that a distinct population known as the Kuloglus was recognized. Not only Turks immigrated; Bosnians, too, were an integral part of the Ottoman elite, and there were European slaves from a variety of ethnic backgrounds.

The Ottoman presence affected the comparative fortunes of cities. Two in particular predominated. Cairo was selected to be the seat of Ottoman power, and as such, it controlled much of the commercial life elsewhere in Egypt as well; virtually all Egyptian trade of any value had to pass through Cairo. The city also served as the jumping-off point for pilgrims going to and from Mecca. Because many never returned to their homeland, separate Maghribi quarters became part of the cityscape. By the end of the eighteenth century the population of Cairo exceeded a quarter million—half its size before the Black Death decimated the population but ten times the size of the next largest cities, Alexandria and Rosetta.

Cairo's Maghrib counterpart was Algiers. By the middle of the seventeenth century it had a highly prosperous economy supported by piracy and the sale of European slaves, and it housed about 100,000 inhabitants. Algiers, too, was extremely heterogeneous, with residents who came from all around the Mediterranean region, including a fairly substantial number of Jews.

Throughout the Ottoman period Morocco remained an independent sultanate divided between Arab-held lowlands and Berber-held mountains. Although Morocco maintained contacts with the Ottomans and some European states as well, its attention was directed southward, toward the Senegal and Niger rivers, where on several occasions the government attempted to establish a trans-Saharan kingdom based on gold and slaves. A number of slaves were kept within its own borders, and, accordingly, Moroccans absorbed elements of Sahelian and Sudanic culture and genetics. In the seventeenth century both domestic slaves and many newly captured ones made up a large portion of the elite 'abad military units, which were prominent in and around the city of Meknes. Upon being disbanded in the next century, many of the former soldiers stayed on to work as laborers and farmers. Over time they lost their separate status by merging into the rest of the Moroccan population.

The Ottoman hold on North Africa weakened during the eighteenth century. Toward the end a military elite of Mamluk beys took the reins of power in Egypt. Their onerous exactions kept the countryside in turmoil; agricultural productivity declined, and popular revolts flared. Using the pretext of reestablishing political order, the French launched an invasion in 1798. They were driven out in 1801 by a combined British-Ottoman force that completed one of the tasks begun by the French, namely, the crushing of Mamluk power once and for all. This was accomplished in 1805, after which Egypt embarked on an ambitious program of political, economic, and military modernization using the European state as its model. One result was that more and more Europeans and Americans came to live in Egyptian cities, where they served as advisers, technicians, entrepreneurs, and adventurers. Stimulated by the construction of the Suez Canal and a local cotton boom, annual immigration leapt during the 1850s and 1860s. The Egyptian population also grew, especially during the last decades of the century following the construction of a modern perennial irrigation system using dams and barrages.

With prosperity on the rise, Egypt once again focused its attention on Nubia. As both Ottoman and Funj power waned, Nubia had broken up into a number of sultanates, which offered little opposition to an Egyptian force that entered the area in 1821 and quickly drove toward Sennar. The Egyptians also seized much land farther west but were unable to overcome the peoples of Dar Fur. To escape the coming of Egyptian political control, some Arab traders took their ivory and slaving activities south and southwest into the region of the Nile-Congo watershed. But the Egyptian government followed them, and during the 1860s and 1870s a huge area occupied by various Nilotic and Central Sudanic peoples was incorporated within the newly established Egyptian Sudan as the province of Equatoria.

In the eighteenth century fortunes in the Maghrib took a marked downward turn. As profits from pirating and slavery plummeted, the region found itself increasingly unable to compete economically and militarily with European states. The population was in decline as well, for besides the reversal in prosperity, there were episodes of bubonic plague in 1784, 1793, and 1817–18 and widespread famine in 1815. Estimates for 1830 put the population of Morocco at 3–4 million, with Berbers constituting more than 50 percent; the population of Algeria was 3 million, half of which was Berber; and the population of Tunisia was 1 million plus, with few Berbers. Tunisia was by far the most urbanized: Tunis had a population of 120,000, and Sousse, Sfax, Gafsa, and Qayrawan were also quite large. The population of Algiers had fallen to 50,000 at most, while Constantine held 25,000. With 100,000 residents Fes was Morocco's largest city.

As far as population is concerned, the next half-century proved uneventful in Tunisia and Morocco. For Algeria, however, the story is quite different. The train of events began in 1830 with a French invasion. A regency was established; and although there was no official intention to bring in French colonists, 25,000 had arrived by 1840, many of them derived from the ranks of the Parisian poor. Most settled within the safe confines of Algiers and other cities, but those choosing the countryside found their livelihoods and lives under assault by Berbers. The French government responded by sending military expeditions against the Berbers, many of whom fled to Morocco. By 1846 the number of colonists had surpassed 110,000, with only slightly more than one in ten engaging in agriculture. In 1851 the total was slightly more than 130,000, with 30,000—nearly a quarter—in agriculture. This trend continued when, following another revolt in 1871, large areas were seized from the Berbers and given over to additional colonists. A new civil government was installed, making much of the Algerian Maghrib part of France.

As the nineteenth century drew to its close, the French extended their territorial conquests into the desert and also into Tunisia and Morocco. Elsewhere, the scramble for Africa was under way. The north of Morocco and portions of the western desert eventually went to Spain, and Italy succeeded the Ottomans in Tripolitania and Cyrenaica. Neither Spain nor Italy, however, sent many colonists, and thus their contributions to the local population were insignificant compared to those of the French.

6

ETHIOPIA AND THE HORN

Themes of unity and diversity pervade Africa's smallest and, in many ways, most distinctive region. Although the sharp environmental contrasts provided by the great Ethiopian massif and surrounding lowlands have given rise to a plethora of peoples with very divergent life-styles, historical experiences are widely shared.

Language bears this out, in that two subgroupings within Afroasiatic predominate. The most far-flung is Eastern Cushitic, which includes Oromo, Somali, Afar, and Saho—all languages associated with peoples of basically nomadic herding backgrounds. Vying for regional dominance is Ethio-Semitic, whose main representatives are Amhara, Tigrinya, and Tigre. From a Central Cushitic base they were created, as the name implies, by a fusion with the languages of Semitic migrants from the southern Arabian Peninsula. As the speakers of Ethio-Semitic worked their way into the mountainous interior, they eventually replaced all but a few pure Central Cushitic speakers, collectively known as Agaw (table 6.1).

A few other minorities, because of either their isolation or peripheral status, were also untouched by the tides of Eastern Cushitic and Ethio-Semitic expansion. Omötic groups found protection within the rugged, heavily forested country of the southwest, while several clans of Northern Cushitic Beja speakers managed to claim the desert country of the extreme northeast. Even more marginally attached were the various Eastern Sudanic peoples of the western lowlands, such as the Kunama, Berta, and Koman, whose principal involvement with the dominant cultures has been to serve as a source of slaves.

89

Table 6.1 • Languages of Ethiopia and the Horn

Family	Major Representatives
Ethio-Semitic	Amhara, Tigrinya, Tigre, Guarge, Harari, Argobba, Gafat, Jabarti
Eastern Cushitic	Afar, Saho, Somali, Oromo, Sidama, Konso
Central Cushitic	Agaw
Northern Cushitic	Beja
Eastern Sudanic	Kunama, Berta, Koman
Omötic	Bako, Ometo

Religion also fits the regional pattern of unity and diversity, and for the last several thousand years, it has shaped the course of population developments to a degree unmatched elsewhere on the continent, not even in northern Africa. Judaism, Christianity, and Islam each found adherents and provided powerful symbols for the creation, expansion, and maintenance of cultural identities.

ETHIOPIAN ORIGINS

The Setting

With sharply incised river valleys more than 1,500 meters deep and rugged mountains rising more than 4,000 meters high, the Ethiopian massif possesses some of the most physically imposing terrain found anywhere in the world. Over much of the area, however, the scenery is not so dramatic and instead consists of broad, gently undulating high plateaus 2,500 meters above sea level. Fertile soils derived from recent volcanic materials abound, and because of the elevation, rainfall is ample and, except in the extreme north, reliable. It was in this setting that the Central Cushites pioneered their teff and finger millet–based agriculture, and by 4,000 or so years ago small farming communities dotted the landscape from Shawa to Tigray and Eritrea.

Shortly thereafter the first Semitic speakers arrived. If, indeed, the Afroasiatic languages originated in northeastern Africa, then peoples of Semitic background could have been present in Ethiopia as early as 8,000 years ago. The more usual interpretation, however, places their appearance between 4,000 and 3,500 years ago, when small numbers of colonists from southern Arabia are thought to have crossed the Red Sea to settle among the Central Cushites of Eritrea and Tigray. In addition to a language, the colonists brought with them a productive agriculture that involved wheat and barley, oxen, and the plow. With these crops and aids to labor, the population of the area grew.

The status of Eritrea-Tigray as an early center of population concentration received a boost 2,500 years ago with the arrival of a second group of Semitic immigrants, the Sabaean Arabs. These Semites brought a literate cultural tradition and a sea-based trading network that stretched around the northern shores of the Indian Ocean and into the Red

Sea. Spices and gums were highly valued in the civilizations of Egypt, southwestern Asia, and India, and it was their availability from nearby sources that prompted the Sabaeans to add the Eritrean coast and its hinterland to their realm of trade.

The distribution of surviving monuments, inscriptions, and sculptures points to an infusion of new southern Arabian cultural elements and, therefore, an ongoing Central Cushitic–Semitic synthesis, which by the end of the millennium supported an increasingly urban-oriented society. Inland trade centers like Melazo, Yeha, and Matara flourished, while Adulis provided the chief port connecting the Greco-Roman world with India. Also by this time, two distinctive northern Ethio-Semitic languages, Tigre and Ge'ez (later Tigrinya), had come into being. Semitic influences also appear to have spread farther inland, leading to the formation of a cluster of southern Ethio-Semitic languages: Argobba, Guarge, Gafat, Harari, and Amharic.

Judaism was another early Semitic introduction. Some commentators have attempted to trace its arrival to the original diaspora or to find evidence for it in the legends surrounding Solomon and Sheba, but such efforts have little to support them beyond speculation or wishful thinking. What limited evidence is available indicates a southern Arabian source sometime during the first century B.C. Judaism was practiced in this part of the peninsula at the time, and Jewish immigrants probably joined the broader Semitic movement into Ethiopia. Most of them seem to have settled in small agricultural villages in the Tigrayan highlands, where they undoubtedly converted some of the local inhabitants.

Aksum

Among speakers of Ge'ez, the wealth derived from trade generated economic and population growth, eventuating in the Kingdom of Aksum (map 6.1). The capital, which bears the same name, is today a small provincial town, but its impressive array of ruins include stone stelae, rock-cut tombs, and masonry buildings, some of them large enough to qualify as palaces. Unusually for the times, no surrounding wall was ever built, indicating a lack of concern about security. Adulis, now called Zula, remained the prime outlet on the Red Sea, and a number of inland urban sites have been identified that await detailed archeological excavation. Texts refer to an earlier monarchy, and the general area could well have been ancient Egyptians' fabled land of Punt and the source of the biblical frankincense and myrrh. Now, however, what is known with any certainty dates to the first century A.D., when Aksum was already a substantial mercantilist kingdom trading with Arabia, Meroë, Egypt, and Rome. In *Periplus of the Erythraean Sea,* a commercial seafaring guide written in Greek sometime between A.D. 95 and 130, Aksum is referred to as a metropolis located about eight days inland from the coast and as the place where all the ivory from beyond the Nile was collected before being sent to Adulis.

By the second century Aksum had become the most important commercial center in northeastern Africa outside Egypt, eclipsing even Meroë . It controlled an area of undetermined extent, known to the Arabs as Habashat, later transcribed into Abyssinia. Evidence points to a number of flourishing towns containing a wide array of occupational specialties

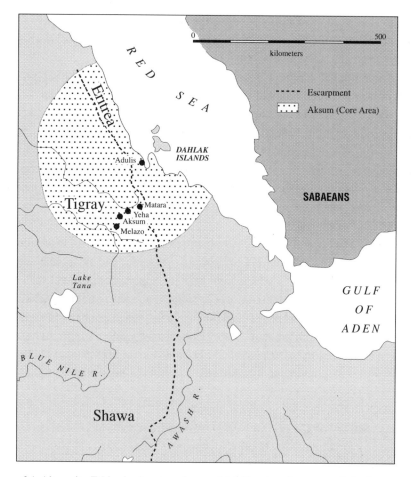

6.1 Aksumite Ethiopia developed around highland trade centers linked to
the port of Adulis on the Red Sea.

and considerable social stratification, including a wealthy elite. At the top of the pyramid
sat a monarch, the *negusa nagast,* the "king of kings." The title suggests that the position
had been won by overcoming other kings, some of whom probably served the negusa
nagast in the capacity of local lords. One estimate places the total population at half a
million when the kingdom was at its peak, but this is no more than a guess. So far, not even
the number within Aksum city itself has been determined.

Sometime during the first half of the fourth century the Monophysite doctrine of
Christianity was adopted as the state religion, and over the next 200 years it gradually
replaced local Cushitic-Semitic polytheisms. Greek and Syriac were early liturgical and
courtly languages, but as Christianity gained converts among the general populace, Ge'ez
supplanted them.

The rise of Christianity sealed the fate of Judaism. It became a minority religion and, in

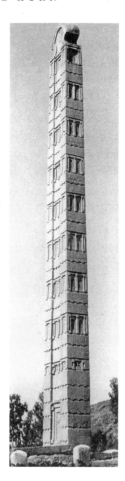

The ruins at Aksum contain a few intact monuments, such as this monolith. (Reprinted, by permission of Greenwood Publishing Group, Inc., Westport, Conn., from David Buxton, *The Abyssinians,* Praeger Publishers, 1970, pl. 42.)

the eyes of the Christians, unworthy of true Israelites, or followers of the Old Testament. Faced with declining fortunes, Jews left Aksum for Lake Tana and the nearby Semien Mountains. Here they seem to have converted local Agaw, creating thereby the nucleus for a new polity. The people would be known as Falasha, although this epitaph was not applied until the fifteenth or perhaps even the sixteenth century, when it designated a particular enemy of the Christian monarchy. The adherents have also been called Black Jews, but their name for themselves is Beta Israel.

Such were the political, economic, and military strengths of Aksum that its influence extended over the area formerly dominated by Meroë, and several times between the third and sixth centuries it was able to add to its share of Indian Ocean commerce by militarily occupying Arabia. Imports included ironware, glass and ceramics, fabrics, wine, sugar, oils, spices, and gems. Among the exports were ivory, gold, emeralds, rhinoceros horns, wild animals, shells, fragrances, and slaves. Supporting trade in this impressive array of commodities was a coinage system using issues in gold, silver, and bronze.

In A.D. 575 Sassinid Persians took control of southern Arabia, an event that sealed

93

Aksum's fate. Several factors, in addition to the loss of preeminence in Indian Ocean commerce, played a role in its gradual decline. One seems to have been population pressure. Aksum had to rely more on local resources, and unfortunately, its ability to produce the most important resource, food, was hampered by the return of more arid climatic conditions. The formative centuries had coincided with a wet phase that nearly doubled the usual three-and-a-half-month growing season. Now the lowlands of the pastoralists were drying up, while drought plagued the highlands. There were too many people for the land to support, as is evidenced by soil erosion due to deforestation and overcultivation, which further depleted the resource base. The southward expansion of the nomadic Beja during the late seventh and early eighth centuries also proved costly. Their continual raiding rendered commercial travel hazardous, and contacts with the coast became intermittent. But by far the most crucial event was the coming of Islam. Its expansion would redraw the population map of Ethiopia and the Horn in profound ways.

ISLAM AND THE RETREAT OF AKSUM

Islam came to the northern Horn early in the eighth century with Arab merchants who traded at the Dahlak Islands. By using religious affiliation to exclude non-Muslim traders they managed to oust Byzantine Greek merchants from the most lucrative contracts. Then they attacked Adulis, sending it to ruin, and carried Islam to the nearby pastoralists—the Cushitic Beja, Afar, and Saho and the Ethio-Semitic Tigre.

Cut off from the ship-borne trade that was the primary source of its wealth, Aksum turned its attention inland. Trade with the Agaw intensified, and by the ninth century the Aksumites had penetrated deep into their territory, spreading Christianity and Ethio-Semitic speech along the way. The growing dominance of Aksum set off a revolt by the Agaw Kingdom of Damot in the 970s that pushed the Aksumites back toward their heartland, where they found refuge in the rugged mountains of Lasta and Tigray. Surrounded by Muslims and Agaw, the descendants of Aksum were effectively isolated from outside contacts, and it was in such a milieu that the insularity of later Ethiopian society had its beginnings. Religion in particular was affected as Old Testament practices and the myth of Solomonic origins became embedded and embellished as key points of dogma.

In the meantime, Islam continued to expand outward from the coast. Inland from Adulis, its progress was hindered by a strong Christian presence in the Eritrean highlands. A much better opportunity for expansion existed at another Muslim-controlled port, Zeila. From Zeila the Awash valley could be followed upstream into the highlands of Shawa without passing through Christian strongholds. A second route ascended the Harar Plateau, going first to Dawaro and then to the small unchristianized Sidama states of the southern rift valleys in the search for sources of gold, ivory, and, most important, slaves. From Yemen to India, there was a constant demand for men to serve in armies and women to serve as concubines, and they could be procured by raiding lands occupied by less politically organized Omötic and Eastern Sudanic peoples. The ports of Berbera, Mogadishu, Marka, and Brava were also tied to this lucrative trade.

Like Adulis several centuries earlier, the ports functioned as centers from which Islam spread to the surrounding population, in this instance, mainly the Somali. By the beginning of the second millennium, the Somali had taken possession of most of the low plateau country south of the Danakil depression and produced, through their migrations, two main branches—the largely pastoralist Dir, Isaaq, Hawiye, and Darod clans of the Ogaden area and northern Horn and the more sedentary Digil and Rahanwiin clans located primarily in the Shabele and Juba River valleys of the south. It was precisely at this point in their history that the Somali elaborated their myths of Arab ancestry going back to Muhammad. These are based on intermarriages between prominent Somali families and local Arabs and symbolize the emergence of the Somali as Muslims. The linguistic evidence, however, shows that the Somali are Africans—specifically, Eastern Cushites.

Conversions took place not only among the Somali but also among other Cushitic and various Ethio-Semitic peoples, including the Harari and Argobba. Toward the close of the twelfth century a chain of Islamic principalities had been established, linking the ports via the Awash valley and Harar with Shawa and the rift valley lakes of the south. The most powerful principality was Ifat, followed by Dawaro, Fatagar, Hadya, and Bali. Within Christian Ethiopia itself a specialized Muslim merchant class known as Jabarti had formed, largely in response to a long-held Ethiopian aversion to trade as an occupation.

CHRISTIAN REVIVAL AND THE AMHARA

Christian Ethiopia did not lie dormant. Reorganized and reinvigorated, it launched upon a new phase of expansion during the twelfth century under the aegis of the Zagwe dynasty. How this Agaw Christian lineage came to power remains unclear, but its accession severed the Solomonic tradition dating back to the fourth century. The Zagwe dynasty shifted the capital to Lalibela in Lasta to confirm the dominance of the southern and western regions and reclaimed portions of northern territory previously lost to the Beja.

Zagwe hegemony did not last long; it ended in 1270, and the myth of Solomonic lineage was reestablished under a dynasty of Amharic origin. Located in the southwestern portion of Wollo and of South Ethio-Semitic linguistic affinity, the Amhara came to define and extend the concept of being Ethiopian. They had accepted Christianity in the ninth century and achieved considerable churchly prominence under the Zagwe. Of the major christianized peoples, they were also nearest to the Muslim traders moving up the Awash valley. Thus religion and commerce combined to place the Amhara at the core of regional developments.

The Amhara made their greatest territorial gains between 1314 and 1344. Many of the smaller non-Christian Semitic and Cushitic peoples and states were conquered, including Damot, and the main Islamic principalities subjugated. After an initial military phase came

150 years when the Amhara sought to consolidate their power and authority throughout the vastly expanded domain. They did so by instituting a feudal-style system in which territorial governors and military garrisons represented royal authority in the dominions. Monks built a complementary and extensive network of monasteries from which they could promote the faith and recruit loyal citizens to the regime. During the fifteenth century the religious paramountcy of the Amhara received official sanction in the final redaction of the *Kebra Nagast* (Glory of kings), the Ethiopian national epic. It reaffirmed Aksum as the spiritual source of the Ethiopian church and the Solomonic dynasty of the Amhara as Aksum's rightful heir.

Considerable variation in the degree of imperial assimilation and control could be found. At the core were Amhara, Begemder, and parts of Shawa and Gojjam provinces (map 6.2). Here, through appointed intermediaries, the emperor ruled supreme. Less closely ruled were Tigray, Wag, and Lasta. In Tigray there was considerable resentment over Amhara preeminence, especially in religious matters, and to mollify malcontents, the emperor allowed a modest degree of political autonomy by recognizing the local authority of leading Tigrinya families. However, this did little to quell a rising tide of Tigrean separatism.

Given the problems of transport and communications, ties with the newly acquired Agaw territories were extremely tenuous. Loyalties in these remote areas still centered on local traditional rulers, and only a strong military presence kept the populace in line so that tribute and taxes could be collected. The same held true for Sidama and other sources of slaves, gold, and ivory in the southwest. The Muslim principalities were even more loosely ruled from the imperial center. They resisted incorporation into Ethiopia and sought to regain their former political, economic, and religious autonomy. Repeated Ethiopian efforts to assert its will kept the northeastern borderlands in what amounted to a perpetual state of seige.

ISLAMIC RESURGENCE

The intensity of the conflicts escalated in the early decades of the fifteenth century under the leadership of Adal, a state controlling the Harar Plateau and surrounding lowlands that was never brought into the Ethiopian orbit. By the late fifteenth century, centripetal forces within Ethiopia had once again overtaken centrifugal ones, and Adal seized the opportunity to raid nearby Christian communities, liberating both territory and wealth and taking numerous captives to sell as slaves. Warfare raged into the sixteenth century, with neither side dominant for very long. The standoff ended when, in 1529, with the aid of Somali and Afar recruits, Adal launched a massive jihad aimed at the heart of Ethiopia, and within two years the Christian armies had been driven deep into mountain refuges. Crucial to the invader's success was Ottoman support, which was mainly in the form of modern armaments, including artillery.

As the jihad advanced, many subject peoples and unconverted or marginally converted

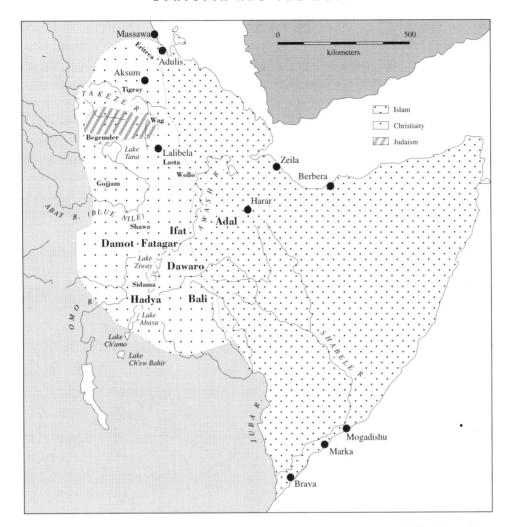

6.2 By the fifteenth century almost all of Ethiopia and the Horn had been divided into either Christian- or Muslim-dominated space.

Agaw joined its ranks, and even some Ethiopian notables saw an advantage in lending their support. By the end of the 1530s virtually the whole of Ethiopia had been conquered, and a new greater Islamic empire seemed to be in the making. An administrative structure was fashioned, and all that remained was to ferret out the remnants of the Ethiopian court and its armies from the northern mountains.

By the beginning of the 1540s, however, the jihad had lost much of its momentum, partly because of the huge area encompassed. In the final analysis, however, a more important reason was the landing of a small Portuguese force near Massawa in 1541 as part of the larger Portuguese strategy to wrest control of the Red Sea from the Ottomans. Although the Islamic armies easily defeated the force the following year, the diversion gave the Ethiopians a respite. In 1543 their revitalized troops joined with the remaining Portuguese in a decisive battle that not only halted the jihad but caused it to disintegrate almost instantly, for reasons that are still unclear.

By the 1550s Ethiopia had regained control over most of its former area, subduing the remaining Islamic principalities and overcoming the always rebellious Damot. Only Adal held out. Faced with economic pressure and religious discrimination, many Beta Israel resorted to tenant farming, while others retreated deeper into the sanctuary of the Semien Mountains or turned to metal smithing, pottery making, woodworking, masonry, or other crafts, displaying skills that both won them renown and evoked fear among the Ethiopians. In spite of the impressive victories, Ethiopia and its Amharic rulers did not experience a new golden age. Before the severed pieces could be put back together again, a new force inserted itself into the picture: the Oromo.

Periodically the contest between Christianity and Islam in Ethiopia turned into warfare. (Reprinted, by permission of the British Library, from J. M. Reid, *Traveller Extraordinary: The Life of James Bruce of Kinnaird,* Eyre and Spottiswoode, 1968, fig. facing p. 145.)

THE OROMO EXPANSION

The origins of the Oromo peoples, formerly called Galla, can be traced to the area of the rift valley and highlands near the headwaters of the Shabele and Juba rivers, where they organized themselves into a series of loosely confederated seminomadic clans. During the early sixteenth century the Oromo embarked on a series of portentous migrations that took them across much of Ethiopia and the Horn (map 6.3). In general, they followed two broad paths, going eastward through Bali and skirting the highland core or heading north and west directly into highland Ethiopia.

The reasons for the exodus once again appear to have resulted from local population dynamics. Undoubtedly playing a role was the seemingly never-ending need of the nomads to find additional grazing lands and water sources to support herd expansion. Furthermore, each newly installed warrior class (an installation took place every eight years) had to prove itself by attacking an enemy for livestock and other booty. In the beginning, such attacks were probably aimed at nearby Eastern Cushitic peoples, who have since disappeared from the ethnic record either because of annihilation or, more likely, assimilation with the Oromo. Possessed of an open and highly flexible social system, the Oromo could absorb others with little difficulty and in this way added yet more Oromo, who made further migrations necessary.

Expansion took the Oromo into a variety of human and natural environments. The very same openness that augmented their number allowed them to adapt, and thus the Oromo became many, all changed in one way or another. Only those who remained behind in the south, notably the Arusi and Borana, stayed essentially the same.

The Oromo clans proceeding north and west encountered the Sidama states. Some of the opposing states managed to fend off repeated attacks, but others were overrun and came under Oromo rule. Political volatility and its inevitable companion conflict became the local norm, effectively cutting the area off from outside contacts until the nineteenth century. By then the Oromo had abandoned nomadic herding for farming and trade-related occupations and had come under considerable Sidama influence. For some, acculturation went so far that they lost their Oromo identity altogether, whereas others adopted a half-Oromo cultural status.

Past Bali in the east, the frontier lay wide open. The rich pastures of the Harar Plateau were especially attractive, and by the early seventeenth century the Oromo had gained control over them, thus ending the long local hegemony of Adal. The years of warfare took their toll, and only the town of Harar managed to hold out as a bastion of Semitic Muslim population. Some Oromo did settle nearby and convert to Islam, but most carried on with their traditional herding way of life.

As the expansion continued in both southeasterly and northeasterly directions, the Oromo eventually found themselves competing with the Somali, Afar, and Saho for grazing and water rights. Conflict flared along a front from the Tana River to Berbera, resulting in frequent shifts of territorial control. In time, however, a general pattern evolved: the

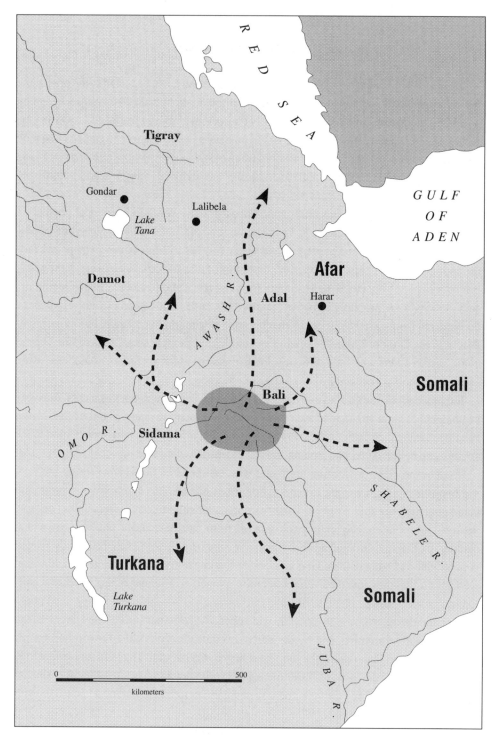

6.3 Migrations took the Oromo across much of Ethiopia and the Horn. They claimed new territory in the semiarid lowlands of the east and south, but those who headed into the highlands often experienced considerable culture change from contacts with Sidama and Amharic Ethiopia.

Oromo occupied the grasslands of the western portions of the low plateaus adjacent to the highlands, whereas the Somali, Afar, and Saho held the eastern lowlands beyond the coast. The Oromo, because of their position, provided a buffer between Christian-held and Muslim-held space that interrupted a competition of nearly a thousand years' duration. The rivalry would be resumed in the nineteenth century.

The Ethiopian reaction to the initial Oromo advances was unconcern. They considered the Oromo primitive and of little consequence, and, in any event, they still had to contend with the Muslim threat. That was finally put to rest in 1579 after a series of victories over Ottoman forces in Tigray; then the Ethiopians turned their attention to their northwestern frontier. By 1620 Beta Israel resistance had crumbled, causing them to lose political autonomy, territory, and members either through death or conversion. Renewed efforts were also made to subdue the remaining unconverted Agaw in Wag and Lasta.

With few Ethiopian troops to resist them, the Oromo quickly spread across the southern and central highlands during the last decades of the sixteenth century and seized control of Shawa and Amhara. They had learned how to use horses and firearms and recruited many disaffected Ethiopian subjects into their ranks, just as the jihad forces had done a few decades earlier. The Ethiopian royal presence evaporated, as symbolized by the relocation of the capital in Gondar, north of Lake Tana. It was safe from the Oromo here but peripheral to the realities of political and economic power in the highlands.

To escape from the Oromo, the imperial Ethiopian court was relocated to the highland fortress of Gondar. (Reprinted from Richard Pankhurst and Leila Ingrams, *Ethiopia Engraved: An Illustrated Catalogue of Engravings by Foreign Travellers from 1681–1900,* Kegan Paul International, 1988, p. 42.)

The Ethiopian cultural presence, however, did not disappear. The Oromo were neither numerous enough nor sufficiently well organized politically to assert control over the territories through which they passed, and many Ethiopian communities survived the Oromo advance because they were located on large flat-topped hills known as ambas or in rugged mountainous terrain. Wars continued into the seventeenth and eighteenth centuries, with the Ethiopians eventually gaining the upper hand, largely by enlisting many Oromo. In the highlands the Oromo took up plow agriculture, and many adopted Christianity and either Amharic or Tigrinya speech. Especially in Gojjam and Begemder, the Oromo became almost totally integrated into Amharic society, even to the point of being accepted within courtly circles. Elsewhere, though no longer nomadic herders, other Oromo held on to their identity, often by adopting Islam as a point of differentiation.

The Oromo migrations upset the balance of power in the highlands, and by the mid-eighteenth century the court in Gondar was little more than token. In previous centuries royalty had been mobile, visiting the provinces on a regular schedule to show their authority. Ruling now in their stead were numerous local warlords, whether of Amharic, Tigrean, or Oromo background, who competed with one another for territorial control and the right to extract tribute from the peasantry. This period is known as *zamana masafent,* "the era of

Many Ethiopian communities survived the Oromo advance because of their defensible locations atop ambas. (Reprinted from Pankhurst and Ingrams, *Ethiopia Engraved,* p. 22.)

princes." Doctrinal disputes and divisions within the church exacerbated the factionalism, and little or nothing suggested the reformation in the making.

Although not directly affected by Oromo incursions, the trade centers along the coast had their ups and downs in response to conditions in the interior. Traders in Massawa and Zeila turned profits from the export of coffee to Europe and from the continuing demand for slaves in southwestern Asia and therefore remained the most active ports on the Red Sea and the Gulf of Oman. Nominally under Ottoman rule, they and other northern centers had mixed Afar, Somali, and Arab populations. Farther south, Mogadishu and Brava still operated, though at a reduced level, and were inhabited mainly by Somalis.

REFORMATION

In spite of the seeming disorganization of the polities, a reformation was about to begin. It would lead to a new political and cultural order, but one harking back to the past. In the 1820s and 1830s Egypt seized territory along the Red Sea coast and sent armies up the Blue Nile River valley. The Egyptian presence generated a supportive Islamic response, most notably among the Somali, for whom religion once again served as a unifying theme. Islam also gained converts from autonomous Oromo groups in the east and south and in Sidama. Repeating a long-established pattern, trade followed an activated Islam, and the ports and the southern interior prospered accordingly.

Within the highlands the zamana mesafent remained in effect past mid-century, but the processes leading to reunification had already taken hold. Imperial reforms meant to replace the old feudal structure of society with a new centralized administration and military were successful at first but ultimately succumbed to still-powerful centripetal forces. Nevertheless, enough changes had been made that a foundation existed for the rise of the modern state of Ethiopia. The Egyptian invasion was repelled, and the capital relocated to Debre Tabor in Shawa, thus once again centralizing the position of the Amhara. Campaigns to reclaim previously lost lands and to extend them quickly followed. At the same time European states were poised to scramble for colonies. A clash of competing imperialisms was inevitable.

7

WESTERN AFRICA

Western Africa begins where the Sahara ends, and because few major topographic features complicate conditions, its environmental zones follow a fairly symmetrical north to south alignment (map 7.1). A short, though erratic, rainy season supports the sparse cover of vegetation that defines the steppelike Sahel, which serves as a transition to the largest and most characteristic region in western Africa—the Sudan. Here is classic savanna, where the rainy season lasts from four months in the north to seven months in the south. Baobab and acacia trees are sprinkled across an open vegetative landscape dominated by bushes, grasses, and other herbaceous growth. Next comes another narrow transitional zone, where savanna and forest intermingle, before the rain forest is reached. It is lowland forest and consists of two discontinuous zones. The eastern zone is essentially an extension of the equatorial rain forest, although the months from December through February are somewhat less wet. Instead of having rain throughout the year, the western zone is monsoonal, with a nine- or ten-month rainy season that brings as much as 4,000–5,000 millimeters of precipitation, peaking in July and August. Separating the two is a drier wedge of savanna and woodland countryside that owes its existence to the oblique way the offshore winds strike land. Finally, there is the coast, fringed with mangrove swamps and pounded by heavy surf.

Four thousand years ago population change across this vast area picked up momentum in response to the slow but unrelenting spread of agriculture. Playing a crucial role in

104

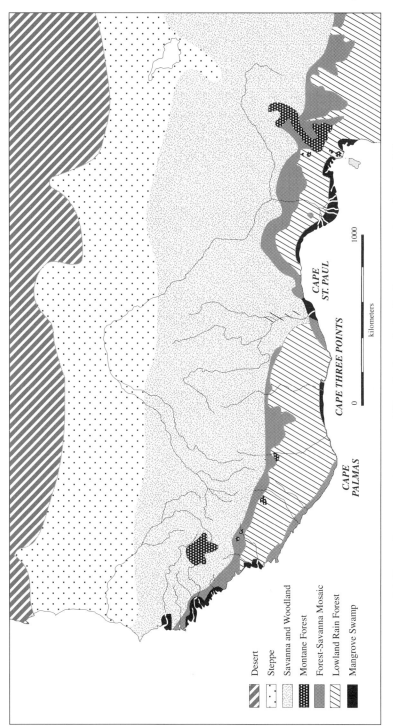

CAPE ST. PAUL

CAPE THREE POINTS

CAPE PALMAS

0   1000

kilometers

Desert

Steppe

Savanna and Woodland

Montane Forest

Forest-Savanna Mosaic

Lowland Rain Forest

Mangrove Swamp

7.1 Vegetation patterns in western Africa display a latitudinal symmetry based on rainfall.

Stands of baobab trees are a common sight on the dry savannas of western Africa. The fruit is edible, and the bark can be used for making ropes and containers. (Photo courtesy of Philip W. Porter.)

events were Saharan nomads, who drifted southward seeking escape from ever worsening desertification. The pressures that their arrival exerted seem to have intensified the pace of agricultural development among various Niger Congo peoples, whose own numerical growth generated further population realignments.

Changes did not come in the form of mass movements, with newcomers seizing control of territory. Rather, the changes resulted from many small, essentially kin-based groups searching for more advantageous places to live. Except for the Guinea Highlands, the Sudanic landscape is dominated by gently undulating plateaus that pose few restrictions to mobility. Nevertheless, significant microenvironmental variations affect crop and live-stock productivity. Soil fertility, water supply, and distribution of disease, particularly sleeping sickness and river blindness, undoubtedly influenced settlement patterns as much then as they did later. The preferred locations developed as population centers, where many of the languages within the Atlantic, Mande, Gur, Kwa, Benue-Congo, and Adamawa-

Ubangi branches of Niger Congo originated (table 7.1). The oral traditions of present-day peoples make frequent reference to specific points of origin, and although these may not be historically precise, they symbolize the strong relation between ethnic identities and particular places.

Other forces besides agricultural development were soon redesigning the population map: iron-making technologies spread, as did, later, the opportunity to participate in interregional and international trade. Trade redefined comparative locational advantage, and in many instances it provided the impetus for the formation of states, which facilitated the growth of population and replaced processes favoring ethnolinguistic differentiation with those that brought convergence.

IRON MAKING

Africa south of the Sahara, unlike the Maghrib and the Nile valley, bypassed an intermediate Bronze Age and went directly from stone-based technologies into those involving iron. Until just recently, it was widely believed by researchers that evidence from Agades showed copper smelting preceding iron smelting. However, this has been disproved, and thus the new interpretation has the two technologies appearing synchronously, but with iron of far greater importance. The earliest dates on record are in the 700–400 B.C. range, with the Taruga site, located along the margins of the Jos Plateau in central Nigeria, having the best documentation. Here slag deposits and at least thirteen iron furnaces have been found in association with the Nok culture, known principally for its pottery and highly detailed terra-cotta figurines. Assemblages point to a sedentary farming population, and, given the location, an association of Nok-Taruga with Benue-Congo yam farmers is reasonable. The homeland of the Benue-Congo languages has been traced to near the confluence of the Benue and Niger rivers, and by the Iron Age considerable internal differentiation had already taken place.

Some paleoarcheologists propose that iron making was invented independently at Nok-

Table 7.1 • Niger Congo Languages

Family	Major Representatives
Atlantic	Woloff, Serer, Fulbe, Diola, Temne, Kisi
Mande	Soninke, Malinke, Bambara, Dyula, Lorma, Kpelle, Mano, Vai, Dan
Gur	Seufo, Grusi, Mossi, Dagomba, Mampruli, Dogon (?)
Kru	Bakwe, Bassa, Krahn
Ijoid	Ijo, Oruma
Kwa	Ewe, Akan, Baule, Aja, Fon
Benue-Congo	Yoruba, Nupe, Igbo, Biram, Jukun, Ibibio, Efik, Tiv, Bantu
Adamawa-Ubangi	Mbum, Bari, Gbeya, Ngabanda, Banda, Zande, Amadi

Abandoned furnaces dot the landscape of western Africa, providing important sources of information about the origin and spread of iron smelting. (Photo courtesy of Christopher R. DeCorse, Syracuse University.)

Taruga. However, roughly contemporaneous and similar sites have also been discovered at Akoujit in western Mauretania and Do Dimmi and Agades in Niger, which suggests the possibility of diffusion from an external iron-making source. Meroë was once widely considered the prime candidate, but the earliest known dates are more recent than those at Taruga by at least 200–300 years. Furthermore, the methods employed at Taruga incorporated sophisticated preheating techniques and an ability to produce steel with a high carbon content, whereas at Meroë the procedures followed Egyptian and Roman styles, using simpler methods of heating and with no carburization.

The Phoenicians are the only other reasonable alternative. They are credited with the introduction of iron making into northern Africa during the first half of the last millennium B.C., and the technologies could very well have followed Libyco-Berber trade routes across the desert to be adopted and subsequently improved on by local smiths.

Whatever the source, once iron making became known, the incentives to adopt it would have been considerable. Iron-bladed hoes, knives, and sickles are far more effective than their stone counterparts, and iron axes undoubtedly facilitated the advance of agriculture into wooded and forested habitats. Also of great significance was the fashioning of iron weapons, specifically spearheads and arrow points. Stone weapons would have been no

108

match for them, and, therefore, the ability to manufacture iron weapons undoubtedly helped determine comparative population success two millennia ago.

In spite of the advantages of iron, the archeological evidence points to a very slow and uneven diffusion of manufacturing technologies that took a thousand or so years to achieve reasonably complete areal coverage. Western Africa is rich in easily mined surface deposits with the required iron content, so the unavailability of raw materials can explain only a small part of the reason why the technologies took so much time to disseminate. Of likely greater significance was that the secrets of iron making were carefully guarded. Over much of western Africa, blacksmiths came to occupy a very special cultural position and were often vested with supernatural powers. Frequently they were, and in some places still are, set apart in hereditary castes, keeping their craft of fashioning earth into objects secret from the rest of the population. Interestingly, blacksmiths are also frequently the featured actors in creation myths, and thus we can hypothesize that at least a few ethnolinguistic identities crystallized around them.

TRADE AND EMPIRE IN THE WESTERN SUDAN

The next population stimulus came from a combination of trade and widening external contacts. Tumuli in both Senegambia and the vicinity of the Niger River bend show evidence of imported wares and the probable existence of localized chiefdoms at least by the early centuries of the first millennium A.D. Numerous megaliths were also left behind in both areas, and the combined evidence suggests a prior period of population growth and incipient social stratification. Further insights can be gleaned from findings at the archeological sites of Dhar Tichitt and Jenne-jeno.

By 900–800 B.C. agricultural expansion and intensification at Dhar Tichitt had given rise to a number of walled villages in secure locations, each containing from 500 to 1,000 inhabitants, who were almost certainly peoples directly related to the later Mande. Around 700 B.C. the settlement pattern changed. There were smaller, more numerous unwalled villages; and because many were in open sites, it is possible that the general social climate had become one of peaceable cooperation, even if unification had not happened. Then from 600 to 300 B.C. the villages were relocated to widely scattered sites in more inaccessible and defensible terrain. The area shows signs of an invasion, with Berber nomads the most likely candidates, and although the previous developmental trend came to an end, another one began that would turn an initial disadvantage into an advantage.

The Jenne-jeno site is located within the inland delta of the Niger River. First settled about 250 B.C., the village grew steadily, covering an area of twelve hectares early in the next millennium. The inland delta had, and has, a highly diverse ecosystem presenting a wide range of specialized food-producing possibilities. Consequently, Jenne-jeno probably started out as a place where local farmers, herders, and fisherfolk brought their produce to exchange with one another. The trade network expanded. No sources of stone, iron, or copper existed nearby, yet numerous artifacts made of all three materials have been uncovered in the archeological debris. The closest source of copper would have been the Aïr, where it has been confirmed that smelting existed at least as far back as the sixth and seventh centuries A.D., whereas the iron most likely came from somewhere farther west. The status of manufacturing at Jenne-jeno is uncertain.

By providing a place for people from all points of the compass to bring products, Jenne-jeno became an interregional trade center. It might have been the first one in the region, but if so, others soon followed, and several of these were the foci for a series of kingdoms and empires in the Sahel and the Sudan. What we know about them is sketchy and comes mostly from oral histories and literate Muslim Arab and Berber travelers, who made their first visits to the Sahel and the Sudan in the eighth century. Nevertheless, what is reasonably clear is that as each rose and fell, the regional population map changed both quantitatively and qualitatively.

Ghana

The first polity we know of to gain prominence was Ghana (map 7.2). Founded by peoples of Soninke (Mande) linguistic background, it followed from later developments at Dhar Tichitt. An accommodation with the Berbers must have been reached because sometime before A.D. 800 an extensive, well-organized state was established. We can have some confidence in this date because Ghana was described by a Muslim Berber visitor near the end of eighth century as flourishing, at least when judged by the wealth of its substantial capital. Known at the time as Koumbi, it is now identified with the archeological site of Koumbi Saleh. Given its location (15° 46′ North and 8° West), its riches must have come mostly from trade. Even back then, it would have been situated near the northern margin of reliable crop cultivation—a liability that was nevertheless more than offset by being strategically placed with regard to two key natural resources, salt and gold, and to trade contacts with the Berbers.

Salt was mined in the western Sahara and then taken to either Koumbi Saleh or Awdaghust, the other important trade center in Ghana, to be distributed to the generally salt-poor savanna and forest regions. The trade had existed for many centuries and undoubtedly played an important economic role at first, but salt soon took second place to gold, derived from alluvial deposits in a region along the Upper Senegal River known as Bambuk. Gold symbolized Ghanaian royalty and therefore must have been an early item of commerce. Eventually, however, external demands as opposed to local ones would define gold's value.

Considerable controversy has surrounded the question of when the trans-Saharan gold trade began in earnest. Although some gold may have found its way across the desert into the mints of the Carthaginians and Romans, the quantity would have been limited. Other sources of gold closer to hand in Spain and the Atlas Mountains were more easily tapped. This began to change during Byzantine times, when the mint at Carthage was turning out enormous numbers of coins. The Arabs continued the trend. They moved the site of the

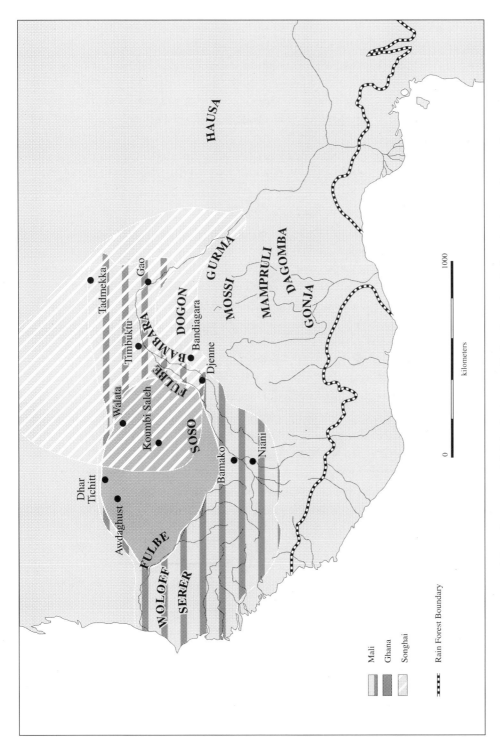

7.2 Powerful empires rose and fell in the western Sudan from the ninth to the sixteenth centuries.

HAUSA

Tadmekka
Gao
GURMA
Timbuktu
DOGON
MOSSI
BAMBARA
Bandiagara
MAMPRULI
Walata
Djenne
DAGOMBA
Koumbi Saleh
FULBE
GONJA
Dhar
Tichitt
SOSO
Bamako
Awdaghust
Niani
FULBE
WOLOF
SERER

Mali
Ghana
Songhai
Rain Forest Boundary

0   1000

kilometers

mint to Qayrawan, and both the Fatamids and the Almoravids built new mints to handle the increased level of production. The demand for gold had exceeded the supply from the traditional sources, and Ghana was on hand to fill the void.

Two other commodities also figured prominently in Ghanaian prosperity. Slaves, captured in war and procured in trade with forest dwellers, accompanied the caravans across the desert, and kola nuts, also from the forest zone, were an important item of commerce within the drier parts of western Africa, where chewing them helped to quench thirst and stay hunger.

The legends reaching the Islamic centers in northern Africa and western Asia earned Ghana the nickname Land of Gold, and it became a destination for increasing numbers of Arab and Berber merchants and holy men. The newcomers added to Ghana's prosperity and prestige, which peaked in the first half of the eleventh century.

Koumbi Saleh had grown to include 15,000–20,000 inhabitants. It was actually a twin city, the prototype of an organizational pattern repeated many times over throughout the Sahel and the Sudan. One city housed the royal court and its retinue, while some ten kilometers away the other served Muslims, who for the most part were non-indigenes, or "strangers." Awdaghust also attracted many Arabs and Berbers, although it was less than half the size of Koumbi Saleh. At the same time that newcomers made their way to Ghana, many Soninke left for other parts of western Africa searching for trade opportunities; the diaspora is still observable in population distributions and is remembered in the oral histories of clans to this day.

Ghana's fall from its pinnacle of power has long been a point of dispute among historians. The decline began during the second half of the eleventh century, and earlier interpretations tended to give primacy to Almoravid invasions, which were the product of intense competition over who would dominate trans-Saharan trade by controlling its most important routes. Armed conflicts between the Ghanaians and the Almoravids certainly occurred from time to time, and in the first half of the eleventh century the Almoravids did manage to seize several strategic desert centers, including Awdaghust, although they never directly invaded Ghanaian territory. The economy of the empire definitely suffered, but other factors also proved instrumental in causing its eventual demise. Of particular importance was the loss of internal cohesion, a result of the incorporation, often by force, of many non-Soninke into the population. When strong competitors appeared on the scene, the fragility of Ghana became evident.

Takrur and Soso

Takrur was Ghana's main rival in the west. Founded by Atlantic-speaking peoples known as Tukulor (a corruption of Takrur) residing along the middle and lower reaches of the Senegal River valley, it became the first African polity south of the Sahara to embrace Islam. The version adopted was that of the Almoravids, who served as a strategic economic and political ally. This cooperation allowed Takrur to challenge Ghana for control of the goldfields in Bambuk and eventually to prevail in the twelfth century. So wealthy and powerful did Takrur become that throughout much of the Arabic-speaking world the name Takrur came to stand for the general region of the western Sudan. Yet Takrur did not have imperial ambitions. Unlike Ghana, it remained spatially confined and ethnically unified, facts that help explain its continued survival for several hundred more years.

In contrast, Soso had a relatively short life span. It is known only through oral traditions, and these are unclear on matters of origin. Some southern Soninke clans in the hill country north of Bamako may have initiated its rise; however, legends claim that the kingdom was founded by a clan of Malinke blacksmiths. Soso adopted a fervent anti-Islamic stance and developed a reputation for the ferocity with which its armies fought. During the first half of the thirteenth century Soso sacked Koumbi Saleh, and when it fell, Ghana faded from history. Farther west, however, another power was on the rise; it would quickly put an end to Soso's brief encounter with fame.

Mali

The formal beginnings of Mali are traceable to another Malinke clan, known as the Keita, who resided in the Upper Niger valley south of Bamako, but its real origins probably go back to Jenne-jeno. During the eleventh century the Keita adopted Islam and started to bring other Malinke chiefdoms under a single kingship centered on the town of Niani. Situated in an area of considerable agricultural productivity and strategically placed along the routes to the goldfields, Mali grew strong enough to overthrow Soso in the 1330s. Expansion continued, and by the end of the fourteenth century Mali encompassed a huge area stretching from the Lower Senegal and Upper Niger rivers eastward to the Niger bend and northward into the Sahel.

Its great size made it an even more diverse state than Ghana. The majority of the people lived in small villages and cultivated rice or sorghums and millets, but some communities specialized in herding or fishing. Trade flourished in the towns, which housed a wide array of craftspeople, along with a growing number of Islamic teachers and holy men. The ethnic mix included Soninke, Woloff, Tukulor, Fulbe (Fulani), Bambara, Bozo, Songhai, Berbers, and Arabs when Mali was at its height. In addition, specialist trading groups arose—the Wangara, Dyula, Marka, and Yarre—who, in their commercial explorations, established a Malinke presence across much of western Africa.

The rise of Mali changed the center of political, economic, and population activity in the western Sudan. Walata and then Timbuktu were successively the principal trans-Saharan trade termini, while Niani prospered as an administrative center. A further aid to the relocation of trade activity was the Arab-Maures advance into the western desert. Their raids and exactions on caravans connecting the Sahel and the Sudan with Morocco eventually led to the abandonment of these routes in favor of ones heading for Algeria, Tunisia, and Egypt. The area near the Niger bend profited in turn, which benefited trade in Gao and aided the rise of Jenne to prominence as a center of Islamic learning.

Widespread internal factionalism during the latter half of the fourteenth century planted the seeds of Mali's decline. It encouraged challenges from non-Malinke portions of the

Islam was brought to the Sudanic kingdoms by Arab and Berber merchants, who stimulated the building of mosques, such as this one in Djenne, Mali. (Photo courtesy of Philip W. Porter.)

empire, as well as attacks by the independent Mossi kingdom, located along the southern border. The Tuareg were able to seize control of Walata and Timbuktu; the Soninke provinces broke away, forming a series of small states; and most critically for later developments in the region, Songhai asserted its independence, setting the stage for what would become the largest and most powerful of the Sudanic empires. Mali held on for a time by reorganizing around its western provinces, particularly those along the Gambia River and in the Casamance, where numerous Malinke colonists had gone. But Mali soon disappeared from the western African scene.

Songhai

The Songhai Empire was founded by people of the same name who may be, as noted earlier, direct descendants of participants in the Late Stone Age aquatic tradition. Apparently in response to the same trade stimulus that prompted the rise of Ghana, a small state formed in A.D. 500–700 around what would become the city of Gao. The state fell within Mali's sphere of influence, but as the focus of trans-Saharan trade shifted eastward and Mali's control of its non-Malinke provinces weakened during the latter half of the fifteenth century, Songhai broke away and set off down its own path of imperial expansion.

Songhai forces first moved upstream to take possession of Timbuktu and Djenne and the lands in between. Military expeditions were launched against the Mossi, driving them from the Niger valley and back to their homeland in the Upper Volta River basin, and following this success, Mali concentrated on halting Fulbe expansion. Once in secure control of the river valley, other expeditions were sent into the lands south of the Niger bend, not so much with the intention of adding imperial territory as to secure the new borders and collect tribute. Similarly, Songhai made no attempt to invade what remained of Mali; vassalage apparently sufficed. But in the north it seized all the former Sahelian possessions of Mali, and in the sixteenth century the Aïr and the saltworks at Taghaza came under Songhai control. Early in the sixteenth century the Hausa states of northern Nigeria were attacked, but despite some initial military success, the invasion failed and with it plans to join western and central Sudan under imperial rule.

Unlike the Soninke and Malinke, the Songhai never sent colonists, traders, or even many administrators to conquered territories. Possessed of a strong desire to maintain cultural purity, they preferred to remain within their homeland and use others as emissaries, intermediaries, and governors.

By all accounts the wealth of Songhai was considerable—at least that enjoyed by many of the merchants and the ruling elite. Salt remained a key commodity in western Africa, although the burgeoning demand for gold and slaves within the Islamic world and the European states of Portugal, Genoa, Venice, Naples, and Sicily fueled an intensified trans-Saharan trade from which Songhai profited as no other Sahelian polity before or since. Luxury goods, such as glass and copper wares, cloth, and perfumes poured in, along with supplies of horses for the famed imperial chain-mailed cavalry. Timbuktu achieved legendary status; besides making economic gains, it attracted an array of Islamic scholars who taught astrology and astronomy, medicine, Arabic grammar and rhetoric, history, and geography, in addition to the Quran.

Yet Songhai could not maintain its territorial grip. Once again the demise of imperial order began with internal conflicts, this time between a much more thoroughly islamicized and largely non-Songhai west and the traditional Songhai core region, where Islam was a veneer. Battles over royal succession during the late sixteenth century weakened the military position of the empire, and before matters were settled, a Moroccan invasion force arrived on the scene, in 1591. It had been sent across the desert to secure for the sultan direct control over the sources of gold that were assumed to lie within Songhai itself. As the Moroccans soon discovered, their information was inaccurate, but armed with harquebuses and muskets, they routed the Songhai armies. In spite of reinforcements, the invaders, most of them mercenaries, were too few to thoroughly subjugate the area and create a province of Morocco as intended. Songhai resistance continued into the first two decades of the seventeenth century, and the fighting took its toll of Moroccans, as did disease—particularly, it seems, malaria and dysentery. But Songhai itself had been torn to pieces; not enough was left to put back together again.

With the demise of Songhai, political space fragmented into many smaller and more ethnically homogeneous kingdoms and chiefdoms, like those of the Gonja, Mossi, Mampruli,

Dagomba, Tukulor, Woloff, and Serer. The cities retained a more international flavor, but their fortunes continued to slide as a new transatlantic trade shifted the center of gravity of western Africa southward toward the coast.

It is impossible to say anything with much precision about population numbers for the several empires—little archeological work has been done, oral traditions tend to omit such information, and the written accounts, first by Arab travelers and then by Europeans, allow only for guesses. It is safe to say that the regional population grew significantly while Ghana, Mali, and Songhai existed and that following the demise of Songhai, population declined to a point of relative stagnation until its twentieth-century upsurge. A figure of 40–50 million inhabitants has been cited for Mali at its height, but such a total is implausible. Accepting it means either postulating the existence of a much larger preimperial population—highly unlikely given an agricultural economy dependent on the hoe, human labor, and low-yielding grains—or later growth rates unmatched anywhere in the world at the time. It would also imply a population collapse of extraordinary magnitude, for which no physical or oral evidence has been found. Similarly, although the principal cities undoubtedly were of reasonably good size, the estimates sometimes seen for Niani and Gao, 100,000 inhabitants each; Djenne, 30,000–40,000; and Timbuktu, 80,000, probably err substantially on the high side.

CENTRAL SUDANIC DEVELOPMENTS

The central Sudan extends roughly from the bend of the Niger eastward across the Lake Chad basin to Dar Fur. The physical landscape is essentially a continuation of that found in the western Sudan; the cultural landscape has evolved somewhat differently, however, providing the rationale for its separate designation. As noted earlier, 4,000 years ago the area was occupied mainly by peoples of Nilosaharan and Afroasiatic ethnolinguistic affiliations. The former may have been practicing some cultivation of crops but continued in the main with an aquatic economy based on hunting, fishing, and intensive gathering. Lake Chad would still have been a substantial body of water, perhaps filling much of the current Bodele depression. But it was shrinking and the grain-farming ancestors of the Chadic speakers gradually assumed numerical predominance. They were part of earlier Afroasiatic dispersals across the Sahara, and by A.D. 500 their small, mud-walled family compounds and villages dotted the countryside.

Kanem and Bornu

East of Lake Chad a Nilosaharan presence was being reasserted in the form of southward-drifting herders seeking forage and water for their herds of cattle, sheep, and goats. They arrived in small groups over several centuries. As they mixed with resident Chadic speakers, their nomadic way of life was modified, and although they became more sedentary, livestock continued to be economically important. In surviving oral traditions the prior inhabitants are called So or Sao, and such easterly Chadic groups as the

116

Kotoko, Buduma, and Musgu may be their direct descendants. The nomads must have gained some kind of social and political ascendancy because their language and traditions of origin prevailed. The Zaghawa, who, according to Arab sources, ruled over the area between Lake Chad and Dar Fur around A.D. 1000, would thus represent the last in a long line of Nilosaharan nomads who had the eastern Lake Chad basin as their destination.

The synthesis of Chadic and Nilosaharan speakers produced the Kanuri, founders of the Kanem state, with its capital at Njimi (map 7.3). Kanem's original wealth developed from a productive agricultural economy complemented by salt mining at Bilma. Although earlier contacts with northern Africa were undoubtedly made, it was during the eleventh century that the involvement of Kanem in trans-Saharan trade became regular. The caravans proceeded via the Fezzan to Tripoli, mainly to exchange slaves for horses. The horses were needed for cavalry contingents, which formed the backbone of the military power of Kanem, but unlike in the western Sudan, no nearby source of gold could be tapped for payment. An ample supply of slaves, however, existed among the less-organized groups to the west and south, and they made up the exports for purchasing horses and other northern products. As elsewhere in the Sudan, Islam followed trade, and it spread rapidly, not just among the ruling class but also among the Kanuri populace at large, more or less mirroring the conversion of Takrur.

Kanem reached its apogee during the mid-thirteenth century, when its territorial hold extended through the desert to Fezzan. In the period of reorganization that followed, the focus of Kanuri activity shifted west of Lake Chad, as is symbolized by the construction of a capital at Ngazaragamu. The resident Chadic peoples were either pushed out or absorbed, and a new state, Bornu, came into being. The former state of Kanem fell under the control of people remembered as the Bulala, either an internal faction or possibly invaders of Central Sudanic background, but in the second half of the sixteenth century Bornu moved against the Bulala and recaptured some territory. By this time most of the former Kanuri-occupied lands east of Lake Chad had been lost, primarily to Shuwa Arabs, who, along with other bedouin, had claimed the grazing lands from here to Dar Fur. West of Lake Chad, however, Bornu, under Kanuri leadership, remained the dominant power for several centuries more.

Hausa States

The only serious rivals facing Bornu were the Hausa, the most westerly, and far and away the largest, of the Chadic-speaking groups. Hausa origins can be traced to the western part of the Lake Chad basin, and the Hausa reached their present distribution around A.D. 1500, undoubtedly with the aid of pressure from Bornu. Settlement followed the long-established nucleated Chadic pattern, and by the thirteenth and fourteenth centuries several of the villages had grown into cities that controlled the surrounding countryside for a radius of fifty to sixty kilometers. Those accorded initial prominence were Gobir, Katsina, Zaria, and Kano, followed by Biram, Daura, and Rano. Together these make up the seven "true" Hausa city-states, as contrasted with seven later ones considered "bastards." Each city had

117

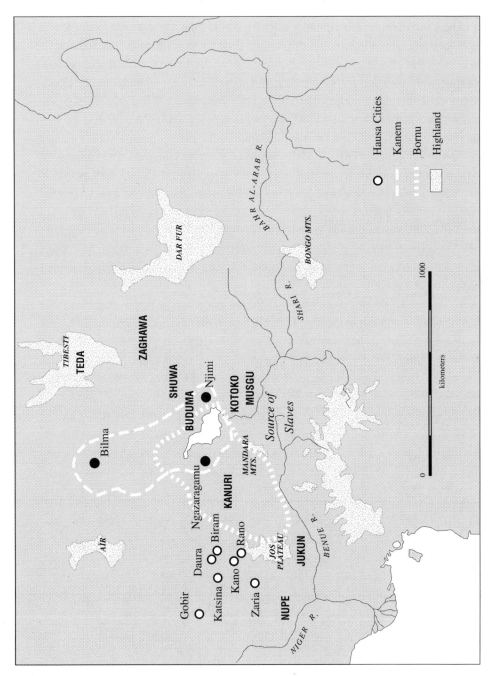

7.3 The area around Lake Chad supported the rise of imperial Kanem and Bornu, whereas the Hausa states developed farther west.

a surrounding wall; within were the residences of the ruling family, a market, quarters for various traders, the shops of numerous craft specialists, and enough agricultural land to feed the population during a siege. Outside the walls were dependent slave villages, free Hausa villages, and dispersed family compounds.

The city-states never united into a single political entity, and thus the Hausa could not challenge Bornu for hegemony in the central Sudan. Nevertheless, they maintained their territorial integrity: all that Bornu could do was exact tribute. The Hausa were also in competition with the Jukun state to their south, where various Benue-Congo speakers had been brought together during the latter half of the fifteenth century, and they successfully faced Nupe expansion during the fifteenth century.

As the city-states accrued wealth, they attracted non-Hausa, beginning in the fourteenth century: Fulbe, Tuareg, Kanuri, Dyula, Songhai, Arabs, and North African Berbers, among others. Some of the immigrants held on to their cultural identities, but most were assimilated. Ease of assimilation seems to be an old Hausa trait, and it aided their earlier expansion at the expense of Benue-Congo peoples.

Islam strengthened Hausa bonds. The religion arrived rather late in Hausaland, but by the sixteenth and seventeenth centuries being a Muslim had become integral to being a Hausa. Indeed, the name Hausa first dates from this time; before then the people were known by their city-state affiliation. Now, however, it was necessary to distinguish between Muslims and non-Muslims, and Hausa came to signify the former. There are still several small groups of Hausa speakers who have remained unconverted and who are therefore not accepted as true Hausa kin.

In the sixteenth century a Hausa diaspora began that continues to this day. Traders and artisans working with metals, textiles, and leather, the Hausa have traveled throughout western Africa, and in virtually all instances, they have steadfastly retained their language and culture.

TOWARD THE FOREST AND THE COAST

Continuity and Change

Most current vegetation maps of western Africa are based on climatic parameters and therefore show the theoretical extent of the rain forest, unmodified by human activity. More accurate maps registering actual instead of theoretical vegetation depict a highly degraded rain forest—much of it, especially in the eastern portion, converted to what is often called derived savanna. Three thousand years ago, however, the forest was still intact and was the domain largely, if not exclusively, of Late Stone Age gatherer-hunters. Those in the west probably spoke various Atlantic languages; in the east, Ijoid and maybe Kwa-related ones. If any agriculture was practiced, it would have been a highly rudimentary form of vegeculture, quite patchy in its occurrence. The numerous rivers and streams offered rich fishing opportunities, and nothing indicates that any special places attracted unusually large populations. If we add imperceptible natural environmental change to the

119

equation, we have a situation in which the people of the rain forest were free from the sorts of pressures that generated early agricultural developments in the drier lands to the north.

The rain forest of western Africa has yielded only a few important cultigens. Its best-known contributions to the list are supplementary foods such as kola, okra, akee, and the malegueta pepper. All the staples eaten in the area, in fact, have come from outside, with rice in the west and yams in the east being initially the most important. Rice and yams may have replaced other, subsequently lost staples, although a better explanation would have rice and yams spreading into virgin territory and productive enough to limit the search for alternatives. Other staples would eventually appear, but much later and from more distant lands. Sometime early in the second millennium A.D., cocoyams, bananas, plantains, and different yam species from southeast Asia made their way to western Africa, and then in the sixteenth century maize, sweet potatoes, and cassava arrived from the Americas. Both here and elsewhere, the new foods improved productivity and furthered the advantage of cultivators over gatherer-hunters.

Another significant agricultural constraint imposed by the rain forest was the nearly universal presence of tsetse-borne sleeping sickness. Somewhat resistant dwarf varieties of cattle and goats were eventually developed; however, they produce little meat or milk, and nowhere in the rain forest did livestock ever acquire much economic importance. Other human and livestock diseases also posed barriers to settlement, but none seems to have had as great an impact on the population as sleeping sickness.

Still, it was only a matter of time before agriculture would make its appearance. Archeologists have yet to set the date, but a plausible inference is that local people must have planted crops at least by the last centuries B.C., and certainly no later than the first centuries A.D. There are signs of iron making at several sites, dated to A.D. 500, and near the end of the millennium trade with Sudanic peoples was a matter of record, suggesting the existence of reasonably large settled populations. In addition, linguistic geography indicates that a considerable degree of language differentiation had taken place, and oral histories sometimes tell of migrations into previously settled areas.

The agricultural frontier seems to have advanced along two fronts, and both population migration and technological diffusion were undoubtedly involved (map 7.4). Rice cultivation progressed among peoples of both Atlantic and Mande linguistic affiliation. East of the Niger River the yams accompanied Benue-Congo peoples; to the west, the Kwa. The earliest settlements probably consisted of scattered kin-based farmsteads and compounds concentrated on interfluves where a lighter forest cover and better drained soils predominated. But fishing and the availability of sea salt also made certain areas along the the coast attractive. The origins of peoples such as the Kru, Ewe, Itskiri, Ibibio, Efik, and Ijoids most likely lie in just such circumstances.

Centralization and Expansion

Near the close of the first millennium the pace of developments in the rain forest picked up, and as in the Sahel and the Sudan, the major impelling force was trade. As the volume

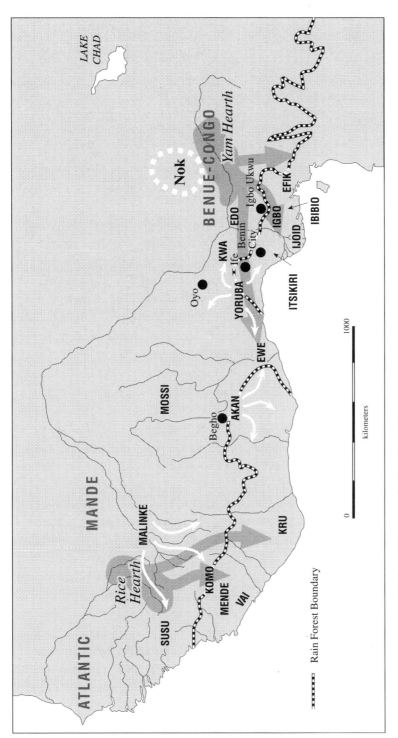

7.4 Two different agricultural traditions, one based on rice and the other on yams, were carried into the rain forests of western Africa. Later, trade opportunities with Europeans drew people toward the coast.

of trade mounted, and longer distances were traversed, processes of political centralization took hold, leading to fundamental changes in the patterns of population density and ethnolinguistic distribution.

The earliest tangible signs of change come from three sites in Nigeria. One is in the southeastern part of the country, where radiocarbon dates from Igbo-Ukwu near modern Onitsha show the presence of a fairly large settled population by the ninth century. A wide array of impressive manufactured objects have been uncovered; many appear to be of local origin, but others came from elsewhere. Among the local items are bronze and copper goods, which, in fact, required imported raw materials to make, while among the imports are items of undisputed Mediterranean origin. Igbo-Ukwu sits squarely within the area considered the homeland of the Igbo (formerly Ibo) peoples, and there is no reason to doubt that their ancestors were its founders.

The second site, Ife, is linked to the origins of the Yoruba, who claim it as their spiritual center. Excavations have uncovered evidence for a townlike settlement created from the fusion of formerly separate compounds that flourished late in the first millennium. Over the course of the next several hundred years similarly structured Yoruba towns were founded both along the northern margins of the rain forest and in the adjacent savanna. Each was positioned to take advantage of north-south trading opportunities and was the center of a small kingdom. Growing prosperity is evinced by the remarkable degree of craft specialization. The bronze and copper artifacts are best known, but expert work was also done in iron, wood, leather, ivory, and cloth. The Yoruba expanded both north and south from their strategic position in the border zone, eventually claiming most of southwestern Nigerian as theirs.

What became known as Benin City can also be traced to A.D. 1000, but unlike Ife, the site lies deep within the rain forest, just west of the Niger River. It was founded by Edo-speaking peoples, whose movement from the savanna into the forest can be followed via a series of earthenwork enclosures. These represent the remains of high-density village settlements, whose inhabitants seem to have cycled through the forest creating cleared patches of land that helped to keep tsetse and sleeping sickness at bay. Larger villages incorporated smaller ones, and by the early fifteenth century a wider Benin state had been forged. Power was highly centralized within an elite commercial class whose trade contacts reached northward to the Hausa city-states and Songhai, westward to the Yoruba, and southward to the fishing communities of the Niger Delta. Warfare provided the means by which Benin extended its territory, and facing superior might, the decentralized and relatively powerless Ijoid peoples had to give way.

Developments were also under way farther west. During the late fourteenth century Begho, in what is now Ghana, developed into a busy market center, particularly for the kola trade, which was controlled from a large Dyula colony with links to Djenne. Political power resided with the Mossi, but the origins of Begho seem to lie with Akan-speaking peoples who were extending their contacts into the forest in a search first for kola and later for gold. A nearby Iron Age site is dated to the second century A.D., and extensive mounds suggest

The Kingdom of Benin supported artists who produced
extraordinarily detailed work in bronze and ivory. (Reprinted
from Margaret Shinnie, *Ancient African Kingdoms,* Edward Arnold,
1969, p. 83.)

the presence by the eleventh century of farming communities speaking proto-Akan languages.

REALIGNMENTS

The Coastal Transition

Until the fifteenth century, settlement at and near the coast consisted mainly of small, kin-based fishing and farming villages. Each was self-sufficient, although canoes carried some interregional trade, and footpaths led to various inland states. The coastal zone was the frontier of western Africa. When European traders appeared on the scene, however, the comparative advantages of interior versus coastal locations shifted dramatically, and within a short time frontier and center reversed position.

Europeans encountered the coast while attempting to bypass Muslim control of trade routes to south and east Asia. After earlier failed efforts by the Genoese and others to circumnavigate an undetermined African land mass, the Portuguese embarked on their sequence of ultimately successful voyages during the fifteenth century. They reached the mouth of the Senegal River in 1444–45, the coast of Sierra Leone in 1460, the mouth of the Volta River in 1471, and the delta of the Niger River in 1473. Although seeking a route to the east, the Portuguese established small trading posts wherever opportunities presented themselves. Typically these were situated either immediately at the coast, on nearby offshore islands, or a short distance up navigable rivers. Specific requirements included the existence of valued commodities and peoples willing to trade them, plus the availability of accessible, safe anchorages.

This combination of needs focused Portuguese attention on three regions. The first stretched from the Senegal River to between the modern cities of Conakry and Freetown. Here an active trade was conducted with Woloff, Serer, and Malinke residents for gums, ivory, dye woods, slaves, gold, and pepper. The second region lay between Cape Three Points and Cape St. Paul, where gold could be obtained from Akan merchants. So available was it that the name Gold Coast soon appeared on maps. To stock and secure their supplies, the Portuguese built the fort of Elmina, the first permanent European structure on African soil south of the Sahara, in 1482.

The third area to capture Portuguese interest was the Niger Delta and its hinterland, with Benin as the lure. Some slaves were obtained to trade for gold along the Gold Coast, but Benin showed little interest in heavy involvement with the Portuguese. It banned the export of slaves, preferring instead to keep them as agricultural laborers and to sell ivory,

Forts, such as Cape Coast Castle in Ghana, were built by Europeans to secure trading rights with Africans. (Photo courtesy of Christopher R. DeCorse, Syracuse University.)

gum, and pepper. For their part, the Portuguese found the delta region rather inhospitable because of heat, humidity, and disease. Consequently, they withdrew to the islands of São Tomé and Fernando Po to found a settler- and slave-based plantation society for growing sugar.

For a time, the Portuguese ignored the Bight of Benin area, which is where savanna interrupts rain forest. Immediately along the coast resided a number of small, more or less autonomous groups of people speaking languages in the Gbe subfamily of Kwa. Ewe villages dominated in the west, while the eastern portion was controlled by several Aja groups. Farther inland were the Fon. A mixed economy based on millet, livestock, fishing, and local trade supported a fairly dense population; however, fringing lagoons and heavy surf made for difficult anchorages, and traders tended to look elsewhere until the seventeenth century.

Virtually all the Portuguese in western Africa were men, and most took local wives, often in polygynous unions. From these relationships arose a distinctive population of traders, the *lançados,* who skillfully negotiated affiliations with chiefs and kings and played the crucial role of intermediaries between Portuguese and Africans.

As Portuguese power waned, other European powers entered the African trade. The first were the Dutch in the 1590s, followed in the seventeenth century by the French, British, Danes, Swedes, and Prussians. French activity focused on the Senegal River and its environs, where they set up a number of outposts. The others had more interest in the Gold Coast, and they built forts similar to Elmina to declare their interest. These forts operated only at the discretion of local African authorities, to whom rent had to be paid.

By the 1620s European competition had expanded into the Bight of Benin. Resident factors represented the parties in trade. Although the area lacked gold, it did have slaves, whose sale soon dominated the export economy to such an extent that another name, Slave Coast, joined the geographic lexicon. The area also earned a reputation as the "white man's grave." To load full cargoes, ships often had to wait offshore for weeks at a time, and the longer they stayed, the more crew succumbed to "fevers," which, as later researchers have determined, were mostly malaria and yellow fever.

During the seventeenth century the trans-Saharan trade rapidly gave way to coastal trade. In addition, recurrent droughts and locust plagues hit portions of the interior, producing food crises that, in several instances, turned into widespread famines. As the balance of trade and subsistence swung toward the coast, population followed suit, and the pattern of urbanization shifted. While cities in the Sahel and the Sudan went into decline, a whole new coastal urban network developed. Africans congregated at the proliferating trade centers, and the more successful—St. Louis, Gorée Island, Rifisque, Bissau, Elmina, Christianbourg (later Accra), Cape Coast, Great and Little Popo, Whydah, Porto Novo, Lagos, Calabar, and Bonny—soon became towns of up to several thousand inhabitants each (map 7.5).

Significant ethnolinguistic changes also took place. For one, the pace of Mande progress quickened at the expense of Atlantic-speaking peoples. On either side of the Gambia,

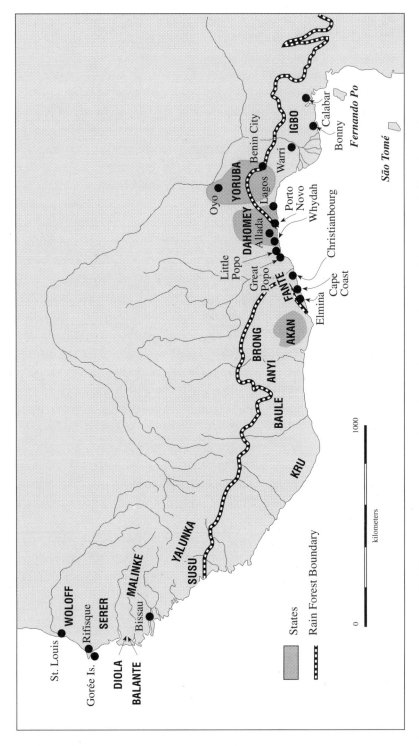

St. Louis

WOLOFF

Gorée Is.
Rifisque

SERER

DIOLA

BALANTE

Bissau

MALINKE

YALUNKA

SUSU

KRU

BAULE

ANYI

BRONG

AKAN

FANTE

Elmina

Cape
Coast

Christianbourg

Whydah

Porto
Novo

Allada

DAHOMEY

Great
Popo

Little
Popo

Oyo

YORUBA

Lagos

Benin City

Warri

IGBO

Calabar

Bonny

Fernando Po

São Tomé

States

Rain Forest Boundary

0

kilometers

1000

7.5 Numerous trade centers existed along Africa's western coast during the eighteenth
century. Most of them were controlled by local African polities.

the Malinke pushed such groups as the Balante and Diola into smaller and smaller pockets of territory. Similarly, in what is now Guinea, the Susu and Yalunka expanded their land-holdings. In other settings, Malinke nobility (the Mani), taking advantage of the breakup of Mali, inserted themselves into positions of authority, and in some instances they induced linguistic shifts among those over whom they ruled. Mande success was closely tied to their mode of political organization—the state—which gave them both economic and military advantages over the largely unstratified and less-organized Atlantic groups. The major exceptions were the Woloff and Serer, whose earlier political achievements helped them hold their positions between the Senegal and Gambia rivers.

Along the Gold Coast the Akan advance continued apace, and during the sixteenth and seventeenth centuries a number of small Akan states attained local preeminence. In the eighteenth century, however, they all yielded to the rising power of the Asante. As the Asante pushed outward in all directions from their center at Kumasi, a complex, wavelike series of migrations followed. For example, Asante pressure on the Brong caused them to move at the expense of the Anyi and Baule, who in turn relocated into the forests of the southern Ivory Coast, where their arrival squeezed others into the south and west. The Asante's main competition for regional hegemony came from the Fante, whose several states managed to maintain control of much of the countryside between the coast and the Asante. The Gold Coast trade still included significant quantities of gold, but to an ever increasing extent, slaves provided the greatest profits.

In southwestern Nigeria the coastal trade both reinforced previous trends and intro-duced new tendencies. Immediately west of the Niger River coastal trade furthered the territorial extension of the Yoruba states, and by the seventeenth century the southernmost ones of Ijebu and Ondo had positioned themselves just inland from the coast. But far and away the most powerful state was Oyo; at one time or another it forced all other states and peoples in the region into a tribute-paying status. Even Benin had to acknowledge Oyo's presence. By the end of the eighteenth century, however, Oyo was losing control, owing to a combination of declining economic fortunes and internal discord. As its hold grew weaker, several tributary delta states, most notably Itsikiri-dominated Warri, built up enough strength from slaving profits to go their own way, and it also lost land in its western provinces to an increasingly powerful Dahomey kingdom.

Dahomey's emergence was tied to highly volatile events at the Slave Coast. Intensify-ing commercial activity during the seventeenth century had given rise to the Aja state of Allada. Centered somewhat inland, for a time it controlled most of the slave trade by being positioned along the routes from the north and from Oyo. By the end of the century, however, Allada had lost out to several better located coastal competitors, especially Whydah. These fell in turn to the Fon kingdom of Dahomey, where the Gbe speakers had elaborated the long-standing kingship system, making it more centralized and militaristic. Muskets aided them in this task, and by the 1720s Dahomey had overrun Whydah and what remained of Allada. The conquest caused considerable economic disruption and population loss, and several decades passed before Dahomey could establish its legitimacy and restore order. When it did, trade once again prospered and, in combination with military might, turned Dahomey into one of the major precolonial powers of western Africa.

The last area of significant trade-induced population activity was along the Bight of Bonny in the vicinity of the Cross River. Because well-organized peoples with whom to do business were lacking at first, merchants stayed away. But the area was populous, and soon a series of small city-states formed under the control of various Efik, Ijo, and Ijaw families. The families had organized themselves into commercial and military houses open to strangers (non-kin), which gave them the capacity to multiply size and strength and to enslave others. As the slave trade entered its final phases, it tended to be more and more concentrated on this part of the coast.

Farther inland, Igbo colonization of the higher lands east of the Niger valley continued unabated. The Igbo never developed anything resembling states, and the impetus for their diffusion apparently had more to do with population growth than trade. Why they experienced a population explosion is unclear but may be related to adopting maize and cassava as staple foods and suffering comparatively little from the slave trade. Igbo expansion pushed the Ijo and Ibibio south, the Eko east, and the Igala and Idoma north.

Population and the Slave Trade

By the seventeenth century the slave trade had western Africa in a viselike grip. Persistent demand in the Arab world kept the trans-Saharan routes active, but it was the rapidly growing demand in the Americas that eventually exerted much the greater force. The cumulative human impact of the trade was enormous and deserves the continuing attention it elicits. Here, however, we will restrict our attention to population trends: what the slave trade meant for the patterns of population growth and distribution in western Africa.

Several unknowables in the equation make any calculation of the overall magnitude of the slave trade a highly approximate enterprise. The only figure with much authority behind it is that about 10 million slaves from Africa reached some destination in the Americas. Of this total, probably at least 6 million came from western Africa. The number can be set as a base minimum. To it must be added those captives who died on board ship, the so-called middle passage. The voyage to the Americas could take three or more months; and in cramped, unsanitary conditions, diseases like smallpox, dysentery, and scurvy often ran rampant. Other captives died in holding pens at the coast, on the forced marches, and in attempts to avoid capture, which in many instances involved local wars. Did these causes of death increase the 6 million figure by 50 percent, 100 percent, or even 1,000 percent? Unfortunately, data are so scanty that the multiplier is anyone's guess.

Trans-Saharan numbers rest on even softer ground, and, not surprisingly, the two most thorough studies have offered widely differing assessments. One puts the number of slaves taken between 1500 and 1900 at 8 million, whereas the other arrives at a total of 9 million for the whole duration of the trade, with a peak during the period 900–1400.

Even a minimum combined total would be in the 10 million range, with a higher total more likely—possibly as high as 20 million—for the 300 years between 1500 and 1800. The effects of the loss were not felt uniformly, however; they varied both temporally and spatially. For western Africa, slaving activities during the sixteenth and seventeenth centuries probably had only a very limited impact on growth. The transatlantic trade seldom took more than 10,000 persons per year, and it was active along virtually the whole coast. The trans-Saharan trade was even smaller and was also widely distributed.

Matters were quite different during the eighteenth century when the transatlantic trade averaged 40,000 slaves per year, most of whom were between fifteen and thirty years of age. The magnitude of the loss would indicate that the population of western Africa must have dropped during the century, perhaps significantly. But the net result seems to have been stagnation, or perhaps a slight decline, from an estimated regional total of 25 million people at the beginning of the century. The main reason for the less-than-expected severity of the loss lies in the preference of transatlantic slave traders for men, who they took over women by at least a two to one ratio. Because of the prevalence of polygyny, the vast majority of "extra" women found husbands, and consequently their reproductive potential remained within the region.

On the other hand, the trans-Saharan trade favored young women by a similar two to one ratio, and thus its demographic effects must have been greater than suggested by volume alone. Probably some smaller groups of people disappeared, while the size of others significantly lessened, a circumstance that might help to explain the ease with which the Mande expanded westward. The fate for many of the surplus men was to contribute to the strength of the various Sudanic states by serving either as slave laborers or soldiers. Indeed, by the nineteenth century there was, so to speak, a Sudanic slave mode of production because of the crucial role that slaves played in maintaining and reproducing the social and political order.

As we know, by the eighteenth century the transatlantic trade had become more spatially concentrated. At first the focus was on the Gold Coast, where the Asante were asserting their dominance. The Asante sold off captives taken in their wars with other Akan states, but when captives ran out, they turned inland to Gur groups, many of which seem to have suffered substantial declines in population. Later in the century the Bight of Benin coast was host to the most intense slaving activity. The invasion by forces from Dahomey and the subsequent slaving activity had a severe impact on the Aja, who lost an average 3 percent of their population annually over a forty-year period. Farther east the Cross River delta states raided inland and virtually depopulated the upper portions of the river valley, while the Igbo expanded through their increasing involvement as slave traders in the nineteenth century.

The slave trade thus played a major role in redrawing the population map of western Africa. Whereas some groups either disappeared or declined, others grew. They did so by absorbing peoples seeking protection from enslavement, by using slaves themselves, and by taking into their ranks female captives not wanted elsewhere. Through such means peoples like the Hausa, Asante, Fon, Yoruba, and Igbo secured their future regional dominance.

Finally, we should note that wherever the slave trade appeared, it seriously distorted the workings of local economies. Areas under the constant threat of raids had to make adjustments, many of which involved economic impoverishment. Crafts declined and agriculture suffered. One important negative change was the increasing reliance on cassava as a staple food. Under conditions of uncertainty, cassava provided several advantages to grains and even yams: not much effort was needed to grow it, the tubers could remain unharvested for several years without serious risk of damage, and the crop stored well. Cassava does have a serious problem, however. It is nutrient poor, especially in protein-building amino acids, and without complementary food sources, the diet suffered, especially those of children, who became more susceptible to the various syndromes of protein malnutrition. Unfortunately, future populations bore the consequences of what slavery brought their ancestors.

Distortions also occurred in the economies of the slaving states. The profits from the trade could be so great that most productive activities appeared comparatively unattractive and, as a result, either stagnated or retrogressed. Once again, there would be a future price to pay.

The Fulbe Diaspora and the Spread of Islam

Because of the Fulbe's phenotypic characteristics, especially a tendency toward light skin color and tallness, early interpretations most often sought to locate their origins somewhere else than western Africa—even outside Africa altogether. Modern linguistic and cultural analyses, however, show that the Fulbe are autochthonous. They speak a language (Fulfulde) that is closely akin to Tukulor and seem to be a synthesis of peoples in the Futa Toro region of the Senegal River basin. A plausible scenario is that the Fulbe derive from an essentially Tukulor base modified by the absorption over several centuries of in-migrating Nilosaharan and Afroasiatic (probably Berber) nomads. Whatever the truth, the Fulbe evolved a cattle-oriented way of life and began moving out of Futa Toro by the tenth century. Their initial migrations may have been prompted by a desire to distance themselves from the increasingly powerful islamicized Takrur (map 7.6).

The Fulbe tended to follow river valleys southward into the Futa Djallon Highlands, where they settled among Dyalonke farmers. They also moved along the Niger River valley, where the abundant grasses and waters of the inland delta proved inviting. By the fifteenth century vanguards had reached Hausaland, and 300 years later some groups had made it as far east as Dar Fur. The Fulbe were always minorities within larger polities and generally found a welcome as suppliers of meat, milk, and hides in exchange for grains, vegetables, and manufactured wares. Their presence thus tended to enrich local economies. Nevertheless, the Fulbe could also be a problem. From time to time they raided sedentary communities for livestock, and their mobility and independence posed state systems of government with difficulties in collecting taxes and tribute. By the time of

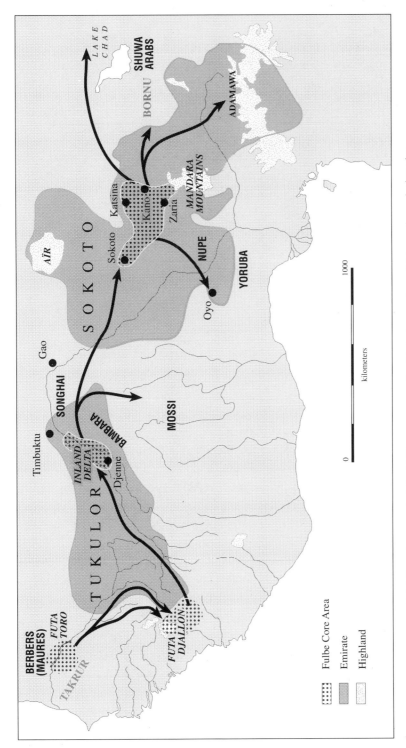

7.6 Migrations carried the Fulbe across much of interior western Africa, where during the nineteenth century they organized several large emirates around jihad movements.

Fulbe Core Area

Emirate

Highland

0   1000

kilometers

BERBERS (MAURES)

FUTA TORO

TAKRUR

TUKULOR

Timbuktu

INLAND DELTA

Djenne

BAMBARA

FUTA DJALLON

Gao

SONGHAI

MOSSI

AÏR

SOKOTO

Sokoto

Katsina

Kano

Zaria

MANDARA MOUNTAINS

NUPE

Oyo

YORUBA

BORNU

SHUWA ARABS

LAKE CHAD

ADAMAWA

Fulbe migrations led them across much of the western Sudan. In the eighteenth and nineteenth centuries they organized jihads that helped make Islam the major regional religion. (Photo courtesy of Thomas Bassett.)

Songhai's ascendancy, the Fulbe were so numurous that they were perceived as a threat, and military force was used to control them.

The diaspora of the Fulbe took some of them into Sudanic towns and cities, creating a long-held distinction between Town and Cattle branches. Fulbe in the towns were exposed to Islam, notably the fundamentalist and militant Almoravid tradition, and by the fifteenth century many of them had become missionary clerics and teachers, directing their conversions toward both their Cattle kin and other nonbelievers. In all likelihood it was Fulbe who effectively proselytized the Hausa.

By the eighteenth century declining economic fortunes in the Sudanic zone accompanied growing concerns among Muslim devouts over the status of their religion. Large areas, like the Mossi states, Nupeland, and Adamawa, remained unconverted, and both scholarship and practice had fallen from their earlier levels. The times were ripe for a jihad, the first notable one of which was launched under Fulbe leadership in 1725–26 in the Futa Djallon. The jihad turned into a Fulbe conquest of the region, and the Dyalonke fled to refuges along the edge of the hills. Many who could not escape entered slavery, either directly under the Fulbe or for sale at the coast.

Additional Fulbe jihads occurred during the nineteenth century, and each one extended their territorial range and control. By far the largest concentration of Fulbe, including both

Cattle and Town varieties, existed in Hausaland, which was targeted in 1804. The various Hausa states vied with one another and thus could offer little organized resistance. Furthermore, the cities had provided a milieu for interaction and cultural exchange among the two peoples, and many Hausa willingly joined the spiritual crusade. The jihad gave rise to the Sokoto Emirate, encompassing all of the states under Fulbe leadership in 1817. Inroads were also made into Nupe and northern Oyo, with both converts and territory being gained. The pacification and unification of this broad area rejuvenated trade, which stimulated urban growth. Kano in particular benefited and soon dominated commercial activity in northern Nigeria.

Attempts to extend the jihad into Bornu failed. The Fulbe armies were met by Shuwa Arab forces from Kanem and defeated. South of Lake Chad, in the lowlands around the Mandara Mountains, the Fulbe experienced greater success. They had infiltrated the area during the eighteenth century, and under the impetus of the jihad the small, unorganized Chadic groups were driven deeper into inaccessible mountain retreats.

Another jihad from 1818 to 1827 led to the formation of the state of Massina, whose territory extended along the Niger River from Timbuktu to Segu. Under the Massina banner, large numbers of Bambara and Songhai came under Fulbe rule. By mid-century, however, Massina was absorbed within the Tukulor Emirate, created by a combined Fulbe and Tukulor jihad that had emanated from the Futa Toro and targeted all infidels throughout the western Sudan. Although encompassing an even larger area than Sokoto, Tukulor could never match its level of prosperity. The trans-Saharan trade had all but ended, and Tukulor was far less closely tied to coastal developments than Sokoto. The population ceased to grow, and the towns and cities continued on their downward path.

By the last decades of the nineteenth century the Fulbe had achieved preeminence across much of the western and central Sudan. Though widely scattered and relatively few in number, they dominated politically, to a large degree because they could claim spiritual superiority. From beginning to end, therefore, Islam propelled the Fulbe diaspora—initially by causing them to seek escape from conversion and later by their becoming the religion's propagators.

Other jihads besides those of the Fulbe left their mark on the Sudan. One of particular significance was the Umarian. In the early 1860s Umarian forces overran the Segu Bambara state, which had arisen during the early 1700s and managed to weather the succession of food crises that marred the century. Although smaller in scale than Mali, Segu bore considerable resemblance to it. The core region contained highly productive Bambara grain farmers, as well as other occupational and ethnic communities. Marka traders operated out of the towns of Sinsani and Nyamina, linking the savanna with the desert and forest, while the Somono fished and ferried commerce along the Niger. Seasonally, Fulbe herders brought their cattle to graze, and smiths, leather workers, and bards formed specialized castes. All the Umarians managed to do was destroy the fabric of Segu society and turn the area into a series of small, warring, feudally structured provinces.

Prelude to Colonization

As the eighteenth century neared its end, the industrializing nations of Europe needed raw materials more than labor. Indeed, the French, British, and Dutch plantation economies in the West Indies were experiencing a slave surplus that drove the profits sharply downward for everyone involved in the slave trade. On another front, a powerful, morally driven abolitionist movement had formed, led by the British. Public pressure forced the enactment of legislation in 1807 outlawing citizens and ships of Great Britain from trading in slaves, and in 1833 slavery was made illegal throughout the British Empire. The two objectives—abolition and the stimulation of "legitimate trade" in valued commodities—became intertwined. As Great Britain and France, in particular, sought to achieve these objectives, they found themselves drawn ever deeper into western African affairs. Their influence on population developments throughout the region became correspondingly more pronounced.

One consequence was the creation in Sierra Leone of a "creole" population. Its origins date back to 1787, when black loyalists who had fled to England during the American War of Independence were resettled around a trading post at the mouth of the Sierra Leone River. Other refugees who first went to Nova Scotia and Maroons (escaped slaves) from Jamaica soon joined them. Disease-induced mortality and a lack of suitable agricultural land threatened the survival of the colony, and it needed military protection from the local Temne, who attacked when they realized that the settlement, now called Freetown, was meant to be permanent (map 7.7).

The fortunes of the colony turned in a favorable direction after Freetown was chosen to be the site of trials of crews captured by British antislaving squadrons. Because of the difficulties of voluntary return or repatriation, many of the freed slaves had little option but to remain in Freetown. Its population boomed, going from 2,000 in 1808, when the British government took over jurisdiction from the Sierra Leone Company, to 34,000 in 1834.

A Krio language soon developed as the medium of everyday communication, but English was also widely spoken, and under the influences of the Church Missionary Society and Wesleyan Missionary Society, both of which played leading roles in the resettlement, a strongly British-influenced culture took hold. Trade, rather than agriculture, dominated creole economic activity, and by mid-century creole traders could be found along the coast wherever economic opportunities presented themselves.

A second new population arose from the efforts of the American Colonization Society, whose objective was to return freed American blacks to Africa—there were more than a quarter million at the beginning of the nineteenth century. Very few seem to have been interested, but a small number of colonists, offered inducements to participate, landed at Cape Mesurado in 1822. Here they proclaimed the founding of Liberia and built the settlement of Monrovia. Although disease took its usual high toll, a trickle of immigrants from the United States, amounting to no more 17,000 by the early 1840s, supported the growth of Monrovia and the establishment of other coastal settlements as far south as Cape

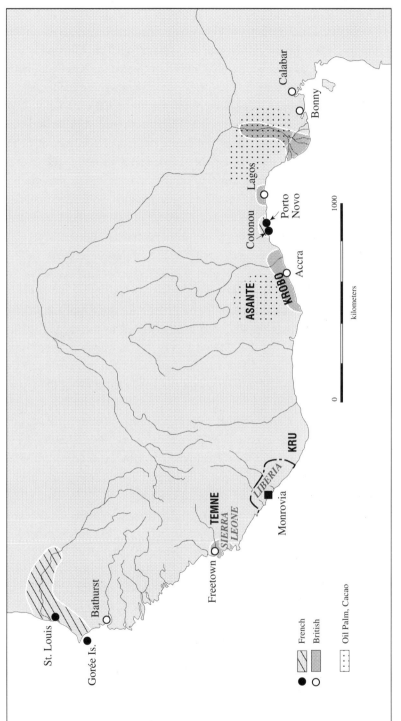

French

British

Oil Palm, Cacao

St. Louis
Gorée Is.
Bathurst
Freetown
SIERRA LEONE
TEMNE
Monrovia
LIBERIA
KRU
Accra
KROBO
ASANTE
Cotonou
Porto Novo
Lagos
Bonny
Calabar

0   1000
kilometers

7.7 By the mid-nineteenth century, peoples in western African were responding to new commercial agricultural opportunities. At the same time, the British and French were poised to begin their scrambles for colonial territory.

Palmas. In 1839 the settlements combined to form the Commonwealth of Liberia, and through strong lobbying, the country secured political independence in 1848. A constitution modeled on that of the United States was drawn up, and, under considerable influence from Baptist missionaries, a heavily Americanized culture found an African home.

The Americo-Liberians, as they were called, often confronted the Kru over matters of local authority. For centuries the Kru had plied the coast in ocean-going canoes, and many hired on as crew aboard European ships. One result was the creation of Kru villages at numerous points along the coast, each one a power to be reckoned with. Inland country remained largely outside Americo-Liberian influence and under the control of small, decentralized communities speaking a variety of Mande and Kwa languages.

The efforts to push legitimate trade centered on encouraging the expansion of cash cropping. Some income could be gained by collecting gum arabic, indigo, and shea butter; European demand for these products was limited, however, and oil palm and cacao quickly surpassed them in value. Oil palm and cacao cultivation spread through the forest areas of southern Nigeria and the Gold Coast, with much of the production coming from large indigene-run plantations. The labor needs of plantations were considerable and were often met by increasing the number of domestic slaves.

Some smallholders also took advantage of the new economic opportunities. Of particular note are the Krobo. For centuries they had been confined to the rugged inselbergs dotting the Accra Plain, but after the abolition of slavery they moved into the surrounding lowlands, vacated during the Asante-Fante wars, and planted them in oil palms. By mid-century the Krobo had become so commercially successful that much of the plain was theirs.

Beyond the new commercial order until after the imposition of colonial rule was most of the rest of the Sudanic zone. So, too, was the coast from the Gambia River to the Ivory Coast, except for small areas attached to Freetown and Monrovia. Overall, the initial phases of cash crop expansion reinforced the established patterns of regional economic and population differentiation rather than changing them.

As France and Great Britain deepened their involvement in western Africa, they selected specific coastal towns as centers of operations, thus providing them with a significant competitive advantage. The French chose St. Louis and Gorée, then Porto Novo and Cotonou. In addition to Freetown, Great Britain developed Bathurst, Accra, Bonny, Calabar, and Lagos, the last being officially annexed to the Crown in 1860. From their position in Accra, the British intervened in the conflicts between the Asante and the Fante confederation, opting to support the Fante because of fears about growing Asante strength. A series of wars began in 1824 and lasted until 1874, when a decisive defeat finally halted Asante expansion. It now became clear to both the French and the British governments that securing a trading position at the coast would necessitate a greater presence, not only at the coast but in the interior as well. For the French this meant using the Senegal River as a corridor of entry, whereas the British looked to the Niger River. The colonial era was about to begin.

8

CENTRAL AFRICA

Nature and history have combined to create a central African region characterized by small polities and low population density. On nature's side there is the vast expanse of equatorial rain forest (map 8.1). As noted previously, gatherer-hunters avoided it until late in the Stone Age, and the earliest farmers in the vicinity stayed away as well. These farmers, who spoke a language or languages in the Central Sudanic family, kept to familiar open woodland country north of the Chad-Congo-Nile watershed to grow millet and sorghum and tend herds of cattle, sheep, and goats. Yet with its poor soils and droughts, this country, too, was less than bountiful. People adapted to its limitations by engaging in land-extensive forms of shifting cultivation around widely dispersed family compounds. As the centuries passed, the repeated burnings, cultivation, and grazing took their toll, and large stretches of woodland were converted into even less productive savannas and thickets. Only in the marshlands of the Shari and Salamat rivers was there a significantly different pattern of settlement. Here abundant fish and richer soils made food more readily available, and permanent villages sprang up wherever dry ground on mounds could be found.

The first farming peoples to enter the equatorial rain forest were Bantu speakers. They grew yams but also relied heavily on fishing, supplemented by some gathering and hunting, and thus their migrations followed the coastal plain or the corridors provided by the many intersecting river valleys in the region (map 8.2). Yet suitable sites for subsistence

137

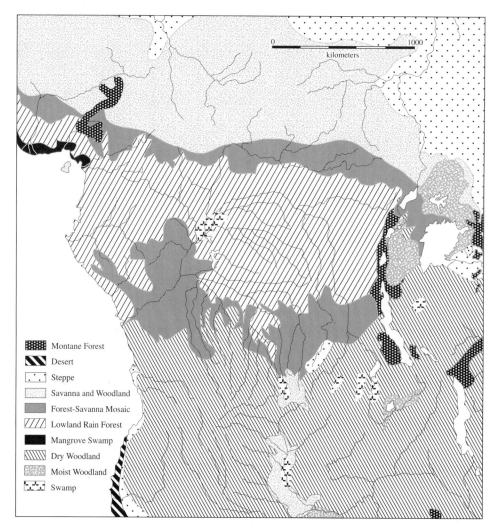

8.1 The vast equatorial rain forest and the large expanses of drought-prone woodlands
to its north and south have helped create a central African region dominated by
small, dispersed polities.

activities were few and far between, and a linear alignment of small, widely scattered
villages was typical.

South of the equatorial forest the Bantu eventually entered the dry woodlands that reach
all the way to the Zambezi River valley and beyond. Here they found soils of even lower
fertility than the ones they had left behind, and the farther south they went, the more
drought became a serious threat. Furthermore, tsetse-spread sleeping sickness was at least
as common as in the rain forest, and so once again human numbers remained on the low
side.

Ethnolinguistic differentiation flourished in such circumstances, but with the passage of

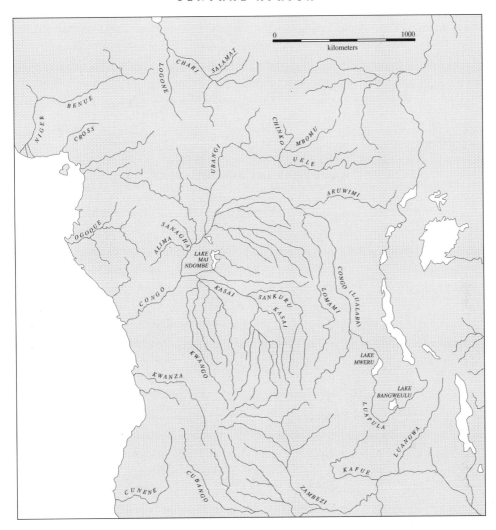

8.2 The river network of central Africa provided corridors for Bantu migrations through and beyond the equatorial rain forest.

time, processes favoring convergence also asserted themselves. Matrilineal kinship systems linked nearby villages into lineages and then clans. Marriage was the key to kinship, and as the links formed, more and more people came to share a common language and a sense of belonging to a broader cultural entity. In many parts of central Africa, lineages and clans were as complex as the social and political organization of people and space would ever be, but in certain locales events unfolded in the direction of wider incorporation. Chiefdoms, kingdoms, and even some empires arose, although nowhere did these match the scale of polities in western Africa. Segmentary pressures constantly intruded; as a result, the size of most polities remained small and their composition variable.

Powerful externally derived forces arrived at the close of the fifteenth century, and as these intensified and spread throughout the region the human landscape was dramatically reconfigured. None of the fragile indigenous societies could effectively control these forces, and the impact on the population ranged from profound to disastrous. Some peoples disappeared altogether, whereas others formed and re-formed in ways that are still poorly understood. When colonial powers arrived, they confronted the most disturbed and violent human circumstances anywhere on the continent.

BANTU ORIGINS AND DISPERSALS

Linguistic evidence points to the Bantu languages as having originated in the vicinity of the Cross River valley near the present-day border between Nigeria and Cameroon. Core vocabulary reconstructions indicate that 5,000 years ago they were practicing a diversified food economy in which the cultivation of yams, legumes, peppers, and gourds was complemented by highly significant contributions from hunting, gathering, and, especially, fishing. Although population growth could not have been very rapid, it apparently was sufficient to induce groups of Bantu to leave their homeland to search for sites capable of supplying their subsistence needs. Movement north and west was impeded by the presence of other, already established agriculturalists, but several other routes lay open.

One direction took some Bantu eastward through the moist woodlands just north of the equatorial rain forest (map 8.3). For various reasons, pressures to keep moving outweighed prospects for permanent settlement. One reason to move on might have been a lack of attractive food-producing sites. Even today, this area remains lightly populated, even by central African standards. However, a somewhat better explanation is that the Bantu were up against a more vigorous expansion of Ubangian peoples. They, too, had adopted yam cultivation and were advancing from the Adamawa Plateau into the country just south of the Congo River–Lake Chad watershed. Along their northern boundary the Ubangians learned about grain cultivation from Central Sudanic farmers, and the knowledge enabled them to colonize both moist and dry woodland habitats—an ability the Bantu still did not have. The Ubangians reached their maximum geographic range 2,000 years ago. Many internal migrations followed, giving rise to groups like the Gbeya, Ngabaka, Zande, Amadi, Banda, and Ngabanda. The days of broader Ubangian expansion, however, had come to an end.

In contrast, Bantu expansion was just beginning. Some people kept traveling east and by 3,000 years ago they entered the fringes of the interlacustrine region in what is now Uganda to begin forming a new population nucleus in one of the richest subsistence environments in Africa. Further Bantu migrations from here will be covered later.

Back west, other Bantu had headed south. They progressed slowly, but 3,500 years ago the Bantu frontier had passed beyond the Cameroon Plateau and into the equatorial rain forest between the Sanagha and Ogooué rivers. Because of opportunities for both on- and offshore fishing, coastal locations were preferred. The settlers often traveled by seagoing

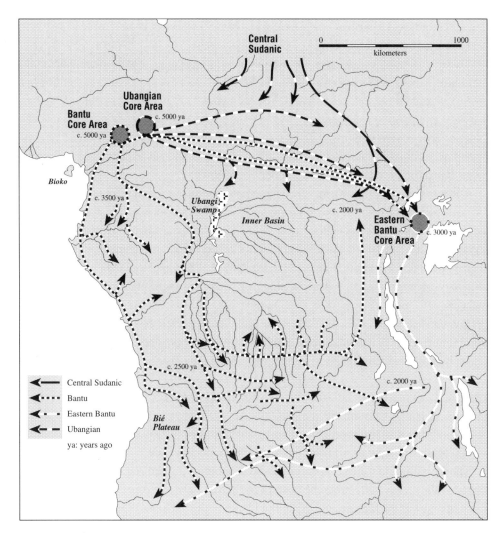

8.3 The peopling of central Africa by farmers started at sources along the northern periphery of the equatorial rain forest and followed numerous and complex routes east and south.

canoe, which took them as far as the the island of Bioko (formerly Fernando Po); there they established a Neolithic culture, isolated for many centuries from later Iron Age developments on the mainland. They also followed overland routes directly through the rain forest. Most traversed the narrow band of country between the rugged upturned plateau, the edge of which serves as the regional watershed, and the swamplands along the Ubangi River.

Bantu entry into the rain forest brought them into contact with pygmoid gatherer-hunters, but because each had different subsistence requirements, little territorial competition took place. By and large, Bantu settlers stayed along the river valleys, living in scattered villages of a hundred or so individuals each. Most of the interior of the rain forest was left to the pygmoids; they could gather and hunt here without fear of serious encroachment. Nevertheless, time was not on their side, for the Bantu were about to acquire two new technologies that would give them a decided advantage.

The first technology to arrive was iron making. It appeared slightly more than 2,000 years ago, probably as a result of diffusion from Nok-Taruga. The cutting capabilities of iron axes made it possible to clear larger fields than before, which meant more abundant harvests and, consequently, greater numbers of Bantu. The digging stick remained the planting tool, so the near-revolutionary impact that iron hoes had on woodland and savanna agriculture was not replicated in the rain forest. Still, as local populations grew, more Bantu villages came to dot the equatorial landscape.

The momentum of movement carried the Bantu settlement frontier south of the narrow western portion of the rain forest during the last few centuries B.C. The frontier did not advance in the common wavelike pattern, with new villages set up just beyond their parent villages. Instead, linguistic evidence indicates a very complex arrangement whereby newcomers from far behind the frontier often led the way. They kept moving until they found suitable unoccupied land; a visual analogy of what happened might be a hopscotch of villages.

Immediately south of the rain forest the Bantu encountered a band of moist woodland similar to that which had provided for their ancestors, but beyond it lay some of the least agriculturally productive lands in Africa. Because of atmospheric stability brought on by coldwater upwellings within the northward-moving Benguela Current, the coastal zone is plagued by increasing aridity, such that beyond Bengo Bay only the river valleys provide suitable settlement sites. Inland, the vast expanses of Brachystegia/Julbernardia woodland rest on infertile Kalahari-sand-derived soils, and here, too, rainfall is scant, reaching as low as 700 millimeters per annum along the Middle Zambezi valley.

The most important area of early population concentration and dispersal was the Lower Congo valley, especially around Malebo Pool. From here one promising nearby settlement option was the high ground of the Bié Plateau. Although characterized by extremely rugged terrain, the plateau had pockets of level ground with comparatively fertile soils, and rainfall was both higher and more reliable than at lower elevations. In addition, good, tsetse-free pastures were on hand. The second settlement option took groups eastward through the narrow belt of moist woodland. Some of the Bantu who headed in this direction went back into the rain forest, following the river valleys in a northerly direction. Seasonally inundated forest covered much of the heart of the Congo basin, and the first settlers avoided it in favor of higher ground, particularly that lying to east of the Lualaba River. About 2,000 years ago, the vanguards moving along this corridor crossed the Aruwimi River, where once again the Bantu encountered Ubangians, as well as some southbound Central Sudanic communities.

It was in this far northeastern corner of the equatorial rain forest that the second technology was acquired: the growing of domesticated bananas and plantains (*Musa* sp.). First cultivated in southeastern Asia, they seem to have reached Africa from several different sources. The earliest varieties probably came as part of the trade with India,

South of the equatorial rain forest, Bantu settlers entered
woodland country characterized by drought, poor soils, and sleeping
sickness. (Photo by Gordon Matzke, Geosciences Department,
Oregon State University.)

meaning that bananas and plantains probably reached Egypt and the Red Sea coast earlier
than 2,500 years ago. A little later they also accompanied Malayan voyagers who touched
points along the east coast on their way to Madagascar. No one really knows how bananas
and plantains managed to find their way into the interior of the continent, but by the first
centuries A.D. they were fast becoming the primary staple crops wherever conditions
permitted. With much higher yields than yams and little effort needed to keep the trees
(actually giant herbs) bearing fruit for years on end, there is little wonder that bananas and
plantains became so popular.

Their widespread use raised previous ceilings on population growth, and the number of
Bantu villages increased even faster than before, with some of communities now moving
away from the rivers and into the rain forest proper. A greater degree of village permanence
also resulted; indeed, permanence was required to reap the advantages of banana and
plantain cultivation.

More and larger Bantu villages spread over a greater area meant intensified contacts
with pygmoid gatherer-hunters, yet widespread conflict still did not take place. A much
more common outcome of the encounters was the establishment of a symbiotic relationship in which a given pygmoid band would regularly establish a camp near a particular

143

Bantu village to exchange meat, skins, medicines, and other products of the forest for pottery, agricultural produce, and iron knives, arrows, and spears. In this way, bands could preserve their autonomy as well as maintain control over a substantial territory. There is no doubt, however, that the Bantu were gaining an upper hand, and the strongest evidence in support of this statement is the complete disappearance of whatever may have been native pygmoid languages. If, as postulated earlier, the languages were of Niger-Congo affiliation, then perhaps the differences with Bantu might not have been all that great, and the transition easy. In any event, the pygmoid languages lost out to those of the villagers. At the same time, the spread of agriculture progressively diminished the capacity of the rain forest to support an independent hunting and gathering existence. In many locales, human activities had degraded forest stands into derived savanna or thicket offering little of subsistence value to the pygmoids. Their response was not to fight or flee but instead to seek an accommodation.

Still other Bantu traveled in a more easterly direction toward Lakes Tanganyika and Malawi, where sometime in the very first centuries A.D. they met Bantu recently arrived from the interlacustrine nucleus. From them they seem to have adopted millets and sorghums, crops much better suited to seasonal rainfall in places subject to drought. These crops filtered back to the west, as did newly acquired cattle, which allowed human settlement to extend to the margins of the Kalahari. Different pottery styles and more efficient iron implements, including hoes, were also acquired, and many archeologists see in this technological complex the coming of a New Iron Age characterized by greater productivity, population growth, and more pronounced regional differentiation.

GROWTH AND DIFFERENTIATION

The West

As a result of the many migrations rippling across the lands east of the Niger River, the northern border of the Bantu eventually came to rest across the Sanagha River in what is now southern Cameroon. Settlements clustered at the coast and along the few riverine sites where it was possible to find an array of food sources. The rest of the far northwestern portion of the equatorial forest was largely bypassed until about the fourteenth century, but even then the number of colonists was small. Although situated close to the cradle of the Bantu, the area north of Cape Lopez had resource limitations that lent it a frontier appearance, with dispersed farmsteads and small villages predominating at the expense of larger social and political units.

Conditions improved south of Cape Lopez, where a complex interweaving of forest, savanna, coastal, and riverine habitats supported a rich food economy with product specialization and riverine trade. The combination encouraged political centralization, which seems to have begun when particular matrilineages grew powerful enough to incorporate others across village lines. Trade was furthered by the creation of markets at the more

Cattle provided the Bantu with an important resource in their efforts to settle the more arid parts of central Africa. (Photo courtesy of Philip W. Porter.)

influential villages, and these in turn attracted more and more people. The most powerful villages enlarged their territorial influence and developed into chiefdoms, with the degree of tribute paying the major determinant of success. Scarcity made humans especially valuable, and they often served as the main method of payment as either slaves or clients. In return for giving up members, small families and lineages received some worldly security otherwise unavailable to them. By the end of the fourteenth century competition for people and other resources had yielded two primary political-economic centers: Loango, along the coast to the north of the Lower Congo River, and Kongo, straddling the banks of the Lower Congo (map 8.4).

Along the coast south of Kongo, the westward-flowing rivers remained the most significant areas of population concentration. The Kwanza River valley supported the rise of the Mbundu peoples, and farther south, the Cunene valley provided an artery for the development of the Ovambo. Inland, the country surrounding the Kwango River became the home of the Yaka and Zombo, while various Ovimbundu-speaking groups occupied the higher ground of the Bié Plateau.

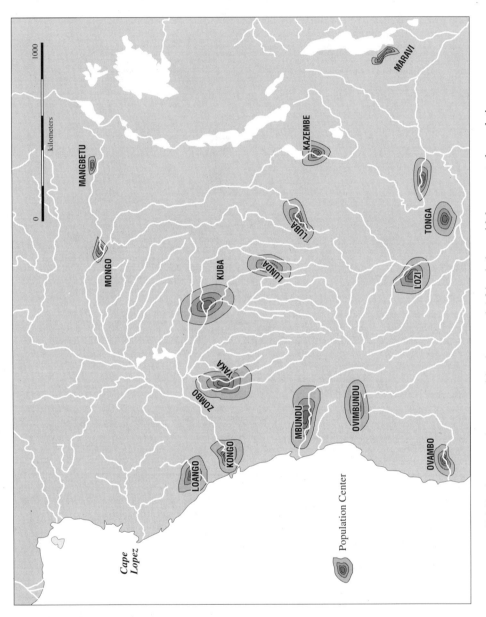

8.4 Environmental opportunities in central Africa led to widely separated population concentrations. Some of these eventually supported the rise of chiefdoms and kingdoms.

The East

The peopling of the eastern reaches of central Africa by farmers proceeded very slowly. A few Ubangian speakers managed to cross the Uele River and enter the northern sections of the equatorial forest, but for the most part they shied away. The Central Sudanic Mangbetu, however, were not so easily deterred. They had mastered the skills of banana and plantain cultivation and by A.D. 1000 were advancing into the Ituri forest lands of the Mbuti pygmoids. Another accommodation between farmers and hunters took place, which in this instance meant that a Central Sudanic language supplanted whatever the Mbuti might have previously spoken.

Some population growth also occurred along the middle reaches of the Lualaba River, where rich fishing grounds existed within a moist woodlands habitat. In addition, the Lualaba was becoming an important trade artery, with tributary junctions serving as strategic sites for village location.

Elsewhere throughout the eastern rain forest, agricultural settlements were very small, very few, and very widely separated. Hunting and gathering remained key subsistence activities among Bantu settlers, most of whom came from the interlacustrine nucleus, and consequently they outcompeted and displaced whatever pygmoid bands may have been there previously. No large population clusters ever developed, and social organization never evolved far beyond patrilineages and certain loosely affiliated associations.

The Interior Basin

Not until the early centuries of the second millennium did Bantu villages converge on the center of the rain forest, and the main impetus came from the east. Once again, pioneers followed the rivers, seeking out habitats in which they could carry on their farming and fishing way of life. An advantageous location existed where the Aruwimi River enters the Congo, and it was from that center that the Mongo language spread in a southwesterly direction to provide much of the forest's interior with a loose cultural affinity. For reasons that will probably forever remain unknown, pygmoids seem not to have survived in independent communities. Possibly they were so few that absorption took place, as is suggested by Mongo genetics and culture.

Assorted migrations converged on the area around Lake Mai Ndomde and the nearby middle and lower portions of the Kasai River valley. This proved to be a fertile environment, and by the last decades of the sixteenth century a federated chiefdom known as Kuba had come into being.

The Southern Woodlands

As in the eastern forest, the agricultural poverty characterizing much of the southern woodland forced many Bantu settlers to depend on gathering and hunting to supplement their diet; thus they competed directly with resident Khoisan. The Khoisan were no match in either numbers or technology, so only a few autonomous bands remained behind in inaccessible retreats.

147

Although this dependence also meant a low population density, a few locales were exceptional. One was located in the Upemba region of the Upper Lualaba River basin, where numerous lakes offered plentiful fish. By the beginning of the second millennium, their exploitation had reached a high-enough level to support a flourishing downriver trade. Some combination of reliable water supplies, rich soils, tsetse-free pastures, and abundant fish and game also favored several other areas, notably the Upper Zambezi floodplain, the Tonga Plateau, the country east of the Middle Kasai River, the Lower Luapula River valley at the south end of Lake Mweru, and the western shores of Lake Malawi, along which several groups coalesced to form the Maravi chieftancies in the seventeenth century.

Although these areas experienced population growth well above the regional norm, political centralization did not immediately follow. In most locales, social organization tended to adhere to matrilineal principles, which can put constraints on the accumulations of wealth and power by requiring that inheritances be distributed to the mother's eldest brother and not to her own children. Accumulation, a prime requisite for centralization, is next to impossible under such circumstances.

In time, nonetheless, centralizing processes did take hold. These seem to have involved several sorts of individuals, such as earth priests, who performed various ancestral and rainmaking ceremonies, and exceptionally skilled hunters. As interregional trade grew in scope, it provided the means for accumulating wealth and helped create a class of "big men" able to ignore conventional inheritance rules. They often bypassed the rules by obtaining pawned wives from impoverished families, and any children born of such unions joined new male-centered lineages. When these lineages became large enough, they provided the base on which localized chiefdoms could be built; the chiefdoms then had the potential to develop into even more extensive kingdoms, which sometimes verged on empire status.

The country surrounding the Upemba basin eventually fell under the sway of the Luba, who had come from the nearby Lomami River valley. Profiting from trade in salt and iron, they developed a patrilineally organized chiefdom by the beginning of the seventeenth century and then capitalized on their location relative to the rich copper deposits lying along both sides of the present-day Zambia-Zaire border. Mining activities date back to A.D. 500, and with the emergence of social elites, copper jewelry became a status symbol in adorning both the living and the dead. As the profits from controlling much of the northward flow of trade poured in, the Luba extended their authority into Upemba. Four chiefdoms joined in confederation, but no unified state ever developed. Still, by the last decades of the eighteenth century Luba language and culture had spread over a wide area.

The Upper Zambezi valley was home to the Lozi, or Barotse, as they are sometimes called. The key to their success was gaining control of the slightly elevated mounds that dot the floodplain. Once they had accomplished this task, the Lozi could take advantage of rich tsetse-free pasturage to increase their most important source of wealth, cattle. By early in the seventeenth century, a Lozi kingship had formed, and over the course of the next century its sphere of influence reached beyond the floodplain into the surrounding wood-lands. The Lozi sent out military expeditions not so much to add territory to the realm as to extract slaves and create tribute-paying satellites. Consequently, Lozi remained more a kingdom than an empire.

Somewhat different circumstances surrounded ascent to power of the Lunda. Inhabitants of the woodlands nearby the Middle Kasai River valley, they adopted cassava as one of their food staples during the late sixteenth century. Because the Lunda continued to cultivate a variety of other crops, cassava, at least in this instance, played an enriching rather than impoverishing role. The population grew, and sometime before the end of the century a Lunda dynasty arose. Instead of seeking immediate territorial aggrandizement, the Lunda increased the number of people at the center of the kingdom, mainly by using captives from groups on the periphery to serve as laborers on cassava plantations. Loaves made from cassava lasted for three to four months, and given the high demand for them, especially among other long-distance traders, the Lunda profited from surpluses that captive laborers helped produce.

By the eighteenth century, however, the Lunda found expansion vital to their continued well-being. Colonies were established between the Kasai and Kwango rivers and within the headwater country of the Zambezi. Later, an even more vigorous colonization effort was launched in an easterly direction. It could not penetrate Luba-held territory, but some Lunda groups eventually reached the Lower Luapula valley, where they organized the Kazembe kingdom during the mid-eighteenth century. Ivory, copper, and salt carried by tributary Bisa traders enabled Kazembe to control an extensive area between Lakes Mweru and Bangweulu, and thus another large swath of the central and southern woodlands became home to Lunda speakers.

RECONFIGURATION

So far, it has been possible to discuss the peopling of central Africa by referring almost exclusively to events internal to the region. Just over 500 years ago, however, powerful external forces entered the area. The most far-reaching emanated from the Atlantic coast, but others from northern and eastern sources also brought important changes with them. Virtually all of these forces arrived in the guise of trade, and by the 1870s nearly every-where and everyone had been touched and irrevocably altered. Those people who were well placed both spatially and politically could profit as never before at the expense of the less fortunately situated, and as the map of power changed, so, too, did the map of local populations. At various times and in various places, numbers both swelled and declined, and groups formed and re-formed. Only the several Tonga peoples occupying the southern plateau of Zambia escaped major involvement.

Atlantic Influences

Once again it was the Portuguese who set the processes of change in motion, and un-like in western Africa, they continued to be prominent regional players from then on.

Initially their attention was focused on the Congo estuary in order to deal with the recently organized Kongo kingdom. In addition to a centralized government with a capital at Mbanga (later São Salvador), Kongo had periodic markets, a kingdomwide shell-based currency, and a trade route to the interior along the Congo River to Malebo Pool, where riverine traffic from throughout the basin converged. By the close of the fifteenth century diplomatic relations between the two courts had been established. One immediate result was the arrival of missionaries, who converted the Kongo to Catholicism and introduced them to Portuguese culture, and within a few years the sons of some Kongo notables left for Portugal to receive formal schooling. However, because there were no major sources of wealth within Kongo itself, official Portuguese interest soon waned in favor of the Gold Coast, India, and Brazil. Commercial activities fell into the hands of individual merchants and adventurers, and once again, a distinctive Luso-African community, the *pombeiros,* came into being.

By 1514 the export of slaves was under way. At first, ivory and beeswax were used to pay for imported textiles, alcohol, metalware, tobacco, and ceramics desired by the Kongo nobility, but these proved to be of too little value. Slaves brought more in exchange, and so the Kongolese court sold off some of their own servants, as well as prisoners destined for execution. They were irrevocably hooked, and when this supply was inadequate, the Kongolese turned inland for other sources. The Tio kingdom of Teke centered on Malebo Pool was a good one (map 8.5), especially when the demand shot up to meet the labor needs of the newly created sugar plantations on the previously unoccupied islands of São Tomé and Principe. The era of sugar prosperity was short-lived, however. First came competition from Brazil, and then in 1574 a slave revolt put an end to the plantation economy, creating an even earlier population of Maroons than in the West Indies.

Within Kongo itself, the Atlantic trade reinforced power at the center, thereby furthering the regional dominance of the kingdom. But as the flow of imports accelerated during the sixteenth century, rival factions developed, and soon centralizing processes were overtaken by traditional segmentation. The pombeiros displayed considerable skill in forming alliances with local dignitaries, and as they did so, the trade monopoly of the Kongo court dissolved. Adding to the diminution of Kongolese authority was the political interference of missionaries, for they, too, played the competing factions game.

The rise of Angola as a trade rival was of even greater significance to the future of Kongo. Angola began with the founding of Luanda in the 1520s by pombeiros attempting to free themselves from Portugal-imposed trading constraints. They managed to achieve independence for a time, but Portugal caught up with them in 1571 by creating the Colony of Angola under a royal charter. The intention was to use Angola both for settlement and for a base to reach valuable silver deposits in the interior. The silver was mythical, and a period of drought doomed the settlement scheme. Nevertheless, the proclamation brought numbers of Portuguese to the new colony, and as an alternative to agriculture, the colonists turned to slaving.

Another drought facilitated the new economic activity. As one bad year followed

150

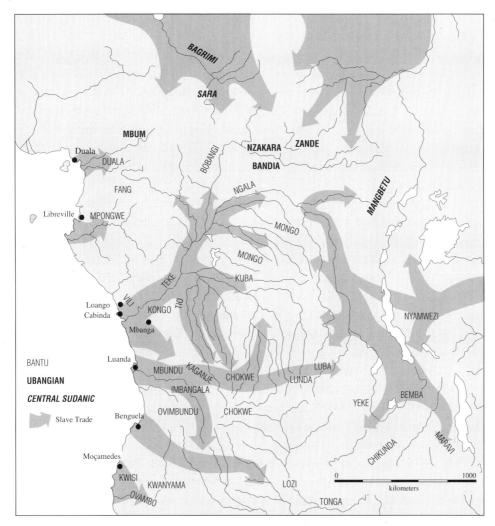

8.5 Central Africa was gripped by forces coming from outside the region, arriving for the most part along with the slave trade.

another in the late sixteenth century, poverty became desperation, forcing more than a few families to sell their own kin, while many others became easy targets for Jaga raiders. In Portuguese, Jaga refers generally to outlaws and brigands, who in this particular instance formed from a warrior class among the Ovimbundu. Another Jaga group, composed mainly of Tio from the Kwango valley, raided Kongo territory in 1568. They arrived during a raging internal power struggle, and the rule of the king collapsed, although Portuguese military intervention quickly restored it.

The economic contest between Angola and Kongo flared into a series of wars in 1622–72, and by their end, Kongo was essentially finished as an important regional entity. It grew progressively weaker at the center, and centrifugal forces reasserted themselves. Many of

151

those who had once identified themselves as Kongo re-formed into other ethnic groupings, such as Mussorongo and Mushikonjo.

The demand for slaves was unabated, and as the sources near Luanda dried up, the search for supplies pushed farther and farther inland. A synthesis of Imbangala and Mbundu produced the Kasanye kingdom astride the Lower Kwango, and it served as a jumping-off point for caravans headed east and south. Guns had been added to the list of imports, and they helped to increase the relative power of the raiders over the poorly organized peoples they encountered along the way. By the early decades of the nineteenth century, slavers had reached the fringes of the Lunda kingdom, and they were invading the forest from the south.

Slaves from around Malebo Pool had also become increasingly scarce, and during the seventeenth century few were brought down the Congo River. Later demands, however, prompted a broader search through the interior basin, and this created new ethnicities out of village alliances formed to protect trading interests. The most active traders were the Bobangi, who controlled canoe traffic from the lower reaches of the Ubangi downstream to Malebo Pool. Others, like the Likuba, Likwala, and Bonga, were formed of peoples banding together to secure tributary routes to slave sources.

During the early eighteenth century slaves began to leave from the port of Benguela directly for Brazil, where the growth in demand had reached virtually insatiable proportions. By the end of the century the trade centered on Benguela had expanded into the Upper Zambezi valley, and once again, obtaining slaves was made easier by devastating drought. From 1785 to 1794 raiders found a steady stream of refugees at their disposal. Later, in 1800 and again in 1805, outbreaks of smallpox similarly reduced community resistance to enslavement.

Although some pombeiros found their way to the Loango coast at an early date, interregional trade in commodities like raffia cloth, salt, and copper remained the main commercial activity. Controlling the traffic were people known as the Vili, the likely originators of the Kingdom of Loango. The Dutch arrived in the 1520s, but at the outset, given their interests in ivory and dye woods, they had a negligible impact on the course of population events. All this changed with the escalating demand for slaves in the late seventeenth century. Portuguese, British, and French traders joined the Dutch, and Loango turned into a busy port. Vili caravans reached the Congo River to obtain slaves from the Bobangi; the Vili's main destination was Angola, however, where a much greater supply could be found. The shift in activity favored the port of Cabinda, and in the eighteenth century it broke away from Loango control. Although significantly reduced in territorial extent, the kingdom held on to its independence.

The area north of Cape Lopez remained peripheral for several hundred more years. Some Dutch ships called occasionally, and in response the Duala moved coastward to open a small port carrying the same name. In the eighteenth century several small kingdoms had arisen on the nearby Bamileke Plateau, but their presence seems to have been unrelated to any advance of the Atlantic frontier.

According to a Dutch rendering, Loango was a large and prosperous city during the seventeenth century. (Reprinted from Basil Davidson, *Black Mother,* Little, Brown, 1961, pl. 19.)

The demographic impacts of the Atlantic slave trade through the eighteenth century are even more difficult to determine in central Africa than in western Africa. On an absolute scale, the numbers are clearly much smaller. In 1500 central Africa may have contained 15 million inhabitants, and the number probably grew to 20 million or so over the next 300 years. There are two reasons why regional population growth could be maintained in the face of a continuing loss across the Atlantic. When the slavers reached an area, the population undoubtedly decreased as people either fled or were taken away in chains or killed. However, the slave frontier seems to have moved on after at most two generations, and then conditions stabilized considerably. Henceforth, those sent off into slavery tended to be misfits, criminals, and others deemed expendable. When they departed, new slaves from the frontier took their place. And as in western Africa, most of those left behind by the slavers were young women, whose reproductive potential helped ensure at least some degree of numerical growth.

The other reason why the population continued to grow relates to the spread of cassava. As we have seen repeatedly, it seems to have set off a minor population explosion wherever adopted, and thus, ironically, cassava both supported the reproduction of slaves and enabled many people to survive.

During the nineteenth century the nature of the trading frontier changed considerably. Slaves remained an important commodity, but after mid-century the transatlantic market shrank to only a fraction of what it had been. Many who were shipped off came from the relatively untouched Gabon coastal zone, where numerous estuaries allowed illegal traders to operate with far less fear of detection than elsewhere. Then, in the 1830s, the activity suddenly gained renewed momentum, with the Mpongwe serving as principal traders. The people who escaped enslavement retreated farther inland, leaving the interior even more sparsely settled than before. Diseases also seem to have played a role, especially smallpox, which spread inland from the port of Libreville, established by the the French in 1848 on the model of Freetown. Filtering into the empty spaces were the Fang, who came south from the Cameroon under the press of Fulbe raiding. The local population density never mounted much beyond the previous very low rates.

Elsewhere the Atlantic slave trade gave way to other commerce. In the equatorial zone, oil palm plantations sprang up near the coast, while timber, ivory, and rubber became highly sought-after inland commodities. As in western Africa, a redirection of the slave economy provided most of the necessary labor. When manufactured items from European factories poured in, interregional trade intensified. The Congo River was an important artery of commerce, and strategic junctions gave rise to trading firms, around which towns of 5,000–10,000 inhabitants developed. The intense competition frequently led to violence, but the societies of the equatorial zone mostly coped, finding ways to adapt to the volatile circumstances. In this they were undoubtedly aided by the great distances that still separated most groups.

Disruption was much more general in the woodlands and savannas of the southern interior. Slave raiding here had become more intense, to supply both transatlantic and ever-growing local demand. Accompanying the hunt for slaves was a frenzied effort to collect ivory. Ovimbundu caravans entered from the west, but the Chokwe eventually gained the upper hand. The Chokwe were late eighteenth-century refugees from the eastern margins of the Bié Plateau who supported themselves by collecting and trading beeswax. Being excellent hunters as well, they turned to procuring ivory and slaves. Most of the original Chokwe were men, and with ivory they purchased women. As the population grew, the Chokwe expanded into the Congo basin as far as the Luba, where rubber collecting had become a highly profitable venture. Although they never formed a centralized state, by 1870 their stockaded villages studded a broad expanse of territory, and even though loosely organized, they could mobilize enough men to take on the forces of the Lunda Empire. Indeed, the Chokwe were more than a match, because internal and external competition soon tore Lunda apart. The one substantial polity able to maintain itself intact until the advent of colonialism was the Lozi kingdom. And it did so by using slaves, who constituted maybe as much as 50 percent of the population of the kingdom by the second half of the nineteenth century.

A very late set of Atlantic influences came from Moçamedes. The aridity of the coast and the sparseness of the population directly inland had discouraged earlier commercial activity until the ivory trade lured some Luanda merchants into establishing a port here in the 1840s. From the port they traveled to the territories of the Kwisi, Kwanyama, and

154

Ovambo but found few elephants, and thus the countryside remained mostly undisturbed. In the vicinity of Moçamedes itself, land was converted to sugar and cotton plantations, and in the 1860s Portuguese fisherman arrived to take advantage of the rich opportunities provided by the the cold upwellings of the Benguela Current.

Other External Influences

External influences filtered into central Africa from directions other than the Atlantic coast. In the fourteenth century the Central Sudanic Bagrimi were subjected to Kanuri slave raiding. When the Bagrimi converted to Islam, the slave frontier was pushed to the Sara, eventually to be stopped at the barrier of the Salamat marshes. A far more active slaving effort was initiated in the late seventeenth century when traders from Dar Fur and Wadai arrived on the scene. Their predations proved costly well beyond the unknown number of slaves captured, for they also appear to have introduced several new devastating diseases. Smallpox and measles created an immediate crisis in many communities, canceling the growth induced by the addition of maize and cassava to the agricultural inventory, while syphilis and gonorrhea left a legacy of infertility that has only recently retreated under assault from modern antibiotics. Augmenting the disruption were occasional forays by Shuwa Arab, Fulbe, and Hausa slave traders.

The Adamawa and Ubangian peoples seem to have been spared the full brunt of this round of assaults, and thus their populations changed mainly in accordance with internal dynamics. Blessed with rich agricultural resources, the Bamenda Hills and Adamawa Plateau supported a dense population. In time, small localized kingdoms emerged, many of which became part of a wider Mbum confederation during the eighteenth century. Farther east, the Zande were expanding from a homeland along the Mbomu and Chinko rivers. They came as conquerers, and the Zande increased rapidly by taking captured women as wives and impressing surviving men into their armies. But no wider Zande state ever emerged; instead, only a very loose confederation of chiefdoms could be put together. With the Zande conquest uncompleted, room for competitors existed. The most dynamic were the Bandia, who created a series of small states along the margins of the equatorial forest, several of which included Zande peoples; also important were the Nzakara, who occupied the woodlands and savannas lying north of the Bandia.

Some slave trading did go on, but it seems to have been less significant than commerce in other commodities until the middle of the nineteenth century. Small numbers of itinerant Jallaba Arabs worked their way south and west, eventually reaching the Zande, while in the Adamawa region trade was controlled by Hausa and Bornu merchants. By the early decades of the nineteenth century more of the intraregional trade had fallen into the hands of indigenous specialists, most notably the Ngala offshoot of the Bobangi along the Middle Congo, with both languages developing into lingua francas.

New waves of destabilization struck around 1850, and only the peoples living along the rain forest margins escaped unscathed. Slaves were once more the most sought-after commodity, and this time the traders arrived heavily armed. From the east came Khartoumers, called that because of the source of their financing. Composed largely of Arabs and some Nubians, the Khartoumers worked out of a series of garrisoned forts stretching from the southwestern Sudan as far as the Zande and Nzakara, and from these strongholds they controlled the surrounding countryside by making deals with local leaders and then turning them into vassals. As a result of their activities, the one state that had arisen in the region, that of the Mangbetu in the remote Ituri-Uele area, fell apart. The west came under assault from the Fulbe. Crucial to their success was an alliance made with the Mbum confederation that gave them some freedom of unopposed movement. The Fulbe used slaves both for their own agricultural purposes and for items to trade with the emirates in Nigeria.

In both east and west the impact of the renewed slaving activities was enormous. Depopulation occurred over enormous areas as people fled or were enslaved or killed in warfare or smallpox outbreaks. In the savannas some people found refuge in the rocky outcrops that dot the landscape, whereas others established palisaded villages or sought the protection of Khartoumer forts and Fulbe settlements. Adopting Islam was even a better way to avoid capture, and consequently it spread throughout the area. Without the intervention of European colonialism, the lands north of the rain forest would certainly have become an integral part of the wider African Islamic world. Instead, they remained incompletely converted and thus peripheral.

The final precolonial intruders into central Africa came from the east: Nyamwezi traders, from the other side of Lake Tanganyika. They were after copper and ivory to ship to the coast opposite Zanzibar; and to carry these goods over the long distances traversed, slaves were used as porters. Upon reaching Kazembe, some Nyamwezi opted to settle nearby and took the name Yeke. They developed a conquest state that incorporated numerous peoples from the area of the Katanga, effectively putting an end to Kazembe suzerainty.

In the 1850s and 1860s Arab and Swahili merchants from Zanzibar also appeared, often in alliances with Nyamwezi, to tap the trade from Kazembe. They also launched slaving expeditions into the Maravi chieftaincies and penetrated the easternmost portions of the equatorial rain forest. From a base at Kasongo Nyangwe, they raided over a wide area looking for ivory and slaves, terrorizing the loosely organized peoples who had up until now been spared destabilizing external contacts.

Two other peoples took advantage of the conditions during the late nineteenth century to extend their territorial range. In the 1870s the Chikunda followed the Zambezi valley to the uplands east of the Kafue River in a search for ivory and slaves, and the Bemba gained control over much of the land between the Luapula and Luangwa river valleys. The soils of this area are some of the most impoverished in Africa, and drought is also recurrent, but in the mid-nineteenth century elephants were abundant, and the Bemba used profits from trading ivory to Arab-Swahili merchants to buy guns so that they could dominate others militarily. Their prowess with arms enabled the Bemba to supplant the Bisa as the preeminent traders in the eastern woodland zone.

156

The natural environment clearly placed severe constraints on the peoples settling most parts of central Africa, but low population density and small-scale polities are not exclusively its doing. Human factors must be added in, especially ones from external sources. By the last quarter of the nineteenth century the forces thus unleashed had seriously eroded the fragile foundations upon which most polities were built. Left behind was a legacy of warfare, disease, and social-political disorder, whose existence reinforced the Darkest Africa image that gave the European powers one of their principal justifications for colonial intervention.

9

EASTERN AFRICA

The phrase "juxtaposed diversity" best describes eastern Africa. Highlands and mountains often rise abruptly from gently rolling plateaus (map 9.1). Some of the uplands, such as the Ruwenzoris and Ulugurus, are massive upthrusts of ancient crystalline rocks, whereas others are the products of Pleistocene tectonic activity. The majority of the volcanoes, including Mounts Kenya, Kilimanjaro, Meru, and Elgon, now lie dormant, but Ol'Doinyo Lengai, near Ngorongoro Crater, and Nyiragongo, in the Virunga Mountains, are still active. Numerous lakes make up for a paucity of rivers. Situated within a shallow basin, Lake Victoria is the largest in surface area. Others follow the crustal gashes of the rift valleys, with the bottom of Lake Tanganyika lying well below sea level. Not as dramatic but of great historical importance is the narrow coastal plain abutting the Indian Ocean. The climate is seasonal, but the lengths of the seasons and even their number vary, producing from arid to almost equatorial conditions. Vegetation correspondingly ranges from desert and semidesert scrub, to variations on the savanna theme, to swamp and grassland, to woodland and forest (map 9.2).

The peoples of eastern Africa are likewise diverse, a condition already observable during the final stages of the Late Stone Age among the several gatherer-hunter populations. The most widespread of the gatherer-hunters apparently had San affinities and occupied the game-rich savannas. Fisherfolk, probably speaking early Eastern Sudanic

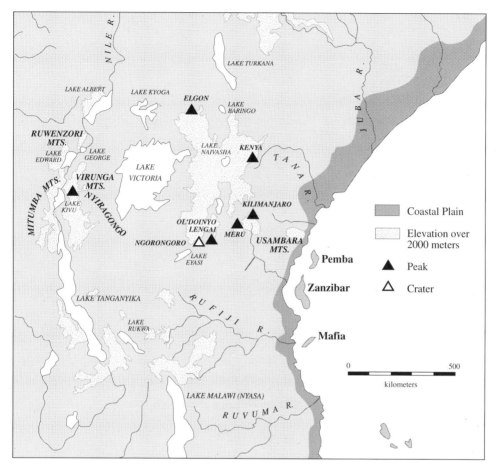

9.1 The topography of eastern Africa consists of a narrow coastal plain and extensive plateaus that are interrupted by mountains, volcanic peaks, and numerous lakes.

languages, exploited lakeshore sites, while some pygmoid groups could be found in heavily wooded and forested habitats. Then, no later than 4,000 years ago, the first farmers and herders made their appearance. They were Cushites from Ethiopia who found the highlands flanking the eastern rift valley to their liking.

At the same time or somewhat later, Central Sudanic speakers moved through the interlacustrine area to an undetermined point farther south. Bantu and Nilotes, on the verge of making an appearance, would be the primary shapers of later regional population developments. What eventually transpired depended on three things: the precise nature of Bantu and Nilotic interaction, the contacts that each group made, and environmental setting. Events created two well-defined subregions, the interlacustrine region and the Swahili coast, and a third, more variable one, which for the sake of convenience I will call the interior mosaic.

159

Although most of eastern Africa's volcanoes have been dormant for many centuries, a few, such as Ol'Doinyo Lengai in Tanzania, have remained active. (Photo courtesy of Becky Thompson.)

INTERLACUSTRINE DEVELOPMENTS

As noted earlier, Bantu-speaking peoples first reached the western margins of the interlacustrine area 3,000 years ago (map 9.3a). Still dependent on yams and fishing, their first settlements congregated at humid lakeshore and riverside locations. Bordering them in drier settings were earlier arrivals: Central Sudanic, Eastern Sudanic, and Southern Cushitic peoples. Paleobotanical findings showing a rapid decline in forest cover suggest that the initial agriculturalists could have reached the lakes as early as 5,000 years ago and certainly no later than 3,000. In any event, from these several sources the Bantu soon picked up sorghum and millet cultivation, along with cattle keeping, and thus gained the means for extending their settlements into the much vaster, seasonally wet and dry climatic zones of eastern Africa.

The Bantu also acquired another asset: iron. Sites from Buhaya west of Lake Victoria have yielded finds that are at least 2,200 years old, and developments were clearly independent of those at Meroë and probably Taruga as well. Once again a link between iron making and population success seems evident, because by A.D. 500 the interlacustrine region

160

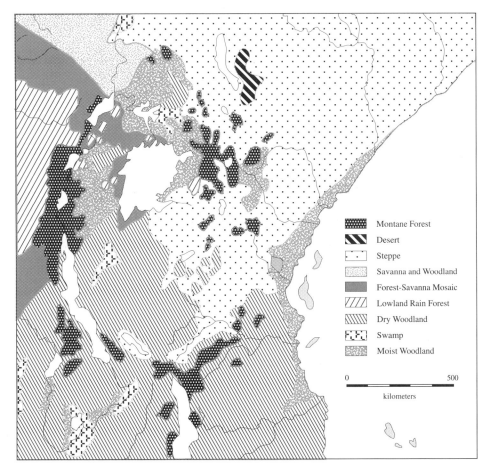

9.2 The complex vegetation pattern of eastern Africa results from how topography influences rainfall.

essentially belonged to the Bantu. Various Central Sudanic peoples still held on at the northern fringes, whereas the Eastern Sudanic and Southern Cushitic peoples disappeared from the area completely—except for what they bequeathed in the way of technologies and loanwords.

In sole possession of a region with reliable rainfall, expanses of fertile soil, lakes and streams for fishing, and grasslands rich in game, the Bantu grew in number—especially after they had plantains and bananas, which arrived earlier than 1,000 years ago. Yet unoccupied space was available, and into it filtered Western Nilotes.

The expansion of the Western Nilotes took place over 400–500 years and did not culminate until near the end of the nineteenth century (map 9.3b). Behind their expansion lay a complex series of population developments within the flat clay plains surrounding the Bahr-al Ghazal and Nile rivers. First came the expansion of the Nuer at the expense of their Dinka neighbors, who, in turn, moved against groups of Lwo speakers, to whom they were

161

The savannas of eastern Africa provided a rich source of game for Khoisan-related gatherer-hunters. (Photo by author.)

closely related, causing many of them to follow the Nile upstream into the savanna country north of Lakes Albert and Kyoga.

Competition centered on two key resources. One was cattle. Although all Western Nilotes have traditionally relied on grains to supply their primary dietary needs, the milk, blood, and meat of cattle made essential contributions, especially during the dry season. The number of cattle owned defined wealth and power; those who had more could dominate those who had fewer. What might have benefited the Nuer was their development of hardy, high-yielding cadatum varieties of sorghum. By allowing them to keep more cattle, the new varieties would have given the Nuer an advantage in the competition with the Dinka for the other key resource—ridge tops, which were sites for permanent villages. The clay plains are inundated during the rainy season, and only a few meters of additional elevation can determine whether land remains above water when the floods come. Of special value were those rare sites also near water during the long, hot dry season that follows the floods.

Some of the villages grew unusually large and supported the rise of localized chieftainships, and these proved crucial to ultimate Nuer success. Armies up to 1,500 men strong could be recruited from different villages, whereas among the less-organized Dinka, villages, for the most part, had to fend for themselves, and fending usually meant flight, not defending, when Nuer forces confronted them. A favored Nuer tactic was to launch attacks at harvest time so that not just territory but also full grain bins could be seized. While using these products of Dinka labor, the Nuer could prepare for the next year's round of conquests. Nuer successes led to a burgeoning population. Captured women and children and

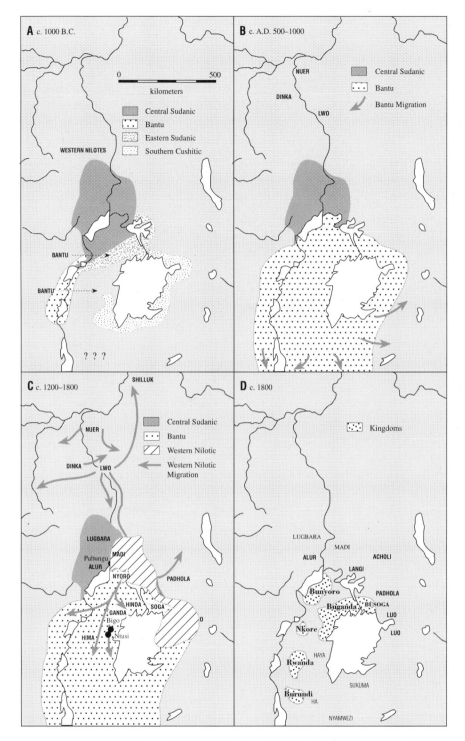

9.3 Central Sudanic, Eastern Sudanic, Southern Cushitic, Bantu, and Western Nilotic speakers all settled in the interlacustrine region of eastern Africa. Eventually several kingdoms became the dominant precolonial polities.

sometimes even whole villages of Dinka left behind during an advance were counted in. Far better for a Dinka to change group affiliation than to die in futile resistance.

Although other factors may have been involved, the redistribution of Nuer and Dinka is probably what induced Lwo migrations. Numerous and complex movements are re-counted in oral traditions, mostly of clan or smaller groups, spanning 400 or more years (map 9.3c). The Lwo traveled with their cattle, setting up temporary camps along the way. Many of the sites at which they supposedly stopped are mythical, but at least one—Pubungu, along the Nile north of Lake Albert—appears to have been regularly used as a point for subsequent dispersals. Well organized and endowed with their valuable cattle, the Lwo succeeded by infiltrating the resident communities of Central Sudanics and gaining political control. Some of their camps became royal courts or capitals of kingdoms, the recipients of tribute demanded from surrounding farmers. In several instances, this pattern of infiltration led eventually to a wider Lwo presence, achieved via a language shift, such as that among the Alur, who were once Central Sudanic speakers.

When Bantu were encountered, the outcome was much different. The first contacts took place northwest of Lake Kyoga, where a Lwo clan known as Bito had established its hegemony within an emerging kingdom among the Bantu Nyoro. Related to the Bito were the Hinda, who formed royal dynasties among peoples along the western side of Lake Victoria, and the Hima, who rose to political power in Rwanda and Burundi. In each instance, Bantu speech and cultural identity prevailed over Nilotic. Indeed, in only one area did the Lwo eventually predominate numerically over the Bantu: in the Nyanza region of Kenya, where the modern-day Luo reside.

The differences in Lwo demographic success may well have been due to preexisting population densities. In what is now Uganda the richest agricultural areas were controlled by the Bantu, and these supported a much greater population density than the less produc-tive semiarid lands inhabited by Central Sudanics. Consequently, for small numbers of Lwo to prevail would have been difficult, no matter how great their wealth in cattle and their political prestige. In contrast, the Nyanza region is not nearly as well endowed agriculturally as the lands on the western side of Lake Victoria or, for that matter, as the highlands to the east, and the Bantu bypassed it for the most part. Only less productive lands more suited to livestock grazing were left for the Lwo to claim, and these lands would have to absorb immigrants for several hundred more years.

Lwo presence and royal lineage are linked in the interlacustrine region. Royal status could be a direct derivative from the Nuer ridge chiefs; the Lwo may indeed have been responsible for its introduction. On the other hand, there is accruing evidence that royal status had been realized before the Lwo arrival. The evidence comes mainly in two forms and points to the existence of several small Bantu proto-kingdoms between the Ruwenzori Mountains and Lake Victoria by 1250. There are repeated references in oral traditions to a royal lineage known as the Bacwezi, or Chwezi, and there are earthworks, the most prominent being at Ntusi and Bigo. The lineages are traceable to very early Bantu legends, while the style of the earthen structures bears considerable resemblance to the one used at later royal courts.

Further confirming a pre-Lwo dynastic tradition is the presumed Bantu origin of the royal property—spear, stool, and sacred drums—of the Alur, Acholi, and several other peoples. Finally, not all Lwo-settled areas developed a royal tradition. The Padhola, for example, maintained a lineage-based system of social and political organization. They had settled the virgin forests west of Mount Elgon and were effectively isolated from Bantu contacts. Similarly, the Luo of Kenya never achieved any degree of political centralization. Although the conditions existed for kingdoms to develop among the Lwo, the Bantu presence in the interlacustrine region seems to have been necessary for their realization.

The matter of royalty's origins brings in the Shilluk. They occupied the western banks of the Nile north of the Nuer and Dinka and developed an elaborate social-political system organized around a divine king, or *reth*. The office is primarily ritual in character and represents the earthly presence of the founding culture hero. How the Shilluk came by their divine kingship continues to puzzle cultural historians, as does their migration history. Some have suggested derivation from ancient Egypt, but there is no evidence that kingship and the Shilluk are anywhere near that old. In fact, the thirty or so dynasties referred to in Shilluk oral traditions fit neatly with the early phases of Nuer-Dinka movements. Thus, the Shilluk could be Lwo who moved north instead of south in the face of disruptive migrations.

In still another interpretation the lines of northward migration are extended even farther. It is posited that the Shilluk were influenced by Bantu ideas of royalty and that they left the interlacustrine region, returning in the direction from which they had originally come. That Lwo migrations were complex and multidirectional is certain, but assuming this complexity in order to find a cultural stimulus is highly tenuous, especially given the rather distant relation between Shilluk and the Ugandan Lwo languages. In all probability, the origins of divine kingship among the Shilluk are better sought in the circumstances of their settlement along the Nile than in a presumed link to lands far away in time and space.

Kingdom formation and consequent interkingdom rivalries dominated the interlacustrine region from the seventeenth century to the close of the precolonial era (map 9.3d). For most of the period, the preeminent power in the north was Bunyoro, but in the nineteenth century it lost ground to Buganda and also to the Ankole state of Nkore. Control of intraregional trade, primarily of salt, iron, hides and skins, and agricultural produce, was the prize in question. In the 1830s Nyamwezi ivory traders showed up, and before midcentury so, too, did some Arab and Swahili merchants, but they never became politically or economically important.

Farther south, the more feudal kingdoms of Rwanda and Burundi were established. From a complicated mix of Hinda, Hima, and local Bantu royalty came the Tutsi. Using cattle as a medium of exchange, the Tutsi instituted a system of clientage with the more numerous cultivators known as Hutu. Also attached in a very tangential way to Tutsi paramountcy were small numbers of pygmoid Twa gatherer-hunters. Movement between Tutsi and Hutu status depended on ownership of cattle and the bestowal of royal favor, but the social-political hierarchy evolved into the most rigidly stratified one of all inter-lacustrine kingdoms.

THE INTERIOR MOSAIC

In the interior of eastern Africa, at various times and in various places Khoisan, Cushitic, Nilotic, and Bantu peoples met one another to produce what is arguably the most complex ethnolinguistic region in the continent. Not until the imposition of colonial order did the shuffling and reshuffling of territory and peoples come to an end.

The train of events started with the departure of Southern Cushites from Ethiopia 5,000 years ago (map 9.4). They followed the eastern rift valley into central Kenya, then spread out into the adjacent highlands. Archeologically their presence is marked by what is called the Pastoral Neolithic (formerly Stone Bowl) Culture. As the name implies, a herding way of life centered on cattle predominated, but grain cultivation can also be inferred from vocabulary reconstructions. Indeed, the presence of Southern Cushitic loanwords among later settlers, especially terms related to agriculture, indicates that the Southern Cushites traveled at least as far east as the Uluguru Mountains, as far west as the southern shore of Lake Victoria, and maybe as far south as the highlands bordering the north end of Lake Malawi. In central Tanzania they have left a physical reminder in the shape of the Iraqw, Gorowa, and Burunge peoples.

Eastern Cushites also made their way south. About 1000 B.C., they took two migration routes from a hearth at the north end of Lake Turkana. The Gabaloid moved along the eastern shore of the lake. Entering an increasingly arid environment, they abandoned agricultural pursuits entirely in favor of hunting, gathering, and fishing. Some of them, like the modern El Molo, stayed at the lake to fish. Others continued south into the forests surrounding the northern slopes of Mount Kenya, where they remained as gatherer-hunters under the name Yaaku or Qwaku. Whether or not Southern Cushites were already there is unclear. Still other Gabaloids seem to have taken the Tana River valley to the coast, where they mingled with and eventually absorbed Khoisan-speaking peoples. Later Oromo and Somali expansion in this direction incorporated their descendants as specialized occupational castes known as Sanye and Boni.

A second branch of Eastern Cushites, the Baz, tracked the western side of Lake Turkana. They managed to survive only for a short time, succumbing to the more vigorous expansion of Southern Nilotes. The Baz, however, left a substantial legacy. To the Southern Nilotes they bequeathed livestock-raising techniques adapted to semiarid conditions and such cultural practices as penile circumcision and clitoridectomy, a prohibition against eating fish, and a cycling age-grade system of social organization.

By 500 B.C. the Southern Nilotes from northwest of Lake Turkana had entered central Kenya, where they divided the space with Southern Cushites (map 9.5). The Southern

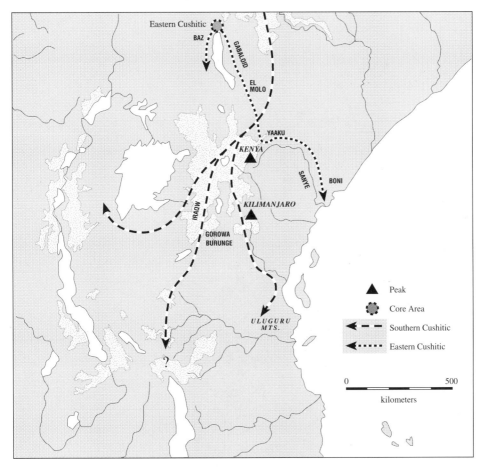

9.4 Southern and Eastern Cushites introduced food-producing economies into the evolving mosaic of interior eastern Africa.

Nilotes took control of the savannas and lower forest zones in the western highlands, where Elmenteitan archeological sites show that they practiced transhumance with cattle and cultivated sorghum and millet. Higher up in the montane forests are Eburran sites, indicating that gatherer-hunters held sway. These people may have been Southern Cushites, but whoever they were, their niche was eventually taken over by Southern Nilotes, represented by the surviving Okiek. In contrast, the drier rift valley and eastern highlands remained the domain of Pastoral Neolithic Southern Cushites.

With the passage of time the Southern Nilotes split into several regional branches. One, the Kitoki, headed for Lake Victoria; another, the Kenya-Kadem, for the Cherangany Hills and beyond. A third remained in west-central Kenya and gave rise to the Dadog and Kalenjin peoples. The Dadog pushed southward into what is now Tanzania, there to encounter still other Southern Cushites as far south as the present city of Dodoma. In

167

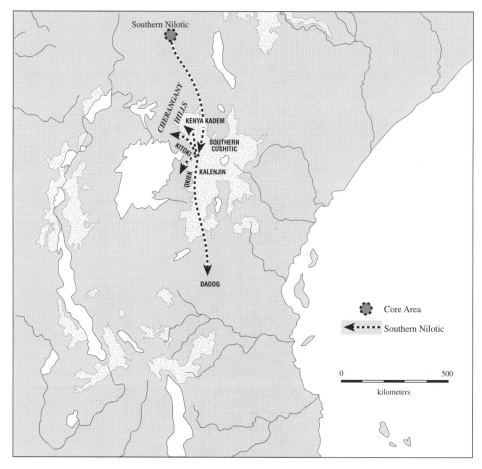

9.5 Southern Nilotic migrants sought the highlands in western Kenya, and from there other streams headed west and south.

contrast, the Kalenjin stayed put, as is inferred from the plethora of sirikwa holes—shallow, lined pits in which livestock were kept—that dot the landscape.

Adding to the turbulence of the interior was the arrival of the Bantu (map 9.6). Immediately east of Lake Victoria they met the Kitoki Southern Nilotes and quickly, it seems, displaced them from around the Kavirondo Gulf and adjacent uplands. The Kalenjin were another matter, and the stream of Bantu migrants moved around them, eschewing the semi-arid plains in favor of other highland areas—Mounts Kilimanjaro and Meru, the eastern rift uplands south of Mount Kenya, the Pare and Usambara mountains, and the Taita Hills—where habitats suitable to the cultivation of grains, along with yams, plantains, and bananas, could be found.

The resident Southern Cushites lost out to peoples who would become the Shambaa, Pare, Chaga, Taveta, Kamba, and Kikuyu-Meru-Embu. They were not overrun; rather, they were slowly absorbed by newcomers with more productive food economies and larger

168

populations. But the presence of the Southern Cushites was not eradicated. They left their mark in the oral traditions of the Bantu, loanwords, irrigation works, and the interesting case of the Mbugu of the Pare Mountains, who speak a language that is essentially Southern Cushitic in vocabulary and Bantu in grammar. The language seems to be quite old, but how it came to be structured as it is remains a mystery; about all that can be stated with confidence is that the Mbugu are a living example of Southern Cushitic–Bantu interactions that span two millennia.

Another early Bantu migration route skirted Lake Tanganyika on both sides. Upon reaching the southern end of the lake, one path turned east into a region that ethnographers term the Tanganyika-Nyasa Corridor. Here a variety of Bantu groups formed, differentiated largely by their agricultural systems. The Nyiha, Safwa, Lambwa, and Nyamwanga of the high plateau country relied on cereal-based agriculture, whereas the Nyakyusa of the warmer slopes leading down to Lake Malawi became plantain and banana cultivators par

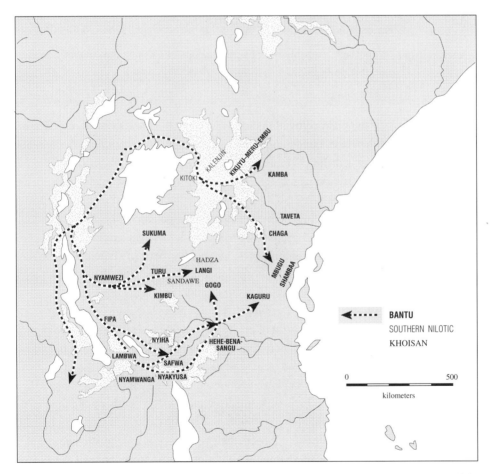

9.6 Bantu colonizing the interior mosaic of eastern Africa first settled the agriculturally rich highlands and only later converged on the less productive center of what is now Tanzania.

169

Ancient irrigation channels, probably built by early Southern Cushitic inhabitants, line the slopes of Mount Kilimanjaro. (Photo by author.)

excellence. Some of the grain cultivators then moved eastward and northward into lower elevations to form the Hehe-Bena-Sangu linguistic cluster. Expansion into the semiarid center of Tanzania created the Gogo and Kaguru groups. They added a cattle-keeping component to their cultivation of sorghum and bulrush millet, most likely from contact with Eastern Nilotic Maasai.

Very gradual incursion into the center by Bantu also occurred directly east of Lake Tanganyika. Malaria-ridden swamps, poor woodland soils, drought, and sleeping sickness made this area uninviting to farming peoples, but small groups of settlers seem to have found widely scattered parcels of reasonably productive land, and from these peoples arose the Nyamwezi, Kimbu, Fipa, Sukuma, Turu, and Langi.

The movement into the center of Tanzania that began in the sixteenth century represents the last phase in the Bantu displacement of previously established inhabitants. Two groups of the Khoisan gatherer-hunters actually managed to survive as distinctive peoples. The Hadza found protection in the dry and tsetse-infested lands surrounding Lake Eyasi, while 150 kilometers to their south the Sandawe held out by slowly incorporating crop cultivation and animal husbandry into their subsistence economy. The number and range of the Southern Cushites were considerably reduced, and if any Central Sudanic groups still existed by then in this part of eastern Africa, their only trace is a linguistic one.

The most dramatic migrations shaping the interior mosaic were those of the Eastern Nilotes (map 9.7). Starting from near the Nile in the southern Sudan, the Eastern Nilotes proceeded to gain control over most of the semiarid rangelands of present-day Kenya and

170

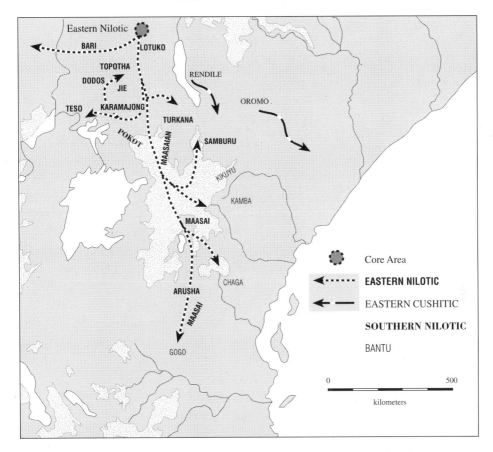

9.7 Far-ranging Eastern Nilotic migrations profoundly influenced population developments wherever they touched.

Tanzania, plus several adjacent areas. Their progress profoundly influenced everyone they met. Of course, the Eastern Nilotes were also changed in many important ways, so that wherever they appeared, a complex interweaving of cultural patterns ensued. We can see this in the numerous branchings of the Eastern Nilotes.

The first branching occurred 3,000 years ago and led to the formation of the Bari-speaking peoples. During subsequent centuries the Bari moved westward across the Nile south of the Sudd into territory held by various Central Sudanic–speaking groups. Loan-words indicate old and enduring contacts between the speakers of the two languages, and it seems plausible that pressure from the Bari induced some Central Sudanic groups to move into the interlacustrine region.

Southern Cushites in the other branch slowly headed southward, and by A.D.100–500 they themselves split into the Teso-Turkana and the Lotuko-Maasaian divisions. The Lotuko-Maasaians interacted with Eastern Cushites around the juncture of the present-day borders of Ethiopia, the Sudan, Uganda, and Kenya. Reciprocal loanwords are common,

171

and it was from the Eastern Cushites that the Lotuko-Maasaians presumably developed their aversion to eating wild game. Also, there is archeological evidence from the Namora-tunga sites west of Lake Turkana indicating an Eastern Cushitic presence before the arrival of the Lotuko-Maasaians. These are burial cairns similar to those still constructed by the Eastern Cushitic Konso of Ethiopia, and the manner of disposing of the dead is unlike that found among any non-Cushitic people. In addition, accompanying rock art displays geo-metric designs that bear a strong resemblance to designs currently made by Eastern Cushites.

The Lotuko settled in the vicinity of the Kinyiti River in the southeastern Sudan, where they have remained to this day, whereas the Maasaian group continued into Kenya. Here they encountered Southern Cushites, Southern Nilotes, and Bantu, all in various phases of expansion and retreat. At the outset, contacts with the first two were especially important because of competition for the same pastoral lands, and from them the Maasaians adopted some of their distinguishing cultural traits, mentioned previously. The Ongamo hived off and settled along slopes of Mount Kilimanjaro, which brought them into lands held by other Southern Cushites and probably by the earliest Bantu settlers.

In contrast, the Maa branch was poised to begin the most eventful and far-reaching of all Eastern Nilotic migrations. The main thrust carried them through the Kenyan rift valley and into the open savanna and steppe lands that extended from southern Kenya to central Tanzania. By the eighteenth century they had displaced the Kalenjin, who had preceded them just a few hundred years earlier. As they consolidated their hold over this huge territory, the Maa established much more intimate and usually dominant relations with surrounding Bantu, most notably with the Kikuyu and Kamba of central Kenya. Ulti-mately, however, it was the Bantu-speaking Gogo who halted the Maa expansion in the nineteenth century. A secondary movement carried the Samburu Maa back north toward Lake Turkana, where contacts with Eastern Cushites were reinitiated sometime after 1500.

Meanwhile, comparative stability prevailed among the Teso-Turkana. They had played a role, along with the Lotuko-Maasaians, in eliminating the Kenya-Kadem Southern Nilotic presence, but it was not until the seventeenth and eighteenth centuries that they entered into an expansionary phase. Then, from a nuclear area along the Kenya-Uganda border north of Mount Elgon, the Teso broke off and moved westward, establishing contacts with Western Nilotes at the beginning of the nineteenth century. Later they also moved south into interlacustrine Bantu country. Others went northward to form the Ka-ramojong, Jie, Dodos, and Topotha, while the Turkana pushed toward Lake Turkana and encounters with the Samburu and Eastern Cushitic Rendile and Oromo. In a reversal of usual trends, the Southern Nilotic Pokot have more recently expanded at the expense of the Karamojong.

The subsistence economies of the Eastern Nilotes underwent considerable diversifica-tion in the course of their migrations. The Bari probably come closest to representing Eastern Nilotic society at the original point of departure, with their transhumant livestock herding supplemented by contributions from fishing and the cultivation of sorghum and

172

Unlike most other Southern Nilotes, the Pokot were expanding during the nineteenth century. (Photo courtesy of Philip W. Porter.)

millet. Fishing was practiced by the Eastern Nilotes as they moved through Kenya, as is illustrated by the remains found at the Turkwell archeological sites, which date to A.D. 500–1000. Only later did the Ongamo-Maa peoples discard fishing under Southern Cushitic and Southern Nilotic influences. After reaching areas with higher rainfall and greater agricultural productivity, the Teso and Ongamo settled down, becoming cultivators for the most part, whereas the Maa developed nomadic herding to the fullest extent possible, at least when measured in terms of how much it dominated subsistence. But even some among the Maa, notably the Arusha around Mount Meru, eventually adopted a farming way of life.

What was the nature of the interactions between the Eastern Nilotes and those with whom they came into contact? Usually the interactions have been pictured as hostile, with the Eastern Nilotes, especially the Maa, playing the aggressor. That conflicts occurred can hardly be doubted. There would have been competition for crucial livestock needs, such as water, salt, and forage, and it is clear from oral traditions and more recent history that intergroup livestock raiding has been a fact of life for a long time. Nevertheless, the norm was apparently gradual displacement, absorption, or coexistence, not continual conflict. Displacement and assimilation are what happened to the Southern Cushites and Kalenjins who preceded the Maasai into Tanazania. Stripped of their herds, they took up gathering and hunting and became known by the Maasai word for hunter, Dorobo. To this day,

173

the Maasai display contempt for them, but no hostility. In fact, the ethnic boundaries are highly permeable. A Dorobo can become Maasai by obtaining cattle and adopting Maasai customs, and, similarly, a Maasai can become a Dorobo by losing cattle and resorting to hunting and gathering. Cultural identity is much more a function of life-style than gene-alogy.

Coexistence is evident in the trade relations that developed between the Maasai and the Bantu Kikuyu and Chaga and other agriculturalists. Milk and skins were regularly ex-changed for flour and tobacco, and some intermarrage occurred. In one instance, in fact, intermarriage became essential: between the Samburu and Eastern Cushitic Rendile. The Rendile have an age-grade system that effectively makes many women ineligible for marriage until they are in their thirties. To remedy the shortage of potential brides, Rendile men often look for wives among the neighboring Samburu, whose women can marry at a much younger age. The arrangement has been peaceable, involving the normal exchange of bridewealth. Were relations not friendly, it is highly doubtful that Rendile culture could have survived.

The warlike image of many of the Eastern Nilotes formed because of a combination of factors. One was the existence of warrior age-grades and the bellicose appearance of the young men in them. Armed with spears, shields, and knives and often displaying an ag-gressive demeanor, they seemed ready to do battle. Another concerns the expansion under way among some Eastern Nilotes when they were first encountered by European travelers; and according to European historical experience, how did expansion occur if not by military means? Yet a third reason involved stories told by Arab and Swahili traders along the coast who wanted to discourage travel to the interior and thus protect their trade monopolies. Finally, during the eighteenth and nineteenth centuries the Maa Iloikop (Kwavi) and Maasai fought over who would control the most important grazing grounds and watering sites. The fierceness of the battles, from which the Maasai emerged victo-rious, contributed to the evolving militaristic stereotype of the Eastern Nilotes.

Two other events in the nineteenth century had a significant impact on population developments in the interior. First, the Ngoni peoples arrived from southern Africa (map 9.8). Organized essentially in military fashion, the Ngoni fought their way north along both sides of Lake Malawi between 1840 and 1845. The streams of migrants converged to the northeast of the lake and formed two conquest states in the 1860s. As the Ngoni advanced, smaller, less-organized peoples either perished, fled, or were assimilated. Particularly hard hit were the plateau lands on both sides of the Ruvuma River. Much of the area was virtually depopulated. Contributing to the destruction were the Ndendeule and Nindi. Both had been conquered by the Ngoni but then broke away to begin their own careers as raiders. The Hehe-Bena-Sangu peoples also responded by creating military organizations to resist the Ngoni and, in the process, forged alliances between small chiefdoms. No large king-doms or states developed, however, and for most of the rest of the century, conditions along the southern margins of eastern Africa remained in turmoil and, therefore, unfavorable to population growth.

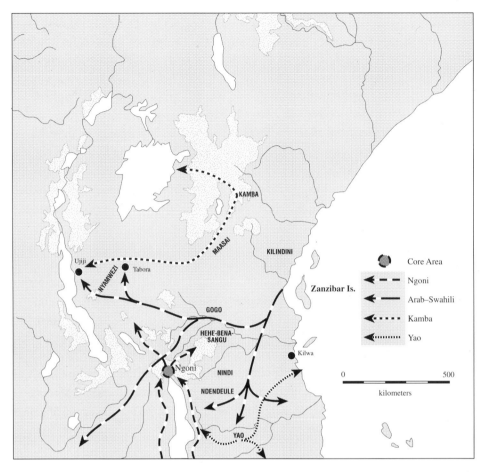

9.8 Extensive political disruption followed the migrations of the Ngoni in the nineteenth
century. At the same time, Arab-Swahili, Kamba, and Yao traders linked the interior of
eastern Africa with the coast.

The second event that affected population growth involved the expansion of trade from
the coast, with ivory as the most valued commodity in the beginning. Only after 1860 did
slaves become an important item of commerce, both to meet the labor needs of newly
established plantations on Mauritius and Réunion and to satisfy the ongoing demand for
domestics in the Arabian Peninsula. The main caravan routes crossed central Tanzania
without taking much of a toll on local populations. They were protected by Gogo warriors,
who exacted heavy tribute on any caravans that attempted to cross their territory. Therefore, most caravans opted for routes south of the Gogo, either heading into the turbulent
woodlands between the Ruaha and Ruvuma rivers for cargo or going on to the slave
emporia of central Africa. Farther north, the waterless nyika bushland backed by the
Maasai similarly blocked Arab-Swahili movement into the heavily populated highlands.

Growing trade contacts with the coast prompted three peoples to seize the role of

175

intermediary. Since at least the eighteenth century, the Kamba had been engaged in long-distance trade, exchanging their poisoned arrows, which were highly prized, for iron, salt, cattle, and other commodities. When the demand for ivory escalated, the Kamba found themselves in a position to respond. They quickly gained control of the northern routes to the coast and sent expeditions into the rift valley and westward to Lakes Victoria and Tanganyika, where some of them stayed on as permanent traders.

The Nyamwezi seized the trade opportunity in Tanzania. They led many of the caravans bringing ivory to the coast opposite Zanzibar, and in their hunt for goods, they, too, spread throughout the interior. Unlike the Kamba, the Nyamwezi eventually became involved in the slave trade, as we saw earlier, and in so doing opened their territory to Arab and Swahili merchants. The merchants congregated at Tabora and Ujiji, which became the first true towns in the interior.

From an even earlier date, the Yao had been bringing ivory from the woodlands east of Lake Malawi to Kilwa to exchange it for various manufactured items, which then found their way into central Africa. After 1850 the combination of profits and disturbed conditions led them to join the ranks of active slavers.

No true states or even kingdoms on a par with those of the interlacustrine region ever developed in the interior. Over much of the area the poor agricultural resource base kept the population density low, and even trade failed to stimulate centralizing tendencies. Instead, power shifted among leaders whose prominence lasted for only short periods of time. The only exception of note occurred in the more fertile lands of the Usambara Mountains, where a statelike entity known as Kilindini managed to unite several small Shambaa chiefdoms in the late eighteenth century.

THE NILOTIC IMPULSE

Although few in number, the Nilotes had made a considerable mark on the interlacustrine and interior regions of eastern Africa by the close of the precolonial era. They occupied large stretches of territory, imparted a substantial cultural legacy, and, directly or indirectly, influenced political and economic developments. Still, the motivation for their various migrations remains obscure. Once again, population pressure has frequently been mentioned as the initiating force, but if it played a major role, number of animals rather than number of people would have been more important to the calculus. Archeologists have yet to provide any evidence of notable growth in human population density associated with a Nilotic presence, but some sites do indicate the presence of fairly sizable populations of domesticated animals. Large herds of grazing wildlife also competed for forage. Recent events in Africa have demonstrated how quickly the carrying capacity of natural rangelands can be diminished by excessive grazing, especially when years of low rainfall follow one another. Migration to find pastures and water is the nomadic herder's response, and for the Nilotes the opportunities for access to needed resources were located almost exclusively to their south.

A population crisis, however, is not needed to induce nomads to move. Routes and cycles of herd movement tend to change, producing a spatial drift that over time can markedly alter population distribution. This drift is increased by what appears to be an almost natural tendency for nomadic societies to segment. As numerous Nilotic oral traditions attest, intergroup conflict is inevitable, and moving away to prevent it is better than staying and fighting, if the option is available. The violent Iloikop and Maasai wars, for example, occurred when the rangelands had been fully occupied. There was nowhere to turn except on one another.

Livestock grazing needs might well explain the impetus for Southern and Eastern Nilotic migrations, but for the Western Nilotes, the scenario was slightly different. The limited number of potential village sites in the southern clay plains of the Sudan led to struggles over their control. Out of such struggles came a redistribution of the population and an embryonic representation of power and its privileges by the Nuer ridge chiefs. This emergent power structure was elaborated on by Lwo who moved into the interlacustrine region and had contact with the nascent Bantu kingdoms. Land could not have been the issue. Bantu cultivators had little need for the lowland savannas and highland grasslands; there was more than enough space to accommodate the needs of herders. Instead, the right to rule seems to have been at stake. Only so many positions of authority existed in a given locale, and once these were filled, aspirants had to look elsewhere. In other words, they had to migrate if they wanted to attain power and the privileges that go with it. This, too, is population pressure, but of a very different kind from that usually portrayed.

THE SWAHILI COAST

The Swahili are among the most distinctive peoples in Africa, and their coastal location is the primary reason why. It provided a setting where multiple cultural influences came together to produce a society characterized by (1) mercantilism based on Indian Ocean trade; (2) town dwelling; (3) a unique architecture using coral and stone; (4) Islam; (5) literacy in an African language with an Arabic script; (5) a sense of belonging to a wider civilization; and (6) social stratification, with ruling elites who stress their Persian and Arab lineages. Influences from southwestern Asia have clearly been significant to Swahili identity, but it is equally obvious that the Asian elements are essentially a veneer glued onto a solid Bantu African framework.

Although the word Swahili is derived from the Arabic word *sawahil,* meaning "coast" and translated as "people of the coast," the Swahili language is of definite Bantu origin. It is related to the Sabaki cluster of Northeast Coastal Bantu that had formed in the Lower Tana River–Lamu Archipelago area around A.D. 500. The original Sabaki lived in small coastal or offshore-island villages where they could both fish and farm. Some Sabaki, however, took up a new economic activity: trading with merchants from the Arabian Peninsula and Persian Gulf. The coastal trade was made possible by the Indian Ocean monsoons, which the dhows could take advantage of; the winds blow reliably from the northeast as far as Cape Delgado beginning in January and then reverse themselves in April.

Regular trade goes back more than 2,000 years. Once again the confirming source is the

Dhows following monsoon winds tied the coast of eastern Africa into a wider Indian Ocean commercial network. (Photo by author.)

Periplus of the Erythraean Sea, which indicates that previous expeditions had been sent to the eastern coast, probably to satisfy Rome's insatiable appetite for ivory. Unfortunately, little information about the area and its inhabitants can be gleaned from the *Periplus,* except notations on several ports and on Arab merchants who sometimes intermarried with the local inhabitants. In all likelihood, the very first Africans with whom the Arabs did business were Cushites, but not too long after the writing of the *Periplus* the Sabaki ancestors of the Swahili were in a position to profit from the African side of the trade.

The formative period for the Swahili was the ninth to twelfth centuries, when all of their major towns were established. The first mentioned in Arabic sources are Rhapta and Kambalu. Neither has been located precisely; the best estimates place Rhapta at the mouth of the Pangani River and Kambalu on Pemba Island (map 9.9). They are followed by Pate, Shanga, and Manda, all grouped in the Lamu Archipelago, and somewhat later by Kisimani Mafia and Kilwa Kisiwani farther south, and then Mogadishu, Malindi, and Mombasa, to cite only those that would achieve greatest prominence. Many others, probably more than a hundred, sprang into existence, flourished briefly, then disappeared. Between the towns, Bantu villagers continued to ply a subsistence farming and fishing way of life.

Each town operated independently and in competition for the growing Indian Ocean trade, initially under the control of Sassinid Persians, whose capital was at Shiraz. In addition to ivory, exports included ambergris, tortoiseshell, leopard skins, mangrove poles, gold, and, of course, slaves. The slaves went to the Arabian Peninsula and India to work as domestics and to southern Iraq, where they were employed as laborers to reclaim

178

As the ruins at Ghedi along the Kenya coast indicate, the fate of many
Swahili cities and towns was to be abandoned after a brief period of prosperity.
(Photo by author.)

marshes for agricultural development. Imports consisted largely of cotton, beads, and chinaware.

The founding of each of the towns is associated in legend with the arrival of the Waungwana (literally, "free born"). Myths have sprung up around them, but some were probably real persons who left established families to look for trade opportunities elsewhere. Whatever the origins of the Waungwana, profits from trade helped turn them into a ruling elite. They constructed separate quarters built of stone and coral, where they fashioned genealogies and a "civilized" urban culture quite different from the culture of nearby villagers. They dressed in free-flowing garments that covered the whole body, ate off china plates using utensils, and spoke a new language—an early version of Swahili.

The commercial high point for most of the towns lasted from the twelfth to fifteenth centuries, and populations grew accordingly. Gold had become an increasingly important commodity, and Mogadishu and Kilwa Kisiwani were the main outlets at first. Kilwa Kisiwani may have had as many as 20,000 inhabitants at its apogee in the first half of the fifteenth century, while at the turn of the century an increasingly important Mombasa probably housed 10,000. By this time, a fairly rigid social system was in place. At the top were the wealthy Waungwana; under them were merchants and traders, most of whom

179

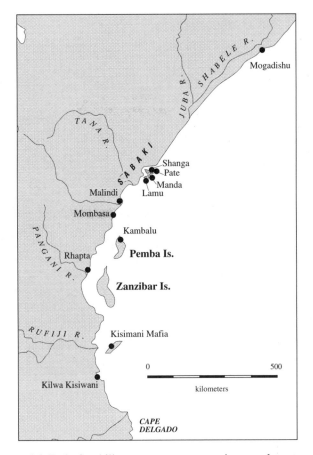

9.9 Early Swahili towns were at strategic coastal or
offshore locations.

came from Yemen and the Hadramat; further down but numerically superior came the free Africans, most of whom farmed and fished; and slaves occupied the bottom rung.

Two other events also proved key to the emergence of the Swahili. One was the coming of Islam. It may have been introduced as early as the tenth century, but active conversions and mosque building had to await the passage of two more centuries. As elsewhere in Africa south of the Sahara, Islam accompanied traders, who served as models, this time for the Waungwana. After the elite took it up, the pace of adoption quickened, and by the fifteenth century Muslims dominated the towns.

The other event involved the Waungwana claim of Shirazi descent. Although a few traders from Shiraz may have been resident for a time in coastal villages, no Persian settlement as such ever occurred; thus the Waungwana claim was a fiction. It was proffered, so it seems, to validate the Waungwana right to rule. In fact, it may have been consciously developed so that Waungwana could differentiate themselves from the many Arab Muslims in their midst. Whatever its source, the myth of a Shirazi background became an important ingredient of Swahili identity.

180

In the sixteenth century Swahili prosperity came to an end, and the towns entered into a decline that lasted for more than two centuries. The main reason revolves around the arrival of the Portuguese. Although the Portuguese had little interest in the east coast other than as a way station on voyages to Asia, they wanted to make sure that no local or foreign power could interfere with them. That they achieved autonomy with so few of their own number on hand—no more than fifty were permanently resident north of Cape Delgado by the close of the sixteenth century—was almost entirely due to the disunity of the towns. Each competed against the others for trading favors, and the Portuguese used a classic divide-and-rule strategy. The result was a succession of intrigues and skirmishes that reduced the volume of trade well below its previous levels.

Events in the hinterland created further trouble for some of the Swahili towns. Just prior to the arrival of the Portuguese, Oromo expansion had reached what are now southern Somalia and northern Kenya. The Oromo raided the towns on a regular basis, causing the total abandonment of some, and many Swahili fled to the greater security afforded by towns farther south. Oromo incursions also triggered numerous coastal Bantu migrations, one result of which was the formation of peoples known as the Mijikenda. From a source area known in their traditions as Shungwaya, located somewhere between the Tana River and Bir Gao, the forerunners of the Mijikenda (literally, "nine towns," each being associated with the origins of a particular subgroup, such as the Pokomo and Giryama) reformed in the coastal hills between the Tana and Pangani rivers (map 9.10). It took several hundred years before the various peoples stabilized their location, and meanwhile, trade with the interior was badly disrupted.

Some revitalization of Swahili economy and society was under way by the close of the seventeenth century. With assistance from Oman, the Portuguese were expelled, except for a brief and uneventful return in 1728, and thus political control returned to the various towns, which resumed their competitive ways. Mombasa, with its superior harbor, emerged as the predominant center, and although for the next hundred years or so, prosperity remained modest by fourteenth- and fifteenth-century standards, conditions slowly improved.

Once again, events in the interior affected the fate of the Swahili. Continuing Oromo raids kept the Somali coast turbulent. In Malindi and farther south, however, the immediate hinterland had stabilized considerably by the beginning of the nineteenth century. Direct trade was possible with Kilindini in the Usambaras, and Kamba, Nyamwezi, and Yao traders tapped trade in the Kenya Highlands, the interlacustrine area, and central Africa. With expanding trade, the number of Omani Arabs in the towns increased, taking a huge leap forward with the decision in 1832 to transfer the capital of Oman from Muscat to Zanzibar, which until this time had been a minor settlement. Ivory and slaves had become so important to Indian Ocean commerce that being close to the source was considered the key to maximizing profits. Furthermore, the establishment of plantation-style clove production on Zanzibar and Pemba made their economies even more dependent on slaves. By the 1840s, caravans from the interior were arriving along the adjacent Tanzanian coast on a

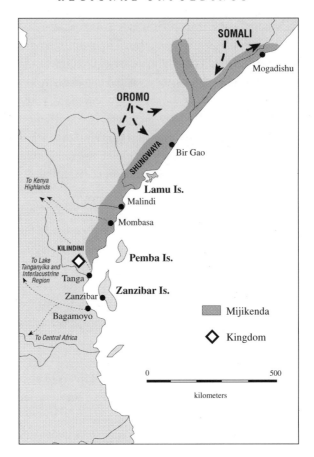

9.10 The northern Swahili coast was upset by Oromo
and Somali incursions during the eighteenth century.
In the nineteenth century, Omani Arabs revitalized
Swahili trade and culture by locating their
capital at Zanzibar.

regular basis and the commercial opportunity prompted more Arabs and also some In-
dians, the financiers of the Omani venture, to migrate across the channel and help found
such towns as Tanga and Bagamoyo.

Arab culture rubbed off on Swahili culture. Very nearly all Arabic words in Swahili and
the formalization of an Arabic script date from the nineteenth century, and Arab styles of
building, especially on Zanzibar, replaced the original Swahili style. A more Middle
Eastern form of Islam was implanted, and as Arab affluence and prestige grew, increasing
numbers of Swahili claimed Arab descent. Although Arab men did marry Swahili women,
most genealogies claiming Arab ancestry are fictionalized. As with the Shirazi claims,
these were apparently adopted to legitimate a separate Swahili identity.

182

Unlike other coastal areas, the coast of eastern Africa remained largely uninfluenced by a precolonial European presence. Explorers, missionaries, merchants, and diplomats all showed up at various times, but they were few in number, and their effect on the population was minimal until the signing of the Anglo-Zanzibar Treaty in 1873, which outlawed the slave trade. A clandestine trade lingered for a while, as it did elsewhere, but by the end of the decade the slave trade had reached an end. The Swahili coast now awaited the coming of the British and Germans to launch it and the rest of eastern Africa into the colonial era.

10

SOUTHERN AFRICA

Agricultural technologies crossed the Zambezi River two thousand or so years ago with the migrations first of Khoikhoi herders and shortly thereafter of Bantu farmers and herders, who also brought iron working with them. For the most part, the two peoples did not compete directly with one another. Instead, their different economic systems led them into different environments. While Bantu were claiming areas of summer rainfall suited to the growing of sorghum and millet, Khoikhoi sought the winter rainfall country of the far southwest and the semiarid grazing lands surrounding the Kalahari. Some San gatherer-hunters survived among both, but in places marginal to Khoikhoi and Bantu needs. This neat pattern unraveled in the seventeenth century, when Europeans settled at Table Bay and then moved inland, first pressuring the Khoikhoi and remaining San and then confronting the Bantu. In a reversal of several thousand years of directional influences, the ensuing clashes pitting Bantu against Europeans and Bantu against Bantu had effects that rippled northward, influencing population developments as far away as Tanzania.

THE KHOIKHOI ADVANCE

The Khoikhoi constitute one of the most intriguing ethnographic puzzles in Africa, partly because of a long-applied classification scheme that collapses economy and language together—the Khoikhoi are herders, the San gatherer-hunters—and partly because

184

the Khoikhoi have often been portrayed as immigrants, perhaps from as far away as Egypt. Both views, however, are incorrect. The Khoikhoi language belongs to a larger Khoe linguistic category that includes the languages of several groups, such as the G/wi and Nharo (Naron), who were formerly considered San, and serological-phenotypical investigations show no close links with any known northern peoples. Indeed, they confirm that the Khoikhoi are variations on a southern African theme of considerable antiquity. The fact that the Khoikhoi are taller than the San is best explained by their milk-based diet, with its high protein content, compared with the totally wild-food diet of the San, and somewhat less seasonal hunger stress over their history.

Linguistic studies point to the Middle Zambezi valley as the locale where the Khoikhoi originated slightly earlier than 2,000 years ago, with the acquisition of livestock playing a key role in their development. In a possible scenario, migrations took some Khoikhoi into the Kalahari and the swamplands of the Okavango Delta, where environmental conditions forced them to abandon herding and return to gathering and hunting for subsistence (map 10.1). Whether San were already present is problematic. We know that at least some of them arrived later, having been forced out of more productive habitats farther east and south. Meanwhile, other Khoikhoi followed much better watered routes that took them into the veld country across the Limpopo River. Here they met newly arrived Bantu for the first time, and faced with competition from people having more productive mixed Iron Age economies, the Khoikhoi veered off to the southwest. Eventually they found two productive habitats that became focal points of settlement: one along the Orange and Vaal rivers and the other in the vicinity of the Cape of Good Hope.

Still unanswered is the question of how the Khoikhoi acquired their livestock. No indigenous southern African species could have been domesticated, and, in any event, the animals show clear signs of northern derivation. Sheep were the first animals taken up, probably borrowed from Bantu who had filtered into the southern woodlands. Here they encountered some Khoe, leading to a southward diffusion of sheep. As for cattle, their later acquisition makes contact with Bantu from eastern Africa more plausible. Still, a Central Sudanic source for domestic animals also has to be considered. A few colonists could have actually reached the Zambezi River valley, where some archeological evidence suggests the presence of pre-Bantu farmers. Khoikhoi languages contain what appear to be Central Sudanic loanwords for livestock and livestock keeping, and several enigmatic groups of gatherer-hunters have survived into modern times. One group, the Damara, speak a Khoe language; another, the Kwisi, Herero Bantu; while, a third, the Kwadi, have an uncertain linguistic status. Could they be the descendants of Central Sudanics who had to resort to gathering and hunting after losing their livestock and lands to more numerous Khoikhoi and Bantu?

Without crops but with herds of sheep and cattle, the Khoikhoi were better able to exploit the scattered and seasonally available food resources of the Karoo bushlands and Kalahari scrub than the San. The San lost ground, and some groups retreated to less contested ground in the Kalahari and the Okavango Delta. The area near the Cape was the

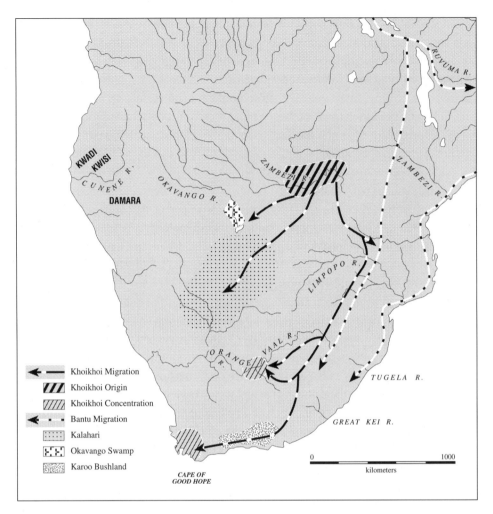

10.1 Food-producing economies advanced across the Zambezi River accompanying both Khoikhoi and Bantu migrations.

major exception. The Khoikhoi did not push out the San; rather, lush forage and abundant and diverse wild-food resources allowed both ways of life to coexist, at least for a while longer.

BANTU DEVELOPMENTS

By covering nearly 3,000 kilometers in less than 500 years to reach southern Africa from eastern sources, the Bantu accomplished one of humankind's most remarkable migrations. At Lake Malawi the path diverged. One group veered off along the Ruvuma River toward the coast, reaching present-day Natal by the end of the third century A.D. The other group continued along the shores of Lake Malawi through what is now eastern Zimbabwe

186

and reached the northern Transvaal around A.D. 500. In both instances, the migrants relied on hunting and fishing to supplement their cultivation of millet, sorghum, and cowpeas. They also tended sheep and goats and some cattle, although cattle had not yet become nearly as important as they soon would.

There are several reasons for the swift Bantu advance. First of all, few human or natural barriers existed to deter settlers. Indeed, migrants could follow open corridors with no one other than scattered bands of San and maybe a few Central Sudanic communities to oppose them. For the most part, however, the soils had limited natural fertility. Cultivation could be supported for only a few years before yields diminished. Because of the abundance of land, people had little incentive to stay in one place and develop more productive, labor-intensive systems of farming to extend the duration of cultivation. They could simply move into yet other virgin territory. The same applied to hunting grounds. When game thinned out, a new area to exploit lay just over the horizon.

People came in behind those who moved on, and the newcomers concentrated on cattle herding. Economically, cattle provided milk for the diet and manure for fertilizer and fuel, and socially they represented the most valued currency in bridewealth transactions. The thesis that newcomers brought the emphasis on cattle is supported by evidence from Leopard's Kopje archeological sites in the southwestern and central portions of the Zimbabwe Plateau. What the data show is a rather rapid change in pottery styles around A.D. 1000, along with indications of an already well developed cattle-based economy. Some researchers posit invaders, but the changes could just as well have been triggered by the arrival of no more than a few cattle-rich families. Possession of large numbers of animals would have put such families in a position to achieve cultural ascendance, then, within decades, numerical dominance as they extended their range of influence. Other archeological sites in southern Africa lend support to this interpretation. They show little or no evidence of a sudden intrusion by outsiders: the changes occur so gradually that the elaboration of the cattle-keeping theme and the appearance of new pottery styles are best seen as representing the adaptations of local peoples to new opportunities.

The development of a more productive mixed farming and herding economy favored population growth. Just how fast it grew, however, depended on local circumstances, which varied considerably; and because substantial distances separated the main growth centers, considerable linguistic differentiation took place. The beginning stages can be glimpsed by looking among the Toutswe remains in eastern Botswana. By A.D. 700 small settlements, probably extended-family-type units or the like, were scattered across the landscape on the richer soils near reliable sources of water. Between 900 and 1300 larger settlements appeared on hilltops, away from water and on thin, unproductive soils. The largest were spaced about 100 kilometers apart, and the only feasible explanation for their location is defense. They give the impression of having been residences of ruling groups to whom others attached themselves—in the residences and in smaller, nearby settlements—in order to exchange food and other commodities for the protection provided by the numbers congregating around a central core. A distinctive ethnolinguistic polity appears to have been in the making, probably one belonging to the Sotho-Tswana group. Others like it would give rise to the Shona, Tsonga, Nguni, and Herero (map 10.2).

Shona

Although the origins of the Shona can probably be found in the Leopard's Kopje culture area, it was later trading activities that stimulated their growth and expansion. Initially, copper and ivory constituted the principal commodities sent to the Mozambique coast, but they soon became secondary to gold. Gold-bearing strata occur at many places along the western margins of the high plateau of Zimbabwe, and some of the mines that tap the reefs near the surface are ancient. They might, in fact, represent the sources for the legendary gold of Ophir, although most of the diggings date from the thirteenth century and correlate with the rise of the first major Shona state, centered on the city of Great Zimbabwe. Its imposing array of stone ruins and trade artifacts testify to the presence of a wealthy ruling class having at one time presided over a polity of considerable spatial extent.

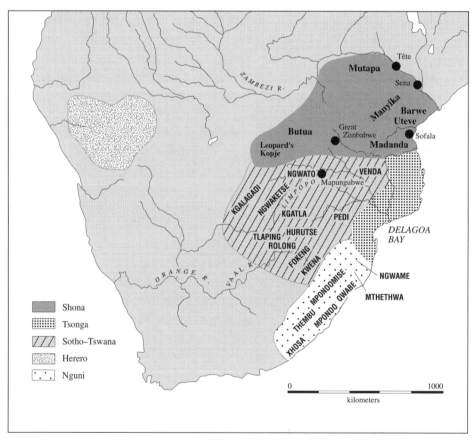

10.2 By A.D. 1500 the combined effects of linguistic differentiation and convergence had produced five Bantu clusters in southern Africa.

Yet the original site of Great Zimbabwe is not distinctive in any way. The city began as a small agricultural village surrounded by stone-walled terraces, of which there were many across the southern portions of the high plateau above 1,000 meters by the twelfth century. Likely predecessors of Great Zimbabwe exist at the earlier sites of Schroda and Mapungubwe in the Limpopo valley. Schroda was founded in the ninth century, and excavations have uncovered imports indicating trade contacts with the coast. Mapungubwe was also involved in long-distance trade, and building arrangements show that power was concentrated in a ruling elite. It dates from the late eleventh to early thirteenth centuries and thus may well have been the immediate predecessor of Great Zimbabwe.

An ability to capture much of the gold trade explains the rise of Great Zimbabwe to preeminence later in the thirteenth century, and for 200 years it grew and prospered. Many luxury items, including silks and carpets, have been discovered, and stone construction flourished. Walls, cattle kraals, and field boundaries were added to terraces; much finer work was later done on courtyards, a royal residence, a conical tower, and, finally, a surrounding wall. Early in the fifteenth century Great Zimbabwe contained an estimated 11,000 people, and some fifty similar, though smaller, settlements fell within its orbit.

The gold trade followed overland routes to Kilwa, as well as the small port of Sofala at the mouth of the Zambezi. Sofala, founded as an outpost of Swahili and Arab traders from Kilwa, was south of where reliable monsoons allowed for a round-trip to Arabia and the

The ruins at Great Zimbabwe have revealed evidence of a prosperous Shona kingdom that lasted for 200 years between the thirteenth and fifteenth centuries. (Photo by Gordon Matzke, Geosciences Department, Oregon State University.)

189

Persian Gulf within a year. The advantage of Sofala was its closeness to sources of gold, and thus it made a useful depot for safe, temporary storage.

Great Zimbabwe, regardless of all these advantages, slipped into a decline in the mid-fifteenth century. An oft-cited reason is overpopulation caused by depletion of soil and woodland resources, but a better reason can be found in a shift of trade routes toward the Zambezi River valley. In addition to gold, supplies of salt and copper existed nearby, giving the valley a strategic advantage over Great Zimbabwe. Sealing their comparative fates was the arrival of Portuguese traders, who built up Sofala and established trading posts at Sena and Tête in hopes of getting closer to the gold that they were after.

By the early sixteenth century the location of Great Zimbabwe had become highly peripheral, and the Shona abandoned it when they turned their attention northward to create a new state known as Mutapa. At its height, Mutapa presided over a large area extending from the plateau to Sofala. Its ascendancy did not last long. The Portuguese used their common tactic of playing off factions within the state against one another in their efforts to control the gold trade. Soon Mutapa, too, was in decline, although unlike Great Zimbabwe, it managed to survive as a fairly wealthy, but territorially much reduced, state.

In the meantime, the locus of power on the plateau had shifted back south, to Butua, a place linked to Great Zimbabwe in Shona tradition. Under the leadership of the Changamire dynasty during the latter part of the seventeenth century, Butua expanded its territorial holdings and managed to seal off most of the high plateau from others, including the Portuguese, whom they confined to the Zambezi valley. In addition to seizing the profits from gold and other commodities, the Changamire instituted a tribute-paying system that brought more wealth to its rulers and also provided a mechanism for organizing the vast territory that they controlled. The government must have been effective, because a period of peace and general prosperity ensued that lasted through the eighteenth century.

Other Shona states—Barwe, Uteve, Manyika, and Madanda—controlled lands east of the high plateau. Although smaller and less wealthy than Great Zimbabwe, Mutapa, and Butua, their endurance attests to competent administration. They helped implant a Shona presence over a wide area.

The main competition for the Shona states came from the Prazos, a mixed group of adventurers who convinced the Portuguese Crown to give them land grants along the Zambezi. They operated from a series of fortified settlements, using slave armies to extract human and other commodities from the surrounding countryside. Most of Shona-held territory, however, remained beyond the Prazos' reach.

Tsonga

The Tsonga developed from the earliest Bantu migrants who followed routes along the coastal plain through what is now Mozambique. Their economy was based on fishing, shellfish collecting, and grain cultivation, and they lived on small, scattered farmsteads extending from the coast into the woodlands. Unlike other Bantu in southern Africa, the Tsonga never relied heavily on cattle keeping—no doubt because much of their territory was tsetse infested, and cattle were subject to outbreaks of nagana. Delagoa Bay provided good harborage, and when Portuguese and other Europeans arrived, its advantages became even greater. Copper and ivory were the main items in demand. To meet the demand, more and more Tsonga came to reside in the vicinity of the bay, while others spread to the interior in an ever-widening search for trading opportunities. Although the Tsonga never established formal colonies, their influence—linguistic, genetic, and cultural—extended well beyond their initial settlement area. Except at Delagoa Bay, the Tsonga population was so scattered that no slave trade as such ever materialized.

Sotho-Tswana

Although the origins of the various Sotho-Tswana peoples may also go back to the Leopard's Kopje cultural sites, the focal point of their formation and subsequent dispersal has been traced to the highveld near the Vaal River, which is free of malaria and well watered. The presence of thousands of stone occupation sites dating back to the first centuries of the second millennium A.D. indicate a mainly sedentary and densely settled population. The first distinctive Sotho-Tswana groups to appear were the Fokeng and Kgalagadi, followed by the Rolong and Tlaping and then the Hurutse, Kwena, Ngwato, Ngwaketse, Kgatla, and Pedi. These names refer to founding lineages and illustrate the pervasive role of segmentation in Sotho-Tswana life. Each lineage eventually produced one or more offshoots, some of which would then incorporate others. Although chiefdoms occasionally developed around particular individuals, segmentation kept larger states from forming.

At first there were many small, dispersed villages similar to those found at Toutswe. In general, villages of several hundred or so individuals were typical of the southernmost

The Tswana built large stockaded towns holding upward of several thousand inhabitants. (Reprinted from Leonard Thompson, *A History of South Africa,* Yale University Press, 1990, pl. 3.)

Sotho, but in the north, large villages—perhaps more accurately, towns—with as many as 15,000–20,000 residents eventually dominated the countryside. Each had economic and political autonomy and was divided into wards that maintained lineage affiliations as the basis of social-spatial organization.

Large villages like these are an anomaly in Bantu-speaking Africa, particularly because they did not arise from trade and the presence of a ruling elite, as among the Shona. One school of thought stresses access to grazing and water resources as a possible explanation. Accordingly, where resources were limited, which is certainly the case toward the Kalahari, people concentrated around a few favored sites. Concentration might have happened where water and forage were abundant but is unlikely to represent the whole story; once again, defense motives have to be given some weight. The highveld of the Transvaal and the eastern margins of the Kalahari provide little in the way of defensive cover against raids aimed at valuables, particularly cattle. Large gatherings of humans would be one response to insecurity, and therefore what the town represented was the merger of separate villages for purposes of mutual self-interest. In this sense, the Sotho-Twana villages were the culmination of what began at Toutswe. Once it was perceived that self-interest was better served elsewhere, however, lineage wards broke away to form new towns.

There were two exceptions to the nonstate tradition of the Sotho-Tswana. Near the headwaters of the Olifants tributary to the Limpopo River, the Pedi established a confederation under a paramount chief during the latter decades of the eighteenth century. The reasons are unclear, but control of the ivory trade might have played a pivotal role. The Venda, situated in the Soutpansberg Mountains, provided the other exception. Here the stimulus appears to have been Shona migrants from Butua who crossed the Limpopo and re-created a small Zimbabwe-like state early in the eighteenth century.

Nguni

The Nguni derive from a fusion of Tsonga and Sotho elements near St. Lucia Bay shortly after A.D. 1000. The environment here was very different from that in the interior and in Mozambique. Instead of open veld or broad, wooded plains, the pioneers encountered a narrow strip of coast bounded by dense forests incised by valleys extending from the Natal Highlands and the Drakensberg Mountains. No large villages formed at first; rather, there were small, dispersed, and self-sufficient homesteads. Slash-and-burn agriculture cleared the forest as the valleys were followed upstream. The uplands remained hunting grounds for use both by Nguni and scattered bands of San.

The adoption of maize as a staple food crop quickened the pace of Nguni expansion and facilitated agricultural colonization of the upland forests. The area north of the Tugela River seems to have experienced the greatest growth, and by the beginning of the eighteenth century four discernible clusters of chiefdoms had developed. From north to south these were the Ngwame, Mthethwa, Ndwandwe, and Qwabe.

There was less population pressure across the Tugela, but reports from survivors of Portuguese shipwrecks indicate that other Nguni had managed to reach the Great Kei

River. They, too, remained stateless. Among their ranks were the Thembu, Mpondo, Mpondomise, and Xhosa peoples. The Xhosa were by far the largest group, and being on the leading edge of interior expansion, they came face to face with the most easterly of the Khoikhoi: the Gonaqua. When contact began, the Gonaqua provided a refuge for Xhosa families who had lost out in internal power struggles, but after several hundred years of peaceful interaction, the Xhosa prevailed by sheer numerical advantage. Lineage genealogies testify to an absorption of the Gonaqua, as do the clicks in the Xhosa language.

The Xhosa were also the first Bantu to encounter Europeans, who came as small bands of hunters searching for game, as well as for cattle, which they could either trade for or steal. At this stage, the Xhosa welcomed them as suppliers of guns, tobacco, and other commodities. Later on, they became the Xhosa's hated enemies.

Herero

The origins of the Herero remain obscure. Linguistically they are related to the Ovambo, which ties them to the Luba-Lunda peoples of central Africa, all of whom, as we have seen, come from a western Bantu background with a matrilineal tradition and have economies centered on grain cultivation, fishing, and small herds of livestock. In contrast, the Herero have a patrilineal tradition and the most cattle-dependent economy in Bantu Africa. The Herero have some faint genetic similarities to the Nguni and may therefore have adopted their cattle-keeping ways, although no likely points of contact can be identified.

In any event, no later than the middle of the sixteenth century the Herero reached the rich grazing lands of the Namibian Highlands, where they encountered groups of Nama Khoikhoi, then expanding northward at the expense of the San. Conflicts flared over grazing and water rights, with neither side able to gain an immediate advantage. The delicate balance of power tilted when the Nama purchased guns from Cape-based traders. Although the Herero were never fully defeated, their expansion came to a halt, and they lost some ground to the Nama.

REORGANIZATION AT THE CAPE

The Khoikhoi Retreat

The Nama represented the Khoikhoi in flight; their era of ascendancy over the winter rainfall portions of southern Africa had come to an end. But it was not the Bantu who brought about their demise. Instead, the destabilizing forces entered inconspicuously and from a totally different direction. In the 1590s Dutch and English ships called at Table Bay on their way to and from India and southeast Asia. Fresh supplies of water and meat were available, and the port provided a good spot for sailors to recuperate after spending many months at sea. In return for providing mutton and beef, the Khoikhoi obtained such items as knives, iron, copper, brass, and tobacco. Trading relations, however, were highly informal, and captains could never be certain that what they needed would be on hand. To overcome this annoyance, the Dutch East India Company sent out employees to establish a provisioning settlement called Cape Town at the foot of Table Mountain. After their arrival in 1652 Khoikhoi autonomy at the Cape quickly deteriorated.

First came a widening sphere of poverty. Many families sold off too many livestock, and still more animals were lost to theft and warfare in competition for trade. An even more crucial factor was the expropriation of grazing lands and watering sites by free Dutch burghers when they moved inland from Cape Town during the last decades of the seventeenth century. Increasing numbers of Khoikhoi, stripped of their means of support, found it necessary to seek employment either with the Dutch East India Company or on the alien farms now in their midst. Few who took these options ever returned to herding; indeed, many dispossessed Khoikhoi soon found themselves accepting the Dutch language and culture as their own.

Khoikhoi disunity let the burghers advance with ease. Although frontier wars were fought in 1659–60 and 1673–77, both went in favor of the settlers. As the losses mounted, indigenous Khoikhoi leaders, who had tenuous authority to begin with, lost their positions to Dutch East India Company and other European bosses.

Matters turned worse when a smallpox epidemic erupted in 1713. Carried on ships from India, it spread rapidly through Cape Town and then into the interior. Whole bands of

Small groups of independent Khoikhoi still inhabited the vicinity of Table Bay at the beginning of the eighteenth century. They soon disappeared, however, as poverty and disease either killed them, led them to flee toward the interior, or forced them to become workers for Europeans. (Reprinted from Thompson, *A History of South Africa,* pl. 2.)

Khoikhoi died off, and others were so depleted that they could no longer maintain an independent existence. In desperation, survivors sought refuge at the Cape, adding to the ranks of Khoikhoi dependent on the Dutch. Still others retreated farther inland to escape the scourge. Some were able to join less afflicted tribes, notably the Orange River Nama, who split into two groups. The one known as the Great Nama set off toward Namibia; the Little Nama, or Orlams, regrouped on the fringes of the European frontier, often raiding across it for livestock and food. They had managed to lay hands on firearms, and their hit-and-run tactics halted the northward advance of settlers until near the close of the eighteenth century. By this time, however, the Cape Khoikhoi had disappeared. Those who had not either died or migrated became a part of another people officially designated Coloureds.

Coloured Origins

The origins of South Africa's Coloured population lie in the decision by the Dutch East India Company to solve its labor requirements by importing slaves. The first shipments brought small numbers of them from Angola and Dahomey in 1658, and these were joined in subsequent years by larger contingents from Madagascar, Bengal, south India, Ceylon, Indonesia, and Mozambique. Resulting African-Asian sexual liaisons left offspring, as did those involving European men and slave women, whom the men preferred to local Khoikhoi. Some of the latter liaisons eventuated in marriages, and for a while fathers could designate their children Europeans if they so desired. In time, this option was taken away, and the children joined the ranks of free "blacks," as all nonslave non-Europeans became known. Most of those of mixed European descent, however, seem to have been born to prostitutes who served the sailors calling at the Cape, and these children maintained their status as slaves. A highly diverse and distinctive population was thus forming at the Cape, one that would need its own designation in a society moving toward ever greater race consciousness.

Some European men did take Khoikhoi wives or concubines, particularly inland from the Cape, where other women were scarce. From such unions arose the so-called Basters (bastards), who self-consciously adopted the Dutch side of their heritage, including language and religion. The number of Basters grew rapidly during the late seventeenth and early eighteenth centuries—too rapidly, in fact, for natural increase to account for the growth. Swelling their ranks were many Khoikhoi who found a Baster identity superior to their own, which carried the image of "primitive" herders. In a few instances, groups formed around prominent families. Among the most successful were the Rehoboth, who left South Africa for the Aures Mountains of Namibia in the nineteenth century. Here they built a closed and prosperous community within one of the richest pasturelands to be found anywhere on the continent.

Mention must also be made of the Griqua, whose origins are traceable to one of the northern Khoikhoi tribes decimated by smallpox and to some runaway slaves who assembled in the vicinity of St. Helena Bay. Accumulating yet other Khoikhoi, an array of European army and ship deserters, and dissident free blacks from the Cape, some families headed eastward, eventually reaching the area north of the Orange River during the last years of the eighteenth century. Here they mingled with Korana and formed two branches, one more Khoikhoi in culture and the other more European. Both became less migratory and accepted the collective name Griqua, derived from one of their founding lineages, the Chariguriqua. Well known for their fighting skills, the Griqua were a formidable foe for Afrikaner and Bantu alike.

Early European Expansion

When the Dutch East India Company sent employees to the Cape Town area in 1652, it did not anticipate establishing a permanent resident population. Within just a few years, however, this is precisely what had come to pass, and by 1657 land was being allocated to free Dutch burghers so that they could produce wheat and wine. The limited amount of arable land around Cape Town was claimed, and to accommodate demand, the company offered freehold titles along the western flanks of the Hottentot-Holland Mountains and in the Constantia valley of the Cape Peninsula beginning in the 1670s (map 10.3). No size limit was imposed, so individual families took possession of huge areas, averaging 2,500 hectares, primarily for livestock raising and hunting. In so doing, they set a pattern of large-

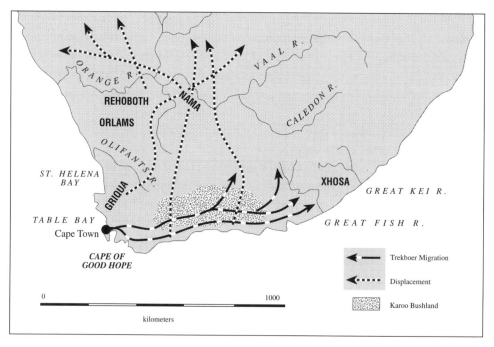

10.3 Trekboer migrations during the eighteenth century displaced Khoikhoi and San speakers and brought them face to face with the more numerous and powerful Xhosa.

196

scale landholding that endured throughout the whole period of European frontier expansion.

By 1717, when the company ceased validating land grants, the Cape settlement incorporated nearly 26,000 square kilometers and held a population of 2,000 Europeans. Those of Dutch descent predominated, but several hundred French Huguenots had arrived in the late 1680s, and occasional Germans, Walloons, and Scandinavians also showed up seeking refuge from the religious wars engulfing Europe. With immigration now virtually at a standstill, this mix provided the essentials from which the Afrikaner nation would arise. Its rapid growth was fueled by an extraordinary rate of natural increase; many frontier families, known as Trekboers, had ten or more living children. European settlers were blessed with abundant rich land, a fairly disease-free environment, and the labor of servants and slaves, so production easily kept pace with population increase.

Aridity north of the Olifants River, plus Griqua and Orlams resistance, halted Trekboer expansion in one direction and refocused it eastward through the bushlands of the Karoo. The main opposition came from "bushmen," composed of Khoikhoi who had lost their herds and some San bands who tried to hold their ground. The Khoikhoi and San stole livestock and burned fields but were outmatched by rifle-wielding commandos on horseback.

The Bantu, however, provided a more formidable opponent for the Europeans: they had numbers and a social-military organization. As noted, the first Bantu contacts with Europeans involved the Xhosa early in the eighteenth century, but it was not until the Trekboers arrived that conflict emerged as a serioius threat. Both economies depended on livestock, and this meant competition for grazing lands, as well as livestock thefts. Wars broke out in 1770–81 and 1793 over possession of the zuurveld (sour veld) west of the Fish River, but neither side prevailed. Caught between the two were the last of the free Khoikhoi tribes, who had fled here earlier in the century. With nowhere else to go and lacking the numbers to compete, they either were absorbed into various Xhosa chieftaincies or became Trekboer servants.

In the meantime, the British, seeking to secure their sea route to India, ousted the Dutch from the Cape. Faced with the destabilizing effects of continuing Trekboer-Xhosa hostilities, the new government sent troops to drive a Xhosa force back across the Fish River in 1811–12, setting off a series of frontier wars that brought Xhosa resistance to an end. The most devastating occurred from 1850 to 1853, and it was followed by outbreaks of cattle lung disease and maize blight. Faced with a desperate situation, many Xhosa and some Thembu joined a millenarian prophetic movement known as the Great Cattle Killing. It carried a promise that the ancestors would return, bringing with them a new age of plenty, if people destroyed their herds and ceased planting. In its wake, untold thousands died of starvation, while others had to migrate in search of wage labor to survive. Large areas were virtually depopulated and, consequently, open to European settlers, now mostly of British and German background. By 1858 only a small fraction of the land once held by the Xhosa remained exclusively theirs.

197

TRAUMAS

Mfecane/Difaqane

While the San, Khoikhoi, and Xhosa underwent the deadly impact of Trekboer expansion, a trauma with even more far-reaching effects hit Natal. The origins of the *mfecane* (Zulu) or *difaqane* (Sotho-Tswana)—translated as "the scattering"—are traceable to the 1790s, when competition over increasingly scarce grazing lands and control of increasingly distant sources of ivory erupted among the northern Nguni. Continuing population growth lay behind the competition, and when the contest was over, the Zulu were on top. Formerly one clan among many, they followed their initial successes with a military and political conquest; in their heyday they had control over an area extending from the Indian Ocean to the foothills of the Drakensberg Mountains between the Pongola and Tugela rivers (map 10.4).

In the course of expansion, the Zulu assimilated survivors from many of the smaller groups of people they had conquered. Although untold numbers of the conquered died, others swelled the ranks of the Zulu *impi,* or army. Still others fled before the Zulu advance; the effects on population size and distribution spread like a disease. Much of interior Natal was temporarily abandoned as people sought refuge farther south. One escape route took survivors along the coast; they migrated in the hopes of settling among the Thembu and Xhosa, who lived beyond the range of Zulu incursions. Some made it to safety, and from them derive the Mfengu, or Fingos. Another route followed the valleys leading into the Drakensberg Mountains, which had remained unpopulated except for San gatherer-hunters. Here, during the mid-1820s, scattered remnants coalesced into the Basotho nation.

Dissension within the Zulu ranks generated breakaways. One splinter group, the Ndebele, moved into the Transvaal, where they engaged in widespread raiding during the 1820s and 1830s. The Ndebele exacted a heavy toll on the Tswana peoples, many of whom were forced to abandon their towns and flee toward the Kalahari. Pressure from the Zulu, as well as attacks from the Griqua and Trekboers, forced the Ndebele toward the Limpopo River. Raiding along the way, they catalyzed the far-ranging Ngoni migrations. Eventually the Ndebele crossed the Limpopo River and settled in southwestern Zimbabwe, setting themselves up as overlords on the resident Shona.

Two other Nguni groups fleeing the Zulu—the Hlubi and the Ngwame—also wreaked havoc in the Transvaal. They forced the Taung into flight, and Taung, in turn, took to a life of preying on others. The Taung were finally defeated and dispersed by the Ndebele. The Hlubi and the Ngwame also defeated the Fokeng, but in this instance survivors re-formed into the Kalolo. Seeking a place to settle, the Kalolo trekked across Botswana into western Zambia, where they seized control of the Lozi kingdom. Though overthrown, the Kalolo bequeathed their language as the foundation for modern Silozi. A second segment of the Kalolo moved into the Shire valley of Malawi, where they helped to organize a state that

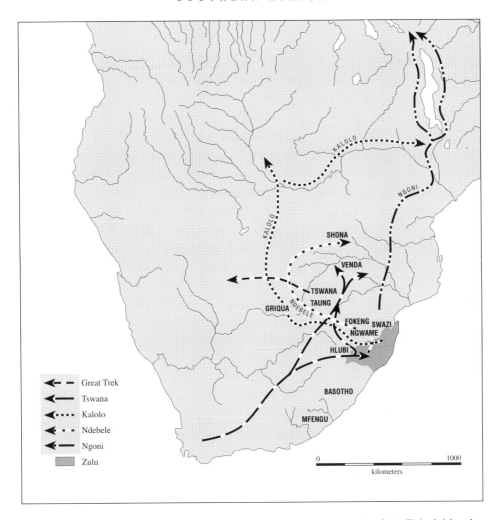

10.4 The population map of southern Africa was redrawn as a result of the Zulu-initiated mfecane/difaqane and the great trek of the Boers.

repelled the Ngoni and kept them moving north. They also fought off Yao and Prazo slave traders, thus sparing the area further violence.

Swaziland also has its roots in the mfecane/difaqane. Various Nguni, Sotho-Tswana, and Tsonga peoples had gathered in the area during previous centuries, but it was the arrival of the fleeing Ngwame that provided the stimulus for the formation of the Swazi state in the 1820s. It crystallized around a kingdom that in the 1850s and 1860s grew strong enough to expand at the expense of the Zulu.

The mfecane/difaqane redrew the population map of the Bantu in southern Africa almost completely. Some groups disappeared; many others were born, mostly from amalgams of various Nguni and Sotho-Tswana elements. Areas both declined and increased in population. But a new equilibrium was never established. Instead, the future brought convulsions that perpetuated instability.

The Great Trek and Its Aftermath

The movement of the Trekboers caused the convulsions. Unable to continue their push to the east because of the Xhosa presence, Trekboers filled the lands in the direction of the Orange River during the first decades of the nineteenth century, driving out the last of the San bands in the process. By 1825 advance groups of Trekboers had crossed the river to discover what appeared to be almost uninhabited country stretching far beyond the horizon. Here were their biblical new lands, those needed to preserve an extensive livestock-oriented way of life and to provide escape from constant wars with the Xhosa and from onerous British rule at the Cape, which by now prohibited slavery. In the early 1830s wagon trains rolled north in a trek that included 15,000 people.

Most of the settlers favored the warm and humid terraces of western Natal, which brought them into direct competition with the Zulu. The Trekboers won a major victory at the Battle of Blood River in 1837, thus securing the area for a while. However, further expansion at the expense of the Zulu proved to be impossible, and when Britain seized control of Natal in the 1850s and encouraged its own colonists to take land, the Trekboers departed.

Their attention shifted to the veld. Malaria and sleeping sickness forced most settlers to leave the lowveld adjacent to the Limpopo River valley; meanwhile, the Venda successfully resisted Trekboer incursions into the nearby Soutpansberg Mountains. To the Trekboers' good fortune, the cooler and relatively disease-free highveld that bore the brunt of the mfecane/difaqane exodus had not yet been effectively recolonized. To secure their new

When the Boers entered the Transvaal, they saw a vast land where they could carry on their pastoralist life-style and be free from British interference. (Photo courtesy of Philip W. Porter.)

patrimony, the Trekboers created a series of republics that evolved into the Orange Free State and the Transvaal. Always land hungry, they annexed large sections of Swaziland and Basutoland by means of conquest and the exaction of concessions. In Trekboer-held territories, Africans were deprived of access to their own lands; they existed only to serve the interests of the new masters.

The British also exerted substantial influence on the population. They encouraged the development of European-held estates in Natal, primarily for the production of sugar cane, and obtained indentured laborers from their Indian Empire to work them. Elsewhere in Natal and the Cape Colony, Britain created native reserves to separate the domains of Africans and Europeans in hopes of pacifying the countryside. In the late 1880s even Zululand fell under British dominion. Protectorates were established over the Swazi, Basotho, and Tswana to secure them from Trekboer encroachment. Many Africans, however, found themselves outside the reserves and became raw material for the labor force of an emergent industrial economy. The stage was set for the rise of a racially divided South Africa whose policies would shape the whole southern African region.

11

CONCLUSION
The End of the Beginning

The peopling of Africa began with the evolutionary debut of the hominids 5 million years ago. They originated during a time of increasing environmental differentiation and occupied niches at ecotones connecting forests with vegetatively open habitats, where they could find a diverse array of foodstuffs to gather and scavenge. Among their key anatomical attributes was a more or less upright posture that freed the forelimbs for tasks other than locomotion, and socially they lived in small bands for protection and probably some measure of food sharing. Physically defenseless compared with their competitors, at least one hominid line developed something crucial to survival: culture. The first cultural act will forever remain a mystery, but three things seem to have been involved in compensating for our ancestors' lack of physical strength and speed: (1) cooperative living arrangements, (2) oral communication, and (3) the ability to use and make tools. We now know that these traits are shared by chimpanzees, but the traits stagnated at an early stage of development. In contrast, our hominid ancestors elaborated them, and as they did so, further anatomical changes occurred, the most notable being an expansion in brain size. As early as 200,000 years ago developments had progressed far enough to yield the first *Homo sapiens*.

Although some people had by now left Africa for Asia and Europe, those who remained behind lived much in the manner of their ancestors. They gathered, scavenged, and hunted, and population numbers grew very slowly—so slowly, in fact, that it took many centuries to add even a fraction of a percent to the total. Being dependent on what nature provided meant that bands usually contained no more than fifty or so individuals, and these bands were few and far between. Still, the tools left behind show a rise in ingenuity in accomplishing a multiplicity of tasks. Skills slowly improved, and adaptations were made to varying raw materials and food-procuring circumstances, producing an ever greater number of toolmaking traditions and, by extension, cultures. Many had appeared by 30,000 years ago, allowing people to extend their settlements over more and more of the continent, including the previously unoccupied tropical rain forest.

Certain other changes began to unfold then. The genetic types responsible for all modern population characteristics were formed. Three of these types, the capoids, tall negroids, and pygmoids were uniquely African, whereas the caucasoid type ranged into southwestern Asia and Europe. Each had evolved within a particular environment, but right from the start, the boundaries overlapped and were permeable, so that a plethora of genetic mixes can be seen and measured today. Only much later, with the rise of racism, would an attempt be made to make anything more out of the intermixing than an interesting problem in human biological evolution.

About 15,000 years ago the protoforms of the modern language phyla of Khoisan, Nilosaharan, Niger Congo, and Afroasiatic also started to take shape. In order, these arose in game-rich southern Africa, within and around the Sahara, along the northern fringes of the equatorial rain forest, and somewhere east of the Nile valley. Two things subsequently happened: the languages broke up into many discrete ones, which ultimately served as important markers of cultural identity, and their locations changed, mostly in favor of Afroasiatic and Niger Congo.

Instigating both processes was the rise of agriculture, which followed upon an earlier phase of intensified gathering, often in association with fishing. Agriculture came in many different versions. One, involving both crops and animals, reached Egypt from a hearth in southwestern Asia 7,500 years ago and from here spread up the Nile into Nubia and westward toward the Maghrib. Others emerged around indigenously domesticated crops within a variety of locales north of the equatorial rain forest, including the highlands of Ethiopia, at lake and riverine sites bordering the southern margins of the Sahara, and along the forest-savanna ecotone. Within the drier habitats of the Sahara and the Horn, livestock provided the basis for the rise of nomadic herding systems of production. Except along the Nile, however, the pace of change was slow, and only very gradually did gathering and hunting give way to agriculture as the primary means of subsistence. In general, agriculture spread from north to south, carried either by migration or cultural diffusion.

Two thousand years ago the course toward reliance on agriculture had been set just about everywhere, and with reliance came a whole new population calculus. In effect, a synergism was created in which production and number of people were correlated. Greater productivity meant more people, and more people meant greater productivity, which, in turn, translated into enhanced group strength and security. Nevertheless, the natural resources to support agriculture varied enormously, and the population map came to reflect this fact. The annual rise and fall of floodwaters turned certain river valleys and lake shores into prime settlement sites, and other centers of population concentration were highlands, especially those with rich volcanic soils. In contrast, much vaster areas of the continent were plagued by some combination of ancient and infertile soils, drought, and various diseases, which kept population numbers low and forced people to move in search of new and better places to farm and raise animals.

An extremely important technological innovation was iron making. Whether derived from external sources or developed indigenously, iron-bladed hoes improved agricultural productivity and iron-tipped spears and arrows gave those who made them a significant advantage over those still reliant on stone. Sources of iron thus became strategic locations, and those who possessed the skill of fashioning tools from earth often served as key personages around whom others gathered.

At different times in different places growing populations and environmental differences created opportunities for trade, and to an ever-increasing extent the ability to control trade came to distinguish the powerful from the weak. Trade started when local networks exchanged food and manufactured items; these networks gave rise to larger kinship networks, and many of these evolved into chiefdoms and kingdoms. People always seem to have been a scarce commodity, and slavery became the way some chose to obtain workers when kinship no longer sufficed. Slaves could be captured, traded for, or obtained as payment from families needing to pay off debts or seeking courtly favors. Women had special value because of their contributions to both production and reproduction.

Those chiefdoms and kingdoms strategically situated took advantage of interregional trading opportunities, and from these arose even more spatially extensive and populous states and empires. Commodities like salt and kola nuts were in demand throughout Africa, but the real potential for wealth derived from foreign demands for the African triumvirate of gold, ivory, and slaves. Peoples of non-African origin came in search of these resources, and they reshaped regional population developments in significant ways. Phoenicians, Ionians, and Romans settled at points along the Mediterranean coast, whereas Arabs connected the monsoonal portions of the east coast to Indian Ocean commerce. In each instance, an urban pattern of settlement was created, with more of an external than an African orientation.

Religion was another important exogenous influence on population. Judaism won some converts in Ethiopia and identified a people with an enduring cultural tradition. Christianity came next, from several different sources, and spread via conversions across much of Africa north of the Sahara. It lasted only in the highlands of Ethiopia and to a lesser extent along the Nile. Islam replaced it. First brought by conquering Arab armies, it reached beyond the Sahara to the Sahel and the Sudan of western Africa and to the Swahili coast of eastern Africa, disseminated by merchants and holy men from a variety of sects. As people adopted Islam, many, especially in northern Africa, became titular Arabs, whereas for others Islam strengthened their own sense of cultural identity.

By A.D. 1500 Africa was a mosaic of different peoples with different sizes of population and varying levels of political organization. Small bands of gatherer-hunters such as the

San of southern Africa and the pygmoids of the equatorial rain forest could still be found. Pastoralists, from Nilotes to Khoikhoi, dominated the more arid portions of the continent, but the vast majority of people farmed and tended livestock, either in larger polities like Mali, Kongo, and Egypt or in clusters of lineage-based units containing no more than several households. But the map was hardly static; it changed constantly as fortunes waxed and waned.

Over most of Africa, segmentary tendencies almost always awaited the weakening of power at the center, whether in the form of an emperor or big man. Consequently, groupings of people constantly formed and re-formed as old alliances gave way to new ones. Almost all African social systems were open and readily absorbed outsiders through the simple process of genealogical incorporation, which turned strangers into kin. Sometimes this occurred through warfare, when one group defeated another in the competition for coveted resources—including everything from gold to water holes—whereas at other times people sought out stronger political entities to protect them from raids, which were usually aimed at their livestock or themselves.

It was this scene of diversity and change that Europeans entered on their way to the wealth of Asia. Always few in number, except in South Africa, where the Afrikaners formed what amounted to a new nation, their influences eventually helped transform the peoples of the continent. Trade relations created a demand for manufactured items from Europe and Asia. Only the powerful could afford them, and possession enhanced their positions of authority, often to the point where autocratic institutions replaced those based on consensus. Now Africans had to pay for the new luxuries, and in many instances the only commodity of value that those in power had to offer was other human beings, sold or exchanged into slavery.

The transatlantic slave trade took the majority, and how that trade and its smaller trans-Saharan and Indian Ocean counterparts affected the peopling of Africa need not be reviewed in detail: it caused dramatic changes almost everywhere. People were lost who otherwise would have remained in Africa, true, but economic and political systems were also impoverished, which had much longer-range implications. Agricultural production dropped, craftmaking skills deteriorated, and authoritarianism reached new heights.

Declining demand and abolitionist sentiments brought the slave trade to an end during the nineteenth century and replaced it with a European-dominated world economy based on so-called free and legitimate trade. Africans made adjustments to the changing circumstances, just as they had so many other times in the past. They adopted new technologies, reorganized their social and economic systems, relocated settlements, and formed different polities. These efforts were interrupted, however, when European competition spilled directly onto the continent during the latter portion of the nineteenth century. Within a few decades virtually all Africans found themselves governed by alien institutions and enclosed within rigid colonial boundaries that severely circumscribed their options. The long beginning of the peopling of Africa had come to an end.

BIBLIOGRAPHICAL ESSAY

There is no purpose to listing all the sources that have informed me about the peopling of Africa. Indeed, given the lengthy gestation of the book, I doubt that I would be able to remember them all, especially from earlier years. Provided here, then, are the most important ones that I have consulted, plus some that would be valuable for anyone pursuing further study. Only English-language titles appear; they are numerous on their own and are accessible to likely readers. After an overview of sources that have general applicability, I will proceed chapter by chapter, with some commentary to show how each source fits into my narrative.

GENERAL SOURCES

Anyone interested in the African past must consult the *Cambridge History of Africa* (Cambridge: Cambridge University Press). It contains eight volumes, five of which are relevant to the time span that I have covered.

vol. 1, *From Earliest Times to c. 500 B.C.,* ed. J. D. Clark. 1982.
vol. 2, *From c. 500 B.C. to A.D. 1050,* ed. J. D. Fage & R. Oliver. 1978.
vol. 3, *From c. 1050 to 1600,* ed. R. Oliver. 1977.
vol. 4, *From c. 1600 to c. 1790,* ed. R. Gray. 1975.
vol. 5, *From c. 1790 to c. 1870,* ed. J. E. Flin. 1976.

Most chapters run between fifty and a hundred pages and encapsulate the state of knowledge in the mid to late 1970s, mostly as seen by leading British scholars. Although much has been learned since then, the overall scholarship is so high that the set remains an essential reference. In citing specific volumes I will use the abbreviation *CHA.*

207

A second valuable reference series is the UNESCO-sponsored *General History of Africa* (Berkeley: University of California Press), hereafter *GHA*. The chapters are shorter and more numerous than in the Cambridge series, and their authors come from varying intellectual backgrounds and include Africans.

vol. 1, *Methodology and African Prehistory*, ed. J. Ki-Zerbo. 1981.

vol. 2, *Ancient Civilizations of Africa*, ed. G. Mokhtar. 1981.

vol. 3, *Africa from the Seventh to the Eleventh Century*, ed. M. Elfasi. 1988.

vol. 4, *Africa from the Twelfth to the Sixteenth Century*, ed. D. T. Niane. 1988.

vol. 6, *Africa in the Nineteenth Century until the 1880s*, ed. J. F. A. Ajayi. 1989.

A third indispensable general reference is the *Historical Atlas of Africa* (Cambridge: Cambridge University Press, 1985), prepared under the general editorship of J. F. Ade Ajayi and Michael Crowder. The maps in the seventy-two plates are excellent summaries of the high points of Africa's past, and I consulted many of them in compiling the maps for this book.

I found some sources particularly useful for a number of my chapters. To avoid constant repetition, let me acknowledge them here.

L. L. Cavalli-Sforza, ed., *African Pygmies*. San Diego: Academic Press, 1986.

J. D. Clark, *The Prehistory of Africa*. New York: Praeger, 1970.

G. Connah, *African Civilizations: Precolonial Cities and States in Tropical Africa*. Cambridge: Cambridge University Press, 1987.

D. Dalby, *Language Map of Africa and the Adjacent Islands*. London: International African Institute, 1977.

J. H. Greenberg, *The Languages of Africa*. Bloomington: Indiana University, 1966.

J. Hiernaux, *The People of Africa*. New York: Scribner's, 1975.

R. W. Hull, *African Cities and Towns before the European Conquest*. New York: Norton, 1976.

P. Manning, *Slavery and African Life*. Cambridge: Cambridge University Press, 1990.

O. E. Miller & N. J. Van Der Merwe, "Early Metal Working in Sub-Saharan Africa," *Journal of African History* 35 (1994): 1–36.

G. P. Murdock, *Africa: Its Peoples and Their Culture History*. New York: McGraw-Hill, 1959.

R. Oliver, *The African Experience*. New York: HarperCollins, 1991.

R. Oliver & B. M. Fagan, *Africa in the Iron Age c. 500 B.C. to A.D. 1400*. Cambridge: Cambridge University Press, 1975.

D. W. Phillipson, *African Archaeology*. Cambridge: Cambridge University Press, 1985.

M. Shinnie, *Ancient African Kingdoms*. London: Edward Arnold, 1965.

CHAPTER 2: BECOMING HUMAN

Human origins are a widely fascinating subject, and a market exists for books that emphasize interpretation over anatomical detail. The following were of most relevance in writing this chapter.

M. H. Brown, *The Search for Eve*. New York: Harper and Row, 1990.

D. Falk, *Braindance: New Discoveries about Human Origins and Brain Evolution*. New York: Holt, 1992.

W. E. Fischer, *The Sex Contract*. New York: Morrow, 1982.

J. Gribben & M. Gribben, *Children of the Ice*. Oxford: Basil Blackwell, 1990.

D. Johanson & M. Edey, *Lucy*. New York: Simon and Schuster, 1981.

R. E. Leakey & R. Lewin, *Origins*. New York: Lodestar Books, 1982.

———, *Origins Reconsidered*. New York: Doubleday, 1992.

C. Stringer & C. Gamble, *In Search of the Neanderthals*. New York: Thames and Hudson, 1993. For more detailed information readers are referred to these sources.

A. Bilsborough, *Human Evolution*. London: Blackie Academic and Professional, 1992.

G. Bräuer, "A Craniological Approach to the Origin of Anatomically Modern *Homo sapiens* in Africa and Implications for the Appearance of Modern Europeans," in *The Origins of Modern Humans: A World Survey of the Fossil Evidence,* ed. F. H. Smith & F. Spencer, 327–410. New York: Alan R. Liss, 1984.

N. Burley, "The Evolution of Concealed Ovulation," *American Naturalist* 114 (1979): 835–58.

K. W. Butzer, "Geo-Ecological Perspectives on Early Hominid Evolution," in *Early Hominids in Africa,* ed. C. J. Jolly, 191–217. New York: St. Martin's, 1978.

R. L. Cann, M. Stoneking & A. C. Wilson, "Mitochondrial DNA and Human Evolution," *Nature* 325 (1987): 31–36.

Y. Coppins, "Hominization: General Problems," in *GHA* 1:400–412.

R. A. Foley & P. C. Lee, "Finite Social Space, Evolutionary Pathways, and Reconstructing Hominid Behavior," *Science* 243 (1989): 901–6.

F. E. Grine, ed., *Evolutionary History of the "Robust" Australopithecines*. New York: Aldine de Gruyter, 1988.

A. L. Hammond, "Tales of an Elusive Ancestor," *Science 83* 4:9 (1983): 36–43.

R. L. Hay & M. D. Leakey, "The Fossil Footprints of Laetoli," *Scientific American* 246 (1982): 50–57.

A. Hill, "Causes of Perceived Faunal Change in the Later Neogene of East Africa," *Journal of Human Evolution* 16 (1987): 583–96.

R. L. Holloway, "The O.H. 7 (Olduvai Gorge, Tanzania) Hominid Partial Brain Endocast Revisited," *American Journal of Physical Anthropology* 53 (1980): 262–74.

F. C. Howell, "Overview of the Pliocene and Earlier Pleistocene of the Lower Omo River Basin, Southern Ethiopia," in *Early Hominids of Africa,* ed. C. J. Jolly, 85–130. New York: St. Martin's, 1978.

N. Howell, "Feedbacks and Buffers in Relation to Scarcity and Abundance: Studies of Hunter-Gatherer Populations," in *The State of Population Theory: Forward from Malthus,* ed. D. Coleman & R. Schofield, 156–87. Oxford: Oxford University Press, 1986.

G. Ll. Isaac, "The Food-Sharing Behavior of Protohuman Hominids," *Scientific American* 283 (1978): 90–108.

D. Johanson & T. D. White, "A Systematic Assessment of Early African Hominids," *Science* 203 (1979): 321–30.

W. H. Kimbel, D. C. Johanson & Y. Rak, "The First Skull and Other New Discoveries of *Australopithecus afarensis* at Hader, Ethiopia," *Nature* 36 (1994): 449–51.

M-C. King & A. C. Wilson, "Evolution at Two Levels in Humans and Chimpanzees," *Science* 188 (1975): 107–16.

R. G. Klein, *The Human Career: Human Biological and Cultural Origins*. Chicago: University of Chicago Press, 1989.

D. Lambert, *The Field Guide to Early Man*. New York: Facts on File, 1987.

R. Lewin, "Africa: Cradle of Modern Humans," *Science* 237 (1987): 1292–95.

P. Shipman, "An Age-Old Question: Why Did the Hominid Lineage Survive?" *Discover* 8.4 (1987): 60–64.

———, "Baffling Limb on the Family Tree," *Discover* 7.9 (1986): 86–93.

J. Shreve, "The Dating Game," *Discover* 13.9 (1992): 76–83.

C. G. Sibley & J. E. Ahlquist, "The Phylogeny of the Hominoid Primates as Indicated by DNA-DNA Hybridization," *Journal of Molecular Biology* 20 (1984): 2–15.

F. Spencer, "The Neanderthals and Their Evolutionary Significance: A Brief Historical Survey," in *The Origins of Modern Humans: A World Survey of the Fossil Evidence,* ed. F. H. Smith & Spencer, 1–49. New York: Alan R. Liss, 1984.

J. E. G. Sutton, "The Prehistory of East Africa," in *GHA* 1:451–84.

C. C. Swisher et al., "Age of the Earliest Known Hominids in Java, Indonesia," *Science* 263 (1994): 118–21.

CHAPTER 3: CULTURAL ORIGINS

Because archeological evidence about the Stone Age in Africa is so spotty, developing general temporal and spatial patterns is much like working on a puzzle—one that will never be completed. Sometimes new pieces fit, but at other times the shape of the puzzle has to be changed to accommodate them. So the attempt at assembly continues; my rendition has been shaped by the following literature.

L. Balout, "The Prehistory of North Africa," in *GHA* 1:568–80.

D. R. Brothwell, "The Skeletal Remains from Gwisho B and C," in *Hunter-Gatherers of Gwisho,* ed. B. M. Fagan & F. van Noten, 37–47. Tervuern: Musée Royal de l'Afrique Centrale, 1971.

J. D. Clark, "The Cultures of the Middle Palaeolithic/Stone Age, in *CHA,* 1:248–341.

R. A. Dart, *The Osteodontokeratic Culture of Australopithecus Prometheus.* Pretoria: Transvaal Museum Memoirs, 1957.

J. W. K. Harris & G. Ll. Isaac, "The Karari Industry: Early Pleistocene Archaeological Materials from the Terrain East of Lake Rudolph, Kenya," *Nature* 262 (1976): 102–7.

A. J. Hausman, "Holocene Evolution in Southern Africa," in *From Hunters to Herders: The Causes and Consequences of Food Production in Africa,* ed. J. D. Clark & S. A. Brandt, 261–71. Berkeley: University of California Press, 1984.

R. G. Klein, "The Ecology of Early Man in Southern Africa," *Science* 197 (1977): 115–26.

D. deLaubenfels, "The Upper Paleolithic Revolution," *Mankind Quarterly* 23 (1983): 329–56.

D. Lubell, "Paleoenvironments and Epi-Paleolithic Economies in the Maghreb (ca. 20,000 to 5000 B.P.)," in *From Hunters to Farmers: The Causes and Consequences of Food Production in Africa,* ed. J. D. Clark & S. A. Brandt, 41–56. Berkeley: University of California Press, 1984.

S. K. McIntosh & R. J. McIntosh, "West African Prehistory," *American Scientist* 69 (1981): 602–13.

F. van Noten, "Excavations at Matupi Cave," *Antiquity* 51 (1977): 35-40.

D. W. Phillipson, "The Later Stone Age in Sub-Saharan Africa," in *CHA* 1:410–77.

R. Potts, "Home Bases and Early Hominids," *American Scientist* 72 (1984): 338–47.

G. P. Rightmire, *"Homo sapiens* in Sub-Saharan Africa," in *The Origins of Modern Humans: A World Survey of the Fossil Evidence,* ed. F. H. Smith & F. Spencer, 295–326. New York: Alan R. Liss, 1984.

K. D. Schick & N. Toth, *Making Silent Stones Speak.* New York: Simon and Schuster, 1993.

C. T. Shaw, "The Prehistory of West Africa," in *GHA* 1:611–30.

A. B. Smith, "Origins of the Neolithic in the Sahara," in *From Hunters to Farmers. The Causes and Consequences of Food Production in Africa,* ed. J. D. Clark & S. A. Brandt, 84–92. Berkeley: University of California Press, 1984.

J. E. G. Sutton, "The African Aqualithic," *Antiquity* 51 (1977): 25–34.

————, "The Prehistory of Africa," in *GHA* 1:451–84.

R. J. Trotter, "From Endangered to Dangerous Species," *Science News* 109 (1976): 74–76.

F. Wendorf et al., The Prehistory of the Egyptian Sahara," *Science* 193 (1976): 103–14.

CHAPTER 4: THE AGRICULTURAL TRANSFORMATION

The subject of agricultural origins has long fascinated scholars in many disciplines, and various theoretical interpretations exist. Each probably contains some grain of truth, but so far I have found that the one put forth by D. Rindos in *The Origins of Agriculture: An Evolutionary Perspective* (New York: Academic Press, 1984) best fits the facts. Here I list other useful general sources.

A. J. Ammerman & L. L. Cavalli-Sforza, *The Neolithic and the Genetics of Population in Europe.* Princeton: Princeton University Press, 1984.

J. R. Harlan, "Agricultural Origins: Centers and Noncenters," *Science* 174 (1971): 468–74.

E. Isaac, *The Geography of Domestication.* Englewood Cliffs, N.J.: Prentice-Hall, 1970.

C. M. Rodrique, "Can Religion Account for Early Animal Domestication?" *Professional Geographer* 44 (1992): 417–30.

C. O. Sauer, *Seeds, Spades, Hearths, and Herds.* Cambridge: MIT Press, 1969.

N. I. Vavilov, "Studies on the Origins of Cultivated Plants," *Bulletin of Applied Botany and Plant Breeding* 16 (1926): 1–245.

For the more specifically African information in the chapter I have relied on the following.

S. Adams, "The Importance of Nubia: A Link between Central Africa and Mediterranean," in *GHA* 2:226–43.

W. Y. Adams, *Nubia Corridor to Africa.* Princeton: Princeton University Press, 1977.

J. Alexander & D. G. Coursey, "The Domestication of Yams," in *The Domestication and Exploitation of Plants and Animals,* ed. P. J. Ucko & G. W. Dimbley, 405–25. London: Duckworth, 1969.

K. W. Butzer, *Early Hydraulic Civilization in Egypt: A Study in Cultural Ecology.* Chicago: University of Chicago Press, 1976.

J. D. Clark, "Prehistoric Cultural Continuity and Economic Change in the Central Sudan in the Early Holocene," in *From Hunters to Farmers: The Causes and Consequences of Food Production in Africa,* ed. Clark & S. A. Brandt, 113–26. Berkeley: University of California Press, 1984.

A. E. Close, "Current Research and Radiocarbon Dates from North Africa," *Journal of African History* 21 (1980): 145–67.

D. M. Dixon, "A Note on Cereals in Ancient Egypt," in *The Domestication and Exploitation of Plants and Animals,* ed. P. M. Ecko & G. W. Dimbley, 131–42. Chicago: Aldine, 1969.

C. Ehret, "On the Antiquity of Agriculture in Ethiopia," *Journal of African History* 20 (1979): 161–77.

————, "Proto-Cushitic Reconstruction," *Sprache und Geschichte in Afrika* 8 (1987): 7–180.

————, *Southern Nilotic History.* Evanston, Ill.: Northwestern University Press, 1971.

C. Flight, "The Kintampo Culture and Its Place in the Economic Prehistory of West Africa," in *Origins of African Plant Domestication,* ed. J. R. Harlan, J. M. J. de Wet & A. B. L. Stemler, 211–21. The Hague: Mouton, 1976.

J. R. Harlan & J. Pasquereau, "Décrue Agriculture in Mali," *Economic Botany* 23 (1969): 70–74.

J. R. Harlan, J. M. J. de Wet & A. B. L. Stemler, "Plant Domestication and Indigenous African

Agriculture," in *Origins of African Plant Domestication,* ed. Harlan, de Wet & Stemler, 3–19. The Hague: Mouton, 1976.

N. Howell, *Demography of the Dobe !Kung.* New York: Academic Press, 1979.

R. B. Lee, "Population Growth and the Beginnings of Sedentary Life among the !Kung Bushmen," in *Population Growth: Anthropological Implications,* ed. B. Spooner, 329–42. Cambridge: MIT Press, 1972.

A. B. Lloyd, "The Late Period, 664–232 B.C.," in *Ancient Egypt: A Social History,* ed. B. G. Trigger et al., 279–348. Cambridge: Cambridge University Press, 1983.

D. Lubell, "Paleoenvironments and Epi-Paleolithic Economies in the Maghreb (ca. 20,000 to 5000 B.P.)," in *From Hunters to Farmers: The Causes and Consequences of Food Production in Africa,* ed. J. D. Clark & S. A. Brandt, 41–56. Berkeley: University of California Press, 1984.

P. J. Munson, "Archaeological Data on the Origins of Cultivation in the Southwestern Sahara and the Implications for West Africa," in *Origins of African Plant Domestication,* ed. J. R. Harlan, J. M. J. de Wet & A. B. L. Stemler, 187–209. The Hague: Mouton, 1976.

M. Posnansky, "Early Agricultural Societies in Ghana," in *From Hunters to Farmers: The Causes and Consequences of Food Production in Africa,* ed. J. D. Clark & S. A. Brandt, 147–51. Berkeley: University of California Press, 1984.

P. Robertshaw & D. Collett, "A New Framework for the Study of Early Pastoral Communities in East Africa," *Journal of African History* 24 (1983): 289–302.

N. M. Sherif, "Nubia before Napata (−3100 to −750), in *GHA* 2:245–77.

A. B. Smith, "Origins of the Neolithic in the Sahara," in *From Hunters to Farmers: The Causes and Consequences of Food Production in Africa,* ed. J. D. Clark & S. A. Brandt, 84–92. Berkeley: University of California Press, 1984.

R. Thelwall, "Linguistic Aspects of Greater Nubian History," in *The Archaeological and Linguistic Reconstruction of African History,* ed. C. Ehret & M. Posnansky, 39–52. Berkeley: University of California Press, 1982.

B. G. Trigger, *Nubia under the Pharaohs.* Boulder, Colo.: Westview, 1976.

———, "The Rise of Egyptian Civilization," in *Ancient Egypt: A Social History,* ed. Trigger et al., 1–70. Cambridge: Cambridge University Press, 1983.

F. Wendorf, *The Prehistory of Nubia.* Dallas: Southern Methodist University Press, 1968.

F. Wendorf et al., "Use of Barley in the Egyptian Late Paleolithic," *Science* 205 (1979): 1341–47.

F. Wendorf & R. Schild, "The Emergence of Food Production in the Egyptian Sahara," in *From Hunters to Farmers: The Causes and Consequences of Food Production in Africa,* ed. J. D. Clark & S. A. Brandt, 93–101. Berkeley: University of California Press, 1984.

M. A. J. Williams, "Late Quaternary Prehistoric Environments in the Sudan," in *From Hunters to Farmers: The Causes and Consequences of Food Production in Africa,* ed. J. D. Clark & S. A. Brandt, 74–83. Berkeley: University of California Press, 1984.

CHAPTER 5: NORTHERN AFRICA

When I started this book, I knew less about northern Africa than about any other region. Fortunately, the region is well covered in *CHA* and *GHA*. The chapters I relied on are:

T. Bainquis, "Egypt from the Arab Conquest until the End of the Fatimid State," in *GHA* 3:163–93.

M. Brett, "The Arab Conquest and the Rise of Islam in North Africa," in *CHA,* 2:490–555.

———, "The Fatamid Revolution (861–973) and Its Aftermath in North Africa," in *CHA* 2:589–636.

M. El Fasi & I. Herbek, "The Coming of Islam and the Expansion of the Muslim Empire," in *GHA* 3:31–55.

W. H. C. Frend, "The Christian Factor in Mediterranean Africa, c. A.D. 200–700," in *CHA* 2:410–89.

A. A. Hakem, "The Civilization of Napata and Meroe," in *GHA* 2:298–325.

P. M. Holt, "Egypt, the Funj and Darfur," in *CHA* 4:14–57.

I. Hrbek, "The Disintegration of Political Unity in the Maghrib," in *GHA* 4:78–101.

———, "Egypt, Nubia and the Eastern Deserts," in *CHA* 3:10–97.

I. Hrbek & J. Devisse, "The Almoravids," in *GHA* 3:336–66.

S. Jakobielski, "Christian Nubia at the Height of Its Civilization," in *GHA* 3:194–223.

D. Johnson, "The Maghrib," in *CHA* 5:99–124.

L. Kropácek, "Nubia from the Twelfth Century to the Funj Conquest in the Early Fifteenth Century," in *GHA* 4:398–422.

R. C. C. Law, "North Africa in the Hellenistic and Roman Periods, 323 B.C. to A.D. 305," in *CHA* 2:148–209.

———, "North Africa in the Period of Phoenician and Greek Colonization, c. 800 to 323 B.C.," in *CHA* 2:8–147.

J. Leclant, "The Empire of Kush: Napata and Meroe," in *GHA* 2:278–97.

N. Levtzion, "North-West Africa: From the Maghrib to the Fringes of the Forest," in *CHA* 4:142–222.

———, "The Sahara and Sudan from the Arab Conquest of the Maghrib to the Rise of the Almoravids," in *CHA* 2:637–84.

———, "The Western Maghrib and Sudan," in *CHA* 3:331–462.

T. Lewicki, "The Role of the Sahara and Saharans in Relationships between North and South," in *GHA* 3:276–313.

A. Mahjoubi & P. Salama, "The Roman and Post-Roman Period in North Africa," in *GHA* 2:465–512.

H. Riad, "Egypt in the Hellenistic Era," in *GHA* 2:184–207.

P. L. Shinnie, "The Nilotic Sudan and Ethiopia, c. 600 B.C. to c. A.D. 600," in *CHA* 2:210–71.

M. Talbi, "The Independence of the Maghrib," in *GHA* 3:246–75.

B. H. Warmington, "The Carthaginian Period," in *GHA* 2:41–64.

In addition, I consulted these sources.

W. Y. Adams, "The Coming of the Nubian Speakers to the Nile Valley," in *The Archaeological and Linguistic Reconstruction of African History,* ed. C. Ehret & M. Posnansky, 11–38. Berkeley: University of California Press, 1982.

———, *Nubia: Corridor to Africa*. Princeton: Princeton University Press, 1977.

A. K. Bowman, *Egypt after the Pharaohs*. Berkeley: University of California Press, 1986.

R. W. Bulliet, *The Camel and the Wheel*. Cambridge, Mass.: Harvard University Press, 1975.

K. W. Butzer, *Early Hydraulic Civilization in Egypt: A Study in Cultural Ecology*. Chicago: University of Chicago Press, 1976.

N. Lewis, *Greeks in Ptolemaic Egypt*. Oxford: Oxford University Press, Clarendon Press, 1986.

P. MacKendrick, *The North African Stones Speak*. Chapel Hill: University of North Carolina Press, 1980.

W. H. McNeill, *Plagues and Peoples*. New York: Anchor Press, 1976.

S. Raven, *Rome in Africa*. Rev. ed. London: Longman, 1984.

A. H. Sayce, "Second Interim Report on the Excavations at Meroe in Ethiopia, II," *University of Liverpool Annals of Archaeology and Anthropology* 4 (1911): 53–65.

R. Thelwall, "Linguistic Aspects of Greater Nubian History," in *The Archaeological and Linguistic Reconstruction of African History,* ed. C. Ehret & M. Posnansky, 39–52. Berkeley: University of California Press, 1982.

B. G. Trigger, *History and Settlement in Lower Nubia*. New Haven: Yale University Press, 1965.

———, "The Myth of Meroe and the African Iron Age," *International Journal of African Historical Studies* 2 (1969): 23–50.

A. L. Udovitch, ed., *The Islamic Middle East, 700–1900: Studies in Economic and Social History*. Princeton, N.J.: Darwin Press, 1981.

A. M. Watson, *Agricultural Innovation in the Early Islamic World: The Diffusion of Crops and Farming Techniques, 700–1100*. Cambridge: Cambridge University Press, 1983.

F. E. Zeuner, *A History of Domesticated Animals*. London: Hutchinson, 1963.

CHAPTER 6: ETHIOPIA AND THE HORN

Less literature is available on Ethiopia and the Horn than on any other part of Africa. There are some excellent studies, however, and they allow us to at least sketch population developments. I have relied on a number of them.

M. Abir, *Ethiopia and the Horn*. London: Frank Cass, 1980.

———, "Ethiopia and the Horn of Africa," in *CHA* 4:537–77.

K. W. Butzer, "The Rise and Fall of Axum, Ethiopia: A Geo-Archaeological Interpretation," *American Antiquity* 40 (1981): 471–95.

D. Buxton, *The Abyssinians*. New York: Praeger, 1970.

M. Hassen, *The Oromo of Ethiopia: A History, 1570–1860*. Cambridge: Cambridge University Press, 1990.

G. W. B. Huntingford, *The Historical Geography of Ethiopia*. Ed. R. Pankhurst. Oxford: Oxford University Press, 1989.

———, ed., *The Periplus of the Erythraean Sea*. London: Hakluyt Society, 1980.

S. Kaplan, *The Beta Israel (Falasha) in Ethiopia: From Earliest Times to the Twentieth Century*. New York: New York University Press, 1992.

D. Kessler, *The Falashas: The Forgotten Jews of Ethiopia*. New York: African Publishing Company, 1982.

Y. M. Kobishchanov, "Aksum: Political System, Economics, and Culture, First to Fourth Century," in *GHA* 2:381–400.

———, *Axum*. University Park: Pennsylvania State University Press, 1979.

D. N. Levine, *Greater Ethiopia. The Evolution of a Multiethnic Society*. Chicago: University of Chicago Press, 1974.

H. S. Lewis, "The Origins of the Galla and Somali," *Journal of African History* 7 (1966): 27–46.

I. M. Lewis, *A Pastoral Democracy*. London: Oxford University Press, 1961.

T. T. Mekouria, "Christian Aksum," in *GHA* 2:401–22.

S. Munro-Hay, *Aksum: An African Civilization of Late Antiquity*. Edinburgh: Edinburgh University Press, 1991.

———, "The Foreign Trade of the Aksumite Port of Adulis," *Azania* 17 (1982): 107–25.

S. Rubenson, "Ethiopia and the Horn," in *CHA* 5:51–98.

W. A. Shack, *The Central Ethiopians: Amhara, Tigrina and Related Peoples*. London: International African Institute, 1974.

T. Tamrat, *Church and State in Ethiopia, 1270–1527*. Oxford: Oxford University Press, 1972.

———, "Ethiopia, the Red Sea and the Horn," in *CHA* 3:98–182.

J. S. Trimingham, *Islam in Ethiopia*. London: Oxford University Press, 1954.

E. Ullendorf, *The Ethiopians: An Introduction to Country and People*. 2nd ed. London: Oxford University Press, 1965.

CHAPTER 7: WESTERN AFRICA

The literature pertaining to western Africa is vast compared with that treating other portions of the continent. The early kingdoms and states, slavery, and the nineteenth century are particularly well covered, and thus I have had to be more selective here than for the other chapters.

M. Adamu, "The Hausa and Their Neighbors in the Central Sudan," in *GHA* 4:266–300.

———, *The Hausa Factor in West African History*. Zaria, Nigeria: Ahmadu Bello University Press, 1978.

I. A. Akinjogbin, *Dahomey and Its Neighbours, 1708–1818*. Cambridge: Cambridge University Press, 1967.

R. A. Austen. "The Trans-Saharan Slave Trade: A Tentative Census," in *The Uncommon Market: Essays in the Economic History of the Atlantic Slave Trade*, ed. H. A. Gemery & J. S. Hogendorn, 23–76. New York: Academic Press, 1979.

V. Azarya, *Aristocrats Facing Change: The Fulbe in Guinea, Nigeria and Cameroon*. Chicago: University of Chicago Press, 1978.

J. Bendor-Samuel, ed., *The Niger-Congo Languages*. New York: Lanhem, 1989.

A. Boahen, J. F. Ade Ajayi & M. Tidy, *Topics in West African History*. 2nd ed. Essex: Longmans Group, 1986.

D. Calvocoressi & N. David, "A New Survey of Radiocarbon and Thermo-Luminescence Dates for West Africa," *Journal of African History* 20 (1979): 1–29.

B. Catchpole & I. A. Akinjogbin, *A History of West Africa in Maps and Diagrams*. London: Collins Educational, 1984.

S. M. Cissoko, "The Songhay from the Twelfth to the Sixteenth Century," in *GHA* 4:187–210.

D. Conrad & H. Fischer, "The Conquest That Never Was: Ghana and the Almoravids, 1076. I. The External Arab Sources" and "II. The Local Oral Sources," *History in Africa* 9 (1982): 21–59; 10 (1983): 53–78.

P. D. Curtin, *The Atlantic Slave Trade: A Census*. Madison: University of Wisconsin Press, 1969.

P. J. Darling, "A Change of Territory: Attempts to Trace More Than a Thousand Years of Population Movements by the Benin and Ishan Peoples of Southern Nigeria," in *Africa Historical Demography*, 2:105–20. Edinburgh: University of Edinburgh Centre of African Studies, 1981.

C. R. DeCorse, "Culture Contact, Continuity, and Change on the Gold Coast, A.D. 1400–1900," *African Archaeological Review* 10 (1992): 163–96.

———, "The Danes on the Gold Coast: Culture Change and the European Presence," *African Archaeological Review* 11 (1993): 149–73.

J. Devisse, "Trade and Trade Routes in West Africa," in *GHA* 3:367–435.

J. D. Fage, "The Effect of the Export Slave Trade on African Populations," in *The Population Factor in African Studies*, ed. R. P. Moss & R. J. A. R. Rathbone, 15–23. London: University of London Press, 1975.

——, "Slavery and the Slave Trade in the Context of Western African History," *Journal of African History* 10 (1969): 393–404.

——, "Upper and Lower Guinea," in *CHA* 3:463–518.

H. J. Fischer, "The Central Sahara and Sudan," in *CHA* 4:58–141.

C. Fyfe, "Freed Slave Colonies in West Africa," in *CHA* 5:170–99.

J. K. Fynn, *Asante and Its Neighbours, 1700–1807*. Evanston, Ill.: Northwestern University Press, 1971.

T. F. Garrard, "Myth and Metrology: The Early Trans-Saharan Gold Trade," *Journal of African History* 23 (1982): 443–62.

H. A. Gemery & J. S. Hogendorn, eds., *The Uncommon Market: Essays in the Economic History of the Atlantic Slave Trade*. New York: Academic Press, 1979.

P. E. H. Hair, "Ethnolinguistic Continuity on the Guinea Coast," *Journal of African History* 8 (1969): 247–68.

D. Henige, "Measuring the Immeasurable: The Atlantic Slave Trade, West African Population and the Pyrrhonian Critic," *Journal of African History* 27 (1986): 295–313.

C. C. Ifemesia, "Bornu under the Shehus," in *A Thousand Years of West African History,* ed. J. F. Ade Ajayi & I. Espie, 284–93. Ibadan, Nigeria: Ibadan University Press, 1965.

L. Kaba, "Archers, Musketeers, and Mosquitoes: The Moroccan Invasion of the Sudan and the Songhay Resistance," *Journal of African History* 22 (1981): 457–76.

M. E. Kropp Dakubu, "The Peopling of Southern Ghana," in *The Archaeological and Linguistic Reconstruction of African History,* ed. C. Ehret & M. Posnansky, 245–55. Berkeley: University of California Press, 1982.

D. Lange, "The Chad Region as a Crossroads," in *GHA* 3:436–60.

——, "The Kingdoms and Peoples of Chad," in *GHA* 4:238–65.

R. Law, "Dahomey and the Slave Trade: Reflections on the Historiography of the Rise of Dahomey," *Journal of African History* 27 (1986): 237–67.

——, *The Slave Coast of West Africa, 1550–1750*. Oxford: Oxford University Press, Clarendon Press, 1991.

N. Levtzion, *Ancient Ghana and Mali*. London: Methuen, 1973.

——, "The Western Maghrib and Sudan," in *CHA* 3:331–462.

P. E. Lovejoy, "The Impact of the Atlantic Slave Trade on Africa: A Review of the Literature," *Journal of African History* 30 (1990): 365–94.

P. E. Lovejoy & S. Baier, "The Desert-Side Economy of the Central Sudan," *International Journal of African Historical Studies* 8 (1975): 551–81.

M. Ly-Tall, "The Decline of the Mali Empire," in *GHA* 4:172–86.

E. A. McDougall, "Salts of the Western Sahara: Myths, Mysteries, and Historical Significance," *International Journal of African Historical Studies* 23 (1990): 231–57.

R. J. McIntosh & S. K. McIntosh, "The Inland Niger Delta before the Empire of Mali: Evidence from Jenne-Jenno," *Journal of African History* 22 (1981): 1–22.

——, "West African Prehistory," *American Scientist* 69 (1981): 602–13.

P. Manning, "Contours of Slavery and Social Change in Africa," *American Historical Review* 88 (1983): 835–57.

——, "The Enslavement of Africans: A Demographic Model," *Canadian Journal of African Studies* 15 (1981): 499–526.

R. Mauny, "Trans-Saharan Contacts and the Iron Age in West Africa," in *CHA* 2:272–341.

N. J. van der Merwe, "The Advent of Iron in Africa," in *The Coming of the Iron Age,* ed. T. A. Wertime & J. D. Mubly, 463–506. New Haven: Yale University Press, 1980.

P. J. Munson, "Archaeology and the Prehistoric Origins of the Ghana Empire," *Journal of African History* 21 (1980): 457–66.

C. W. Newberry, "North African and Western Sudan Trade in the Nineteenth Century: A Re-Evaluation," *Journal of African History* 7 (1966): 233–46.

D. T. Niane, "Mali and the Second Mandingo Expansion," in *GHA* 4:117–71.

R. Oliver & A. Atmore, *The African Middle Ages, 1400–1800*. Cambridge: Cambridge University Press, 1981.

J. N. Origi, "A Re-Assessment of the Organization and Benefits of the Slave and Palm Produce Trade amongst the Ngwa-Ibo," *Canadian Journal of African Studies* 16 (1982): 523–48.

Y. Person, "The Coastal Peoples: From Casamance to the Ivory Coast Lagoons," in *GHA* 4:301–23.

W. D. Phillips, Jr., *Slavery from Roman Times to the Early Transatlantic Trade*. Minneapolis: University of Minnesota Press, 1985.

M. Posnansky, "Archaeological and Linguistic Reconstruction in Ghana," in *Archaeological and Linguistic Reconstruction in Africa,* ed. C. Ehret & Posnansky, 256–65. Berkeley: University of California Press, 1982.

R. L. Roberts, *Warriors, Merchants, and Slaves: The State and the Economy in the Middle Niger Delta, 1700–1914*. Stanford: Stanford University Press, 1987.

W. Rodney, "The Guinea Coast," in *CHA* 4:223–324.

D. Ross, "The Dahomean Middleman System, 1727–c. 1818," *Journal of African History* 28 (1987): 357–75.

A. F. C. Ryder, "From the Volta to the Cameroon," in *GHA* 4:339–70.

R. A. Sargent, "From a Redistributive to an Imperial Social Formation in Benin, c. 1293–1536," *Canadian Journal of African Studies* 20 (1986): 402–27.

P. R. Schmidt & D. H. Avery, "More Evidence for an Advanced Prehistoric Iron Technology in Africa," *Journal of Field Archaeology* 10 (1983): 421–34.

T. Shaw, *Igbo Ukwu: An Account of Archaeological Discoveries in Eastern Nigeria,* 2 vols. London: Faber and Faber, 1970.

D. J. Stenning, "Transhumance, Migratory Drift, Migration: Patterns of Pastoral Fulani Nomadism," *Journal of the Royal Anthropological Institute* 87 (1957): 57–73.

J. F. G. Sutton, "The Aquatic Civilization of Middle Africa," *Journal of African History* 15 (1974): 527–46.

———, "Towards a Less Orthodox History of Hausaland," *Journal of African History* 20 (1979): 179–201.

E. Szymanski, "Africa and the Portuguese Colonization," *Africana Bulletin* 33 (1986): 37–50.

R. F. Tylecote, "The Origins of Iron Smelting in Africa," *West African Journal of Archaeology* 5 (1975): 1–9.

L. E. Wilson, "The 'Bloodless' Conquest in Southeastern Ghana: The Huza and Territorial Expansion of the Krobo in the Nineteenth Century," *International Journal of African Historical Studies* 23 (1990): 269–97.

CHAPTER 8: CENTRAL AFRICA

What central Africa lacks in quantity of literature it more than makes up for in quality. Two books, in particular, are among the best ever written on any African topics. One is J. Vansina's *Paths in the Rainforest* (Madison: University of Wisconsin Press, 1990). I have relied on it extensively for information pertaining to Bantu settlement of the equatorial zone. The other is J.

C. Miller, *Way of Death* (Madison: University of Wisconsin Press, 1988), which details the course and impact of the Angolan slave trade. Another key book is D. Birmingham, *Central Africa to 1870* (Cambridge: Cambridge University Press, 1981). It brings together the pertinent chapters from the *Cambridge History of Africa* into one convenient collection. There are other valuable sources of information as well.

D. N. Beach, "The Zimbabwe Plateau and Its Peoples," in *History of Central Africa,* vol. 1, ed. D. Birmingham & P. M. Martin, 245–77. London: Longman, 1983.

P. R. Bennett, "Patterns in Linguistic Geography and the Bantu Origins Question," *History in Africa* 10 (1983): 35–51.

D. Birmingham, "Society and Economy before 1400," in *History of Central Africa* vol. 1, ed. Birmingham & P. M. Martin, 1–29. London: Longman, 1983.

D. D. Cordell, "The Savanna Belt of North-Central Africa," in *History of Central Africa,* vol. 1, ed. D. Birmingham & M. Martin, 30–74. London: Longman, 1983.

N. David, "Prehistory and Historical Linguistics in Central Africa: Points of Contact," in *The Archaeological and Linguistic Reconstruction of African History,* ed. C. Ehret & M. Posnansky, 78–103. Berkeley: University of California Press, 1982.

C. Ehret, "Linguistic Inferences about Early Bantu History," in *The Archaeological and Linguistic Reconstruction of African History,* ed. Ehret & M. Posnansky, 57–65. Berkeley: University of California Press, 1982.

R. W. Harms, *River of Wealth, River of Sorrow: The Central Zaire Basin in the Era of the Slave and Ivory Trade, 1500–1891.* New Haven: Yale University Press, 1981.

A. Hilton, "The Jaga Reconsidered," *Journal of African History* 22 (1981): 191–202.

P. de Maret & F. Nsuka, "History of Bantu Metallurgy: Some Linguistic Aspects," *History in Africa* 4 (1977): 43–65.

J. C. Miller, "The Significance of Drought, Disease, and Famine in the Agriculturally Marginal Zones of West-Central Africa," *Journal of African History* 23 (1982): 17–62.

M. D. D. D. Newitt, "The Early History of Maravi," *Journal of African History* 23 (1982): 145–62.

D. W. Phillipson, "Central Africa to the North of the Zambezi," in *GHA* 3:643–63.

T. Q. Reefe, "The Societies of the Eastern Savanna," in *History of Central Africa,* vol. 1, ed. D. Birmingham & P. M. Martin, 160–204. London: Longman, 1983.

D. E. Saxon, "Linguistic Evidence for the Eastward Spread of Ubangian Peoples," in *The Archaeological and Linguistic Reconstruction of African History,* ed. C. Ehret & M. Posnansky, 66–77. Berkeley: University of California Press, 1982.

J. Thornton, "Early Kongo-Portuguese Relations: A New Interpretation," *History in Africa* 8 (1981): 183–204.

J. Vansina, "Bantu in a Crystal Ball," *History in Africa* 6 (1979): 287–333; 7 (1980): 293–325.

———, "Do Pygmies Have a History?" *Sprache und Geschichte in Afrika* 7.1 (1986): 431–45.

CHAPTER 9: EASTERN AFRICA

The Swahili past can be reconstructed from a wider array of sources than is usually available, and two recent books—J. Middleton, *The World of the Swahili* (New Haven: Yale University Press, 1992), and D. Nurse & T. Spear, *The Swahili: Reconstructing the History and Language of an African Society, 800–1500* (Philadelphia: University of Pennsylvania Press, 1985)—admirably summarize what is known. I also used supplementary texts.

H. N. Chittick, "The East Coast, Madagascar and the Indian Ocean," in *CHA* 3:183–231.

R. L. Pouwells, "Oral Historiography and the Shirazi of the East African Coast," *History in Africa* 11 (1984): 237–67.

A. M. H. Sheriff, "The East African Coast and Its Role in Maritime Trade," in *GHA* 2:551–67.

J. de Vere Allen, "Swahili Culture and the Nature of East Coast Settlement," *International Journal of African Historical Studies* 14 (1981): 306–34.

J. C. Wilkinson, "Oman and East Africa: New Light on Early Kilwan History from the Omani Sources," *International Journal of African Historical Studies* 14 (1981): 272–305.

For the rest of eastern Africa, researchers must rely on a scattering of sources, although fortunately for my purposes, many of them focus on matters of migration and population change.

S. H. Ambrose, "Archaeological and Linguistic Reconstructions of History in East Africa," in *The Archaeological and Linguistic Reconstruction of African History,* ed. C. Ehret & M. Posnansky, 104–57. Berkeley: University of California Press, 1982.

———, "The Introduction of Pastoral Adaptations to the Highlands of East Africa," in *From Hunters to Farmers: The Causes and Consequences of Food Production in Africa,* ed. J. D. Clark & S. A. Brandt, 212–39. Berkeley: University of California Press, 1984.

J. L. Bernstein, "The Enemy Is Us: Eponymy in the Historiography of the Maasai," *History in Africa* 7 (1980): 1–21.

———, "The Maasai and Their Neighbors: Variables of Interaction," *African Economic History* 49 (1976): 1–11.

C. Ehret, "The East African Interior," in *GHA* 3:616–42.

———, *Ethiopians and East Africans: The Problems of Contact.* Nairobi: East African Publishing House, 1974.

———, "Historical/Linguistic Evidence for Early African Food Production," in *From Hunters to Farmers: The Causes and Consequences of Food Production in Africa,* ed. J. D. Clark & S. A. Brandt, 26–35. Berkeley: University of California Press, 1984.

———, *Southern Nilotic History.* Evanston, Ill.: Northwestern University Press, 1971.

C. Ehret et al., "Some Thoughts on the Early History of the Nile-Congo Watershed," *Ufahamu* 2 (1974): 85–112.

C. Ehret & D. Nurse, "The Taita Cushites," *Sprache und Geschichte in Afrika* 3 (1981): 125–68.

E. E. Evans-Pritchard, *The Divine Kingship of the Shilluk of the Nilotic Sudan.* Cambridge: Cambridge University Press, 1948.

M. Goodman, "The Strange Case of Mbugu (Tanzania)," in *Pidginization and Creolization of Languages,* ed. D. Hymes, 243–54. Cambridge: Cambridge University Press, 1971.

B. Heine, F. Rottland & R. Voser, "Proto-Baz: Some Aspects of Early Nilotic-Cushitic Contacts," *Sprache und Geschichte in Afrika* 1 (1979): 75–91.

A. H. Jacobs, "Maasai Inter-Tribal Relations: Belligerent Herdsmen or Peaceable Pastoralists," *Senri Ethnological Studies* 3 (1979): 33–52.

R. C. Kelly, *The Nuer Conquest: The Structure and Development of an Expansionist System.* Ann Arbor: University of Michigan Press, 1985.

M. Lynch & L. H. Robbins, "Cushitic and Nilotic Prehistory: New Archaeological Evidence from Northwest Kenya, *Journal of African History* 20 (1979): 317–28.

D. Nurse, "Bantu Expansion into East Africa: Linguistic Evidence," in *The Archaeological and Linguistic Reconstruction of African History,* ed. C. Ehret & M. Posnansky, 199–222. Berkeley: University of California Press, 1982.

K. Odner, "Economic Differentiation and Origin of Dorobo (Okiek) Ethnicity," *Sprache und Geschichte in Afrika* 7.2 (1986): 307–22.

B. A. Ogot, "The Great Lakes Region," *GHA* 4:498–524.

————, ed., *Zamani: A Survey of East African History*. Nairobi: East African Publishing House, 1973.

R. Oliver, "The Nilotic Contribution to Bantu Africa," *Journal of African History* 23 (1982): 433–42.

P. Robertshaw & D. Collett, "A New Framework for the Study of Early Pastoral Communities in East Africa,"*Journal of African History* 24 (1983): 289–302.

P. R. Schmidt, "A New Look at Interpretations of the Early Iron Age in East Africa," *History in Africa* 2 (1975): 127–36.

D. L. Schoenbrun, "We Are What We Eat: Ancient Agriculture between the Great Lakes," *Journal of African History* 34 (1993): 1–31.

R. Soper, "Bantu Expansion into Eastern Africa: Archaeological Evidence," in *The Archaeological and Linguistic Reconstruction of African History,* ed. C. Ehret & M. Posnansky, 223–38. Berkeley: University of California Press, 1982.

R. Spencer, *Nomads in Alliance: Symbiosis and Growth among the Rendile and Samburu of Kenya*. London: Oxford University Press, 1973.

J. E. G. Sutton, "The Ancestors of the Interlacustrine Kingdoms," *Journal of African History* 34 (1993): 33–54.

M. Twaddle, "Towards an Early History of the East African Interior," *History in Africa* 2 (1975): 147–84.

R. Vossen, *The Eastern Nilotes. Linguistic and Historical Reconstructions*. Berlin: Dietrich Reimer, 1982.

C. C. Wrigley, "The Problem of the Luo," *History in Africa* 8 (1981): 219–46.

CHAPTER 10: SOUTHERN AFRICA

Twenty-five or thirty years ago the southern African past was recounted as essentially a "white" one. The Bantu presumably did not arrive any sooner, and, according to prevailing Eurocentric views, they really were not important except as obstacles to be overcome. That has all begun to change, and both the longevity and the complexity of pre-European settlement are coming into sharper focus. How far we have come is illustrated in the indispensable *The Peoples of Southern Africa and Their Affinities* (Oxford: Oxford University Press, Clarendon Press, 1985), by G. T. Nurse, J. S. Weiner & T. Jenkins; *The Shaping of South African Society, 1652–1840* (Middletown, Conn.: Wesleyan University Press, 1988), ed. R. Elphick & H. Giliomee; and *Farmers, Kings, and Traders: The Peoples of Southern Africa* (Chicago: University of Chicago Press, 1990), by M. Hall. Other sources that I found valuable are:

A. Barnard, *Hunters and Herders of Southern Africa*. Cambridge: Cambridge University Press, 1992.

D. Birmingham & S. Marks, "Southern Africa," in *CHA* 3:567–620.

J. R. Denbow, "Cows and Kings: A Spatial and Economic Analysis of a Hierarchical Early Iron Age Settlement in Eastern Botswana," in *Frontiers: Southern African Archaeology Today,* ed. M. Hall et al., 24–39. Oxford: British Archaeological Reports, 1984.

————, "A New Look at the Later Prehistory of the Kalahari," *Journal of African History* 27 (1986): 3–28.

J. Denbow & A. Campbell, "The Early Stages of Food Production in Southern Africa and Some Potential Linguistic Correlates," *Sprache und Geschichte in Afrika* 7.1 (1986): 83–103.

R. M. Derricourt, *Prehistoric Man in the Ciskei and Transkei*. Cape Town: C. Struik, 1977.

————, "Settlement in the Transkei and Ciskei before the Mfecane," in *Beyond the Cape Frontier,* ed. C. Saunders & Derricourt, 39–82. London: Longman, 1974.

C. Ehret, "Patterns of Bantu and Central Sudanic Settlement in Central and Southern Africa (ca. 1000 B.C.–500 A.D.)," *Transafrican Journal of History* 3 (1973): 1–71.

R. Elphick, *Kraal and Castle: Khoikhoi and the Founding of White South Africa.* New Haven: Yale University Press, 1977.

T. M. Evers, "Sotho-Tswana and Moloko Settlement Patterns and the Bantu Cattle Pattern," in *Frontiers: Southern African Archaeology Today,* ed. M. Hall et al., 236–49. Oxford: British Archaeological Reports, 1984.

P. S. Garlake, *Great Zimbabwe.* New York: Stein and Day, 1973.

L. Guelke, "Frontier Settlement in Early Dutch South Africa," *Annals* (Association of American Geographers) 66 (1976): 25–42.

A. J. Hausman, "Holocene Evolution in Southern Africa," in *From Hunters to Farmers: The Causes and Consequences of Food Production in Africa,* ed. J. D. Clark & S. A. Brandt, 261–71. Berkeley: University of California Press, 1984.

T. N. Huffman, "Southern Africa to the South of the Zambezi," *GHA* 3:664–80.

R. R. Innskeep, *The Peopling of Southern Africa.* Cape Town: David Philip, 1978.

R. G. Klein, "The Prehistory of Stone Age Herders in South Africa," in *From Hunters to Farmers: The Causes and Consequences of Food Production in Africa,* ed. J. D. Clark & S. A. Brandt, 281–89. Berkeley: University of California Press, 1984.

T. Maggs, "The Iron Age South of the Zambezi," in *Southern African Prehistory and Paleoenvironments,* ed. R. G. Klein, 329–60. Rotterdam: A. A. Balkema, 1984.

J. S. Marais, *The Cape Coloured People, 1652–1937.* Johannesburg: Witwatersrand University Press, 1962.

S. Marks & R. Gray, "Southern Africa and Madagascar," in *CHA* 4:384–468.

P. Maylam, *A History of the African People of South Africa.* New York: St. Martin's, 1986.

R. Oliver & A. Atmore, *The African Middle Ages, 1400–1800.* Cambridge: Cambridge University Press, 1981.

J. D. Omer-Cooper, "Colonial South Africa and Its Frontiers," in *CHA* 5:353–92.

————, "The Nguni Outburst," in *CHA* 5:319–52.

J. B. Peires, *The Dead Will Arise: Nongqawuse and the Great Xhosa Cattle Killing Movement of 1856–7.* Johannesburg: Ravan Press, 1989.

R. Ross, "Ethnic Identity, Demographic Crisis, and the Xhosa-Khoikhoi Interaction," *History in Africa* 7 (1980): 259–71.

A. B. Smith, "Prehistoric Pastoralism in the Southwestern Cape, South Africa," *World Archaeology* 15 (1983–84): 79–89.

L. M. Thompson, *A History of South Africa.* New Haven: Yale University Press, 1990.

J. Vansina, "Bantu in the Crystal Ball," *History in Africa* 6 (1983): 287–333; 7 (1984): 293–325.

INDEX